"It's amazing how perfect the day can be – and out of the blue, life suddenly deals a disastrous blow. Even more amazing is how a young fellow like bill, and his family and friends, can turn it around and make such a positive return to a good life. This is the inspirational story of Bill Fallon, I'm proud to know him."

Merv Griffin
Chairman, The Griffin Group and
former Chairman, Griffin Gaming

"It is unbelievable to see Bill ski again and be able to partici-pate in all the sports he loves so much. After reading this fascinating book about Bill and his remarkable comeback it made me really understand the real meaning of perseverance. This powerful book also made clear that one should not take a healthy life for granted."

Georg Capaul
Head Alpine Coach for the U.S.
Women's Team

"This is a truly inspirational story of courage, perseverance, and personal discovery. I recommend it enthusiastically to everyone who thrills to see triumph emerge from tragedy."

Nader F. Dareshari
Chairman and CEO
Houghton Mifflin Company.

Dedication

This book is dedicated to my wife, Susan,
and my two children, Shannon and Flash,
who have lived the nightmare with me.
Their love and encouragement gave me strength that
I did not know I had.
I am overwhelmed by their compassion,
understanding and tolerance of my anger and suffering.
I would be nothing without them.

A touching example of the depth of my children's love
and compassion occurred only one day
before I sat down to write this dedication.
My true love, Sue, and I had erupted in an angry argument
during one of my brain-damaged moments when my rage
engulfs me and strains our lives together.
I had lost it, and I thought I had lost my wife too.
I was distraught and deeply depressed.
My son, Flash, came out to the hammock where I lay crying,
climbed up and wrapped his arms around me.
He told me he loved me,
then squeezed me so tightly it brought me back from the edge.

Courage
to
Persevere

by Bill Fallon
with Dan Egan

World Leisure Corporation
an Egan Entertainment Network Production

Book was published by World Leisure Corporation
through Egan Entertainment Network
PO Box 1305, Lincoln, NH 03251
Tel. (800) 619-6801

Distributed to the trade in the U.S.A. by
Midpoint Trade Books, Inc., 27 W. 20th Street, Suite 1102,
New York, NY 10011, Tel. (212) 727-0190, fax (212) 727-0195.

Distributed to the trade in U.K. by
Portfolio, Unit 1c, West Ealing Business Centre, Alexandria Road,
London W13 0NJ. Tel. (0181) 579-7748, fax (0181)567-0904.

Distributed to the trade in Canada by
Hushion House, 36 Northline Road, Toronto,
Ontario, M4B 3E2, Canada
Tel. (461) 287-3146 fax (416) 287-0081
Internet: www.hushion.com.

Mail Order, Catalog, other International sales and rights, and
Special Sales handled by Egan Entertainment Network, Inc.
PO Box 988, Campton, NH 03223
Tel. (603) 726-9926 E-mail: info@eganentertainment.com

ISBN: 0-915009-69-2

Preface

I did not set out to write this book, but the more I told my tale,
the more encouragement I received to put the story to paper.
The look I saw in the eyes of listeners finally inspired me.
My co-conspirators and editor kept after me to finish writing
the story, to be upbeat and positive, as if there was a pot of
gold at the end of the rainbow.
Sadly, that is not my reality, but the reality is that my story
gives listeners and readers the courage to endeavor to persevere through any tragedy or hardship.
Miracles do happen and one may happen for you.

Introduction

Most people incur brain trauma during an accident, are immediately disabled and then surgically repaired shortly afterwards. I was not that lucky—there was a lot of time to think about what was happening. The patient recovering from a sudden blow doesn't experience the same psychological trauma as someone who enters the hospital seemingly normal and healthy, but who leaves, after surgery, with severe neurological impairments. The victims of quick deaths don't have time to think about their fate, to become really frightened, to plan for all the things that could go wrong, and to decide how to handle those situations for the well-being of their family.

Many people have a problem accepting that they are sick, even after doctors and lab results indicate a disease or abnormality. Denial and fear are powerful enemies that can destroy a patient's future. If you do not feel as sick as doctors say you are, it is difficult to comprehend the seriousness of your condition. If you compare the symptoms that indicate an arteriovenous malformation (AVM) to the neurological deficits that you will incur to remove it, your immediate reaction is to just live with the headaches. Unless you have seizures or lose neurological functions, it is very hard to believe, let alone accept, the fact that your brain is in serious trouble and that your best choice is to go through the most dangerous surgical procedure possible in order to stay alive. Without the support and knowledge of many friends in the medical field, I might not have risked the cure.

I have met about 10 other AVM patients and discovered that many of them cannot be helped. In some cases, the doctors decide that if the condition is not immediately hazardous to the patient's health, it is better to do nothing. The theory is that medical technologies are advancing so quickly, the near future may bring a treatment that will be more effective and less invasive, thereby resulting in less damage. In other cases, the doctors feel that if they do nothing, then the patient faces certain death, which was the situation in my case.

When you fight a personal battle with a foe that you can't see—death—the only weapon you have is your own spirit and courage. Those weapons cannot be given, you have to conjure them up from within. Never give up hope and always endeavor to persevere.

Acknowledgements

All through the history of humankind, the relationships of fathers and sons have taken different forms. My relationship with my father has its ups and downs—happily, more ups than downs. I owe him a great deal; in fact, I owe him my life. I learned his greatest attributes, practiced them and refined them. I also learned not to make the negatives a part of my character. In true Jack Fallon fashion, I had the ambition, the competitive drive and the strength to overcome my adversities. My father is a great man with great accomplishments and, like a loyal soldier, I learned the lessons he taught me well. I thank him, and I love him.

My mom deserves a seat in Heaven for all her prayers and all the candles she set a match to. She is one of the most loving, generous and faithful mothers a son could have. Mom, I love you!

Pam, my sister, has been through a lot with me. Even though distance separates us, we have always been close. Like the dynamic duo, we stick together and watch out for each other. When I needed her strength to overcome the pain of surgery, she rode out the storm with me. Thanks, Pam, I love you.

My brother, John, doesn't know it, but he had the most delicate and dangerous task of anyone—getting Sue to the hospital and standing by her through early labor before the Flash's arrival. In fact, all my family rallied around me to help me wage my war and conquer my catastrophe. To all of you, thank you!

To the Joneses, Collelas, Howards and Luptons—your support made my success possible, and I will be forever grateful.

Dr. Robert E. Crowell uses his talents and his courage to strive to be his best, at times facing hopeless odds. He has tirelessly worked to save countless AVM/aneurysm patients. I will forever be connected to him; he is a part of my life. I think of him every day and wish him well with my deepest and most sincere gratitude.

Dr. Daryl Gress now lives in the San Francisco area and is the chief neurologist at the hospital known as University of California, San Francisco. He continues his passion to help people with brain injuries. His willingness to help me understand my plight and the extra time he gave me will forever be appreciated.

When I thanked Dr. Crowell for saving me, he denied that it was his success and proclaimed it was the work of Dr. John Pyle-Spellman. I owe JPS a debt of gratitude. I think I saw him only once after surgery, and if I forgot to thank him then, I thank him now. The last I heard he was in New York at Columbia Presbyterian hospital.

Dr. James Schumacher—"the shoe"—he is the man, a very cool dude and an incredibly talented neurosurgeon. Jim is now somewhere with his guitar and scalpel in Florida, performing miracles with brain surgery and treating Parkinson's disease and epilepsy.

Dr. Christopher Ogilvie was appointed to succeed Dr. Crowell at Mass General performing difficult AVM surgeries. He continues the fine work of his mentor, saving lives and leading the battle against a rare and little-understood neurovascular disorder.

Dr. Richard Westmark—"Doogie Howser"—is alive and well in Houston, working his magic in a private practice. I last heard that Richard had saved an astronaut's child and was seen at NASA flying the shuttle simulator and consulting NASA on its medical research for space travel.

Dr. Lotfi Hacein-bey, his wife, Yasmina, and their two children have become United States citizens. They live in Burlington, Vermont, where he is associate professor of radiology and director of diagnostic and interventional neuroradiology at the University of Vermont College of Medicine. Yasmina has finished graduate school and is teaching.

Dr. Karen Rives is alive and well, pursuing her orthopedic practice in the mid-Atlanta area.

Ann Geary and her husband, Bill, are busy raising two young children. The last I heard, Ann was still working part time on Ellison 22.

Barbara Dunderdale and her staff continue to be Angels of Mercy. They were truly wonderful and made my hospital experience bearable. I will forever be grateful to the whole staff for their compassion and tenderness.

Walter Mattson is still running his dojo to support his golf habit. Walter is one of those special people you sometimes have the privilege to meet and call a friend. Walter and my fellow students are never far from my thoughts. Walter will never accept the credit he deserves for teaching me a new way to live or for the critical role he played in my salvation. If Sue and I were to have another son, I would give his name careful consideration. Walter is in my thoughts every day. I cherish the time we had together; Walter taught me life's lessons.

Dr. Christopher Gates, to date, has not fallen asleep in any of our sessions. His role in my life has been one of my most stabilizing influences. Under his care I have grown and matured. I continue to consult him, since my mental health and well-being is a constant balancing act. As strong-willed as I am, I need his help in sorting out the multiple issues that cause me distress and complicate my anxieties.

Ken Hardy has had the difficult task of keeping me from harm's way and teaching me the ways of the glacier and high alpine. Ken has taught me many life lessons over the years. I thank him for his friendship and trust. Ken is one of the finest athletes I have had the honor to ski with. I value the times we have had together, and I will continue to aspire to be one of his guides.

Nader Dareshori, originally a client and ultimately a friend, motivated me to write my story. On his advice, I started to write just as he instructed: "Bill, if you write your story the way you tell it, I am sure it will be read. Your story is inspirational and one that should be told." Nader, I thank you for your encouragement and support.

I owe my friendship with Kevin Deverich to my dad. At his insistence, I entertained a new client and out of that grew a strong bond, one that transcends friendship to brotherhood. Kevin, thank you for providing me the opportunity to get back to work and for helping me regain my self-esteem. I thank you for being not only a friend but a big brother, one who cared to help me when others would not.

I thank Tom Gallagher for seeing that I could make a valuable business contribution, for showing me respect and trust, and for providing me with the responsibility to go out a winner. If he ever needs a good soldier, I will respond to his call to arms. I cherish the time we had working together. My only wish is that he would retire so I could have a playmate.

Merv Griffin's aura and his character is of such high quality that I have only met one other person with that grace and charisma—Jackie Kennedy Onassis. I wish Merv long life and good health.

Dan "the man" Egan—it is a long story to say how we connected, but kindred spirits have a way of finding each other. As fate would have it, Dan and I met skiing. When I discovered he had written a book, I asked him to show me how to publish mine. Dan was able to read 500 pages of stream-of-conscious babble and eliminate the redundancies, organize the chaos and structure my story. In the process we became good friends. I wish to thank him for tolerating me and respecting the originality of my writing. His experience in building Egan Entertainment helped my book materialize. Sue, the kids and I will be eternally grateful. Dan and I dream of buying a Winnabago to use next winter on an extended road trip from ski resort to ski resort, shamelessly promoting my book. Dan, live long and prosper. Maybe one day I will show you a few ski secrets of my own.

It is curious how strangers from faraway places can enter your life and make an impact. I met Trevor Reeves on the chairlift one season when he came from Australia to experience some real skiing in the White Mountains of New Hampshire—not that fairyland powder that ski resorts out west claim to have. Trevor knew he had not really skied until he had mastered the rock-hard, icy, narrow New Hampshire trails. Instinctively he knew how to complete his skiing career to become a great technical skier. Most Aussies go to Canada, Colorado or Utah. As fate would have it, Trevor became a friend. When I asked him if he could fix my computer problem, his reponse was, "Too easy." I had a sick computer that had scrambled the first draft of this book. Trevor fixed the problem, upgraded my computer and added a scanner. He scanned all 350 pages of text, reformatted them and copied them to a new disk. Trevor was an officer in the Australian Navy and is a fine gentleman. If Trevor had not entered my life, this book would not have been published, and I would have missed the chance to have him as a friend.

Incredibly, Joan Paterson was able to tune into my personality after reading the collaborative effort Dan and I had undertaken and handed to her. The remarkable thing is that Joan was able to edit my writing style without losing my personality in the way the story is told. In my first attempt to edit this story, my original editor did not understand me. When Sue and I first saw his treatment of my writing, all we could think of as we read it was that I would not have said or done that. Within six months, we had fired that editor and shelved the book. Happily I can say that Joan, in her wisdom and intuitiveness, has done such a good job of editing that each time Sue read a revised chapter, the story got better and Sue was just as affected as the reading before. As a novice writer, I appreciate Joan's efforts and talents—she has done a fabulous job. I am thankful and proud to have her name associated with my story. If there is ever to be another book, I would enjoy the opportunity to work with her again.

As we travel down our life's path, we meet friends and make enemies (more friends than enemies I hope), but there is one constant in life and that is change. Life is all about change and evolution. Nothing stays the same and no one lives forever. In my lifetime, I have made my share of friends and enemies. I have also made enemies of my friends and friends out of enemies. This is not intentional. We learn to change and adjust; we adapt and overcome; in the process, we gain and we lose.

Friendships are like life—we must accept people for themselves, learn from them and change. Some friendships transcend boundaries and become like the love of a brother or sister. Those kind of bonds, if strong, endure change and catastrophe, triumph and tragedy, and last forever. I am lucky to have more of those kinds of friends; they know who they are and they know I love them, too. To the handful of guys I have known as long as 30 and 40 years, the longevity of our friendship is a testament to the strength and endurance of our bond. To Hot Dog, Tony, Haas, H.L., Pete, Joe and Bill, Bang Bang and the boys of B-25, Art, Arthur, Wayne, Floyd, John, the A-team skiers I ski with, and all the rest—luv ya, man. To all women, I believe that you are God's greatest creations and without your caring, love, strength and nurturing, we men would be lost in the abyss.

Courage
to
Persevere

Chapter 1

Ever since high school I have had headaches. Not run-of-the-mill headaches, but headaches that blur my vision and feel like a red-hot iron rod burning inside my brain, just over my left eye. The pain is so intense I knock myself out with pills and hope that when I wake up, the pain will be gone. Worse than the pain, however, was the news I received on November 29, 1990, a beautiful sunny day in Massachusetts. I was driving my red Porsche 944 Turbo down the Massachusetts Turnpike on my way to close the biggest real estate deal of my life. Months in the making, this deal was going to net me a million dollars in commissions. After 12 years of struggling, bullied around by senior brokers who had it out for me because I was the boss's kid, the big one was coming home. Clients decide who represents them based on the hallmarks of success. I had learned to play the game and was about to enter the big leagues. I was a man on a mission.

I had one stop to make before the closing, an appointment with Dr. Speirings, a headache specialist who had run some tests to determine the cause of my never-ending headaches. Prior to Thanksgiving, he had assured me that I had nothing to worry about. And I wasn't worried—life was grand. As the morning sun shone in my eyes, I became lost in the events that led to this day.

After college I lived in the mountains in pursuit of the outdoor life—hunting, fishing and skiing. My lifestyle made a statement against conformity and city life. I had become a world-class skier, competing first as an amateur in my teens and then as a professional at 18. I have skied with the greatest skiers in the sport and I learned from the champions Paul and Paula Valar. Paul was a Swiss champion and his wife skied on the 1948 U.S. Olympic Team. Then there was Art Fuhrer, the great-grandfather of freestyle, Stein Ericson and Wayne Wong.

Skiing helps me pursue an elusive inner peace that I achieve by conquering each and every run, whether on a desolate glacier in the high alpine or on crowded trails in an eastern ski area. The feeling of control, mentally and physically, is a form of escapism for me, a rebellion against the structured environment of my family—especially against my father, who always put work before his kids. On the slopes my mind focuses on the laws of gravity, physics, geometry and aerodynamics. Skiing allows me to get lost within myself.

During this time I met Sue, who became my wife. A combination of mountain life and the forces of nature brought us together. Sue claims she knew she would marry me when she first saw me ski! Without skiing, I would not have met Sue, and without Sue, I would in all likelihood be dead. I would have sailed farther on stormy oceans, I would have skied faster downhill, I would have driven my car at higher speeds. I would have lived a more reckless life.

When ski season was over, jobs were scarce. Insecurity crept into my life in the form of parental pressure and I decided my headaches were stress related—or perhaps a result of the fast life catching up with me. When I finally bit the bullet in the late '70s and moved to Wayland, west of Boston, to accept a job with my father's real estate company, stress became a major part of my life and my headaches increased in frequency and pain. By this time, Sue was questioning why I suffered from so many headaches.

In 1990, although the market in real estate had gone sour, I was feeling on top of the world. I was earning a reputation as a top-notch broker who could afford life's luxuries. Sue was expecting and our daughter, Shannon, was 5. One day in October, Sue and I were mountain biking on the conservation trails in Wayland when I was struck with the worst headache of my life. I started to become short-winded and Sue noticed I was turning pale gray. It took more than an hour to make it back to our house when it would normally have taken 15 minutes. That day, Sue insisted that I see a doctor, but I shrugged off her insistence.

Sue was pregnant with our second child—we knew the baby would be a brother to Shannon—and wanted to keep biking for exercise. So the next Saturday morning, we hit the trails again. About 45 minutes into our ride, I once again started to complain that my head hurt, so we headed home. Back at the house, the migraine continued and I grabbed a couple of Darvorcets, a pain-killer my doctor had prescribed. Since the light in the room bothered me, Sue darkened the room and I went to bed. The next day, the pain continued; I stayed home from work for three days. This was becoming a pattern.

On the third weekend we went for another bike ride on the same trail. My headache returned, I turned chalk white, and I started sweating. I stopped riding and walked my bike home. It was back to bed for five days, no going to work. Toward the end of the week, my buddies called to arrange a weekend hunting trip. Ignoring Sue's protests, I agreed to go with them on a one-day trip to western Massachusetts.

Every year my buddies Rick Burtt and Chris Haney and I go bow hunting for a day. We use bow season to get away from it all and to scout out a few good hunting areas for a three-day trip during rifle season. Secretly, I hoped that one day spent stalking the elusive whitetail deer would help me relax from the stresses of the real estate profession and make my headaches disappear. On our scouting trip, the three of us split up and I climbed a tree to wait for a deer. Once up there, I started sweating, just as I had the weekend before, and I knew my color had changed. I couldn't move, and I stayed in the tree all day. When I got home that night, Sue said I looked terrible, a total contradiction from what you would expect after a day spent in the woods.

On Sunday, Sue said she was going to call a doctor first thing Monday morning. Insisting that I needed to find out once and for all what was causing my headaches, she contacted a friend, who recommended Dr. Speirings. Unfortunately he had no open appointments until April. Then Sue's friend called the doctor and set up an appointment for the following day, a total inconvenience because I had scheduled a big meeting for that day.

I'll never forget my first appointment with Dr. Speirings. For three hours, we discussed my family history of allergies and medical conditions. Then he suggested an MRI—just to rule out the remote possibility of a tumor. The appointment was scheduled for November 19, two days before my 37 birthday. It sounded routine and, to please Sue, I went along with the program. Friends described the MRI procedure as lying still in a narrow tunnel for an extended period of time. I wasn't worried, I was used to small spaces after 35 years of sailing with Dad, who often requested my presence in the bilge to check the ballast or look for leaks. Besides, Dr. Speirings assured me that there was a 99 percent chance the MRI would show nothing.

The weekend after my MRI was Thanksgiving. We loaded up the car and headed to Wiscassett, Maine, for a family gathering with Sue's side of the family. The pills Dr. Speirings had prescribed helped me feel better and his words kept playing over and over in my mind, "There is a 99-percent chance the MRI will show nothing and that will pretty much alleviate my concern about any serious neurological ailments." By the time we got home after the Thanksgiving holiday, the doctor had left several messages on our answering machine. Listening to them, I became a little alarmed.

On that fateful Monday, I arrived at my appointment with Dr. Speirings, distracted by the real estate closing in the afternoon. Whatever the doctor had to say was all part of the process of pleasing my wife. In Dr. Speirings' office, I heard the good news/bad news—and medical terms like neurological disease, birth defect and cerebral hemorrhage. The good news was that I didn't have cancer; the bad news was that I was dying or would be dead before I was 40. The day was going south fast!

The initial diagnosis was an arteriovenous malformation (AVM) in the left occipital lobe of my brain, approximately 4.5 to 5.5 centimeters in size. An AVM is a knot of arteries and veins that develops where there is a juncture of arteries and veins. A leak occurs under any kind of pressure, physical or stress related, where the veins branch off from the arteries; anything that increases the heart rate can make it leak. AVMs develop in the brain or spinal cord. An AVM in the spine is not that big a deal— loss of blood and maybe paralysis. An AVM in the brain is different—if it blows, you die. I was told that there was an 8 percent chance of dying that would compound annually every year I lived. In short, I was a walking time bomb!

Dr. Speirings suggested I consult a specialist at Tufts and politely deferred revealing any more information as he lacked experience in the field. I thanked him, gave him a look that implied he was a mad scientist and walked calmly to my car. My mind was in shock and already teasing me with the next task of the day—closing my big real estate deal and making a killing on the commission.

Back in my car, I drove fast through the streets of Boston. With the radio blasting, I reassured myself, "No way, I'm fine." The broker in me was in full control, my mind was focused on dollars, big dollars—I didn't have time for AV-whatever and brain defects. This was not happening to a Fallon. And, even if it were, I would get it fixed—no problem. I picked up the phone to call Sue, then hung up. Sue was pregnant; she did not need to be engulfed in a sinkhole of fear. I would figure this out after the deal closed. When I had the money, things would be worked out. I did not believe I was sick or dying—I did not look like a dying man! The news was incomprehensible. I had never heard of an AVM or known anyone who had one. The deal, I had to concentrate on the deal. I had worked too hard to let it go. Nothing a Fallon does can be easy or simple, but what should I do? I needed to talk with someone, someone who could wake me up from this nightmare.

The only person I could think of was Dr. Karen Rives, a source of information who became a friend during my father's fight for survival with rheumatoid arthritis. On the way to the real estate closing, I called her on my car phone and asked her to explain what an AVM was. Dr. Karen immediately said that it was serious and asked if I knew anyone who had one. I replied, "Yes, me." She then asked where I was. "On Huntington Ave on my way to an appointment."

"No, you are not," she said. "You are going to come and see me."

We argued, but Dr. Karen persisted. She begged me to turn the car around, drive directly to Brigham & Women's Hospital and pick up the results from the MRI. I protested, knowing the hours, days and months that had gone into my imminent real estate closing. But Dr. Karen was direct and confirmed Dr. Speirings' words: I could die at any moment. Commissions and real estate deals won't mean a thing then. Sensing her urgency, I caved in and agreed to see her.

As Dr. Karen instructed, I drove to the hospital and grabbed the MRI film from the lab, not an easy task without a doctor's permission. I essentially talked my way through the red tape and walked out with the films under my arm. Then I called Sue from my car phone and she asked a bunch of questions that I didn't know the answers to. I described the thing in my head was like a tumor. Sue screamed and started to cry. We both fell silent as the truth began sinking in. Sue's reaction slapped me in the face, and I thought, "Wow, this is real."

At Dr. Karen's request, I went straight to her office in the Massachusetts General Ambulatory Care Center and waited for her. Dr. Karen was the chief resident orthopedic surgeon and her office was filled with the tools of her trade. Dr. Speirings had not shown me the MRI films and because I am a Type A personality—genetically dominant in my family—I took a look at them. Seeing them made me cry. It didn't take a medical degree to know that a black spot about the size of a lemon in the back of my brain was not a healthy sign.

Dr. Karen arrived at her office with Dr. Kevin Mcgrill, the chief resident in the neurosurgery department. I can't believe how lucky I was in an unlucky situation. Dr. Mcgrill, a tall handsome man with a gentle manner, informed me that Dr. Robert E. Crowell, one of three experts in arteriovenous malformations, practiced at Mass General. They rushed me into Dr. Crowell's office, where he began telling me about a 25-year study in the Netherlands that had discovered, with accuracy, the probability of hemorrhages as a result of AVMs. I heard him speaking, but I was not really listening. Shock and denial had taken over. All I could think of was that I was dying. Dr. Crowell was compassionate but unspecific. Later I came to understand that brain surgery is not an exact science. Just as every patient is different, every result is different. Even if the surgery is in the same lobe of the brain, the results can change. At some point I started to come out of my daze and asked the doctor what to do next. His response was not that comforting: He ordered me to take it easy, not to lift any heavy objects, to leave work immediately, and to go home and enjoy my family.

Then I received my second stroke of good fortune. In mid-December, 10 of the top doctors in the field of vascular neurosurgery were holding their annual conference at Mass General. Dr. Crowell wanted to discuss my case at the conference. In order to do a proper diagnosis, he needed results from another MRI and something called an angiogram. The description of the angiogram was frightening. Doctors tell you enough to raise your anxiety level but not enough to scare the shit out of you. The MRI is a piece of cake; the angiogram is another matter.

Dr. Crowell went on to say that I was one of about 200,000 individuals in the U.S. with this birth defect, which occurs in the seventh to 13th week of the fetus' development, and that 75 percent of patients hemorrhage before the age of 40. If I were lucky, I would die. The size of my AVM was so large that if I survived, neurological deficits would make me a vegetable. He went on to say that my chance of hemorrhage was about 16 percent. At that point I stopped listening. I thanked Dr. Crowell and left the hospital feeling like a zombie. With the sun shining over the Charles River, I drove in silence, wondering what to do and where to go. I called work to make arrangements for someone to make my apologies to my clients and thought about Sue, my angel, Sue. Pregnant Sue. What did the future hold for her, for my unborn child, and for my daughter Shannon, sweet little Shannon?

My job as a broker came before my family, something I had learned from my father, who always put his clients and deals first. Working every minute of every day cultivating relationships with the sole purpose of making a deal or closing a sale had become my life. Money was what I provided to my wife and child. Now all that I had worked for was slipping away because of some rare birth defect. For the first time since I had stopped skiing full time, I contemplated life without my family and their lives without me. I hardly knew myself these days, unlike during the days when I lived in the mountains. As I looked up at the sun, I thought about how the sun's rays light up the crystals in the snow and how that used to illuminate my soul and spirit. That mystical quality was missing from my life. I had let it slip away, and I wondered whether it would ever come back.

By the time I arrived home, Sue had picked up Shannon from her afternoon school program. While Sue and I hugged, cried and sat in shock, we tried to keep Shannon from becoming alarmed. I spent most of that night on the phone talking to Dr. Karen, asking questions and trying to get a grip on what it was all about. The next day I set up meetings with co-workers and clients and started to divest my duties. My dad's reaction was, "It's not as bad as you think, you'll be all right." Needless to say,

I moved ahead with the pressing issues—my living will and letting go of work.

On Tuesday, Sue and I decided that the only option concerning work was to take a leave of absence. Our weekly department meeting was at 8 a.m. That took care of part of the problem—assembling the brokers for the sales meeting and informing them. Then I had to assign responsibility for my accounts, answer questions about my condition and get the hell out of the office before I lost control. Leaving work was not that difficult—the real estate market was down and the pressure was burning me out. The reality of the transition would sink in later. In the meantime, ski conditions were getting good and I love to ski more than anything else in the world!

Courage to Persevere

Chapter 2

Dr. Crowell scheduled the angiogram for December 7, 1990, my own personal Pearl Harbor day. For me, the angiogram is a devastating experience. Just prior to my first one, I was sitting in the pre-procedure room, wearing one of those short hospital gowns that open in the back, when Dr. Karen walked in and said, "Guess what? You've tested positive for AIDs!" The oxygen in the room was immediately sucked out by the gasps from the other patients. "Ha," said Dr. Karen, "only kidding."

As I was recovering from that amusing joke—my anxiety level was way up by now—an Asian doctor named Golden Pan came in. In an attempt to relieve my apprehension, I asked whether his nametag was a joke. He brushed off my humor by talking about the risks involved, informing me that I risked a hemorrhage and/or paralysis while undergoing the angiogram. I signed the releases reluctantly—as if there were a choice. Then it was off to the X-ray room. With six X-ray machines, half a dozen technicians, and an equal number of doctors milling about preparing to start the procedure, the room resembled a garage filled with mechanics. Soon I was hooked up to a few IVs and feeling no pain, due to the Valium pumping into my arm. As soon as I was positioned on the table, my hospital gown was removed and the female nurse began shaving my private parts—an extremely humiliating few moments.

An angiogram reminds me of the Walt Disney movie "Fantastic Voyage." Overhead to my left was a large white screen lit from the back. On this screen there were three black-and-white X-rays of my skull. As I moved, so did the X-ray pictures. "Kind of neat," I thought, and then I felt a wet sensation in my groin area and heard a "ssssht ssssht" noise. By this point my adrenal gland, a terrific organ that secretes hormones to give you the ability to power through any situation, was really putting out a lot of stuff.

I could hear the doctors talking and that funny sound—ssssht tap! This procedure is a slow and meticulous operation that can take about four hours. The doctor inserts a very fine catheter into the femoral artery in your groin. Then the doctor has to push the catheter up into your brain through the arterial system. The three X-ray screens on my left indicated the location of the catheter in my body. A fourth screen, in red and white, showed what the camera lens in the very tip of the catheter could see. It literally shows the doctor the way from inside the artery. The ssssht sound is the doctor pushing in the catheter; the tap sound is the doctor knocking out the air bubbles. Having an angiogram is analogous to riding a roller coaster with nitroglycerin in your head. I consider myself an expert on this subject since over the next six months, I would undergo this procedure six times.

Soon after the angiogram started, Dr. Karen came in and noticed that the Valium was no longer soothing me. Although the nurse administered more, it seemed an eternity before it took effect. As the temptation to sleep was growing, the medical team persisted in asking meaningless questions. It didn't occur to me then, but they needed me to stay alert to tell them how I felt, a critical issue when you realize the doctor has a small margin for error or the patient is as good as cooked. Then I felt a pain— actually more like a cramp that kept growing in intensity. When I could have sworn that Hulk Hogan was standing on my chest, I decided to let the doctor know about it. The 12 people in the room froze, reminding me of the TV commercial for Merrill Lynch back in the '70s.

"Where is the cramp?"

"In my chest!"

Tap, sssht, tap—the cramp subsided. Later I found out that the cramp was a result of the catheter going the wrong way into my heart, a deadly act and another good reason to have a patient awake during an angiogram.

It seemed like a lifetime, but after two hours elapsed, the doctor was entering my brain with the catheter. I could hear what sounded like little bubbles popping behind my ear. Glancing at the screen, I could see the catheter highlighted behind my ear, a weird sensation. Then the doctors injected a dye into my veins that felt like warm blood going through my brain. The dye highlighted the malformations and painted a clear picture of where the AVM was located. I must have been allowed to finally fall asleep because things seemed to go by quickly from then on. I was told the worst was over. This was such a relief that I must have stopped producing adrenaline and the Valium really kicked in. I was wasted, but could still feel the doctor placing a lot of pressure on my femoral artery to stop the bleeding. Then he sent me off with a sore groin to enjoy a good Valium buzz in the recovery room. When I awoke, I convinced myself that this was the worst of things to come. How naive I was—this was only the beginning.

Of all the unpleasantness I was to endure over the next two years, the angiograms and two angioplasty procedures were worse than the two brain operations that took 18 hours and 24 hours each. I can never quite find the appropriate way to verbalize the impact these procedures had on my body, mind and soul. From this very first angiogram, something within me changed. My body hurt from the procedure; my brain reacted to the intrusion of the catheter, the dye and, later, the glue and human hands. Ultimately, my inner being felt invaded. My soul and spirit started to crack. Even today, these cracks leak the pain of who I was into who I became.

The month of December is always a joyous time for our family, with the celebration of Shannon's birthday, Christmas and skiing. I must have turned into a zombie that year because I don't remember much about the holiday season. I do know I made hundreds of phone calls to Dr. Karen, who had moved to Milwaukee for a year to begin her foot and ankle studies. Most were inquiries about the reality of the situation or discussions about my emotions—fear, denial, guilt and anger—and the one question that constantly ran through my mind, "Why me?" I still don't have an answer for that one.

Fear was a prominent emotion. What was there for me to fear? Death? Well, yes; however, for me, death is not an end or a beginning. I believe that we have energy within us that resembles electricity. The laws of physics teach that pure energy disperses or moves from one form to another; therefore, energy doesn't die. Biology teaches that signals from the brain to parts of the body are electrical. The human body is 98 percent fluids and most fluids conduct energy. If this is true, where does this energy go when the body that carries it dies? Is life after death Heaven or Hell or Rebirth? My theory is that life as we know it is a phase in the existence of a human being. This thought was the reason I didn't fear dying. Life is the beginning of our consciousness and the electricity in our brain becomes the vehicle of thought. If thought is electricity and electricity is a form of pure energy, our consciousness cannot die—it must change from one form to another. We must continue in some other form. Hence, if life as we know it is a beginning without an ending, what is there to fear? My rationalization kept me from completely falling apart. I was frightened, but it was the fact that I might live that I feared. The deficits that could result from my disease if I lived scared me more than death.

I also feared the loss of privacy—every aspect of my life exposed. I would be faced with all of the issues that normally confront the elderly: estate planning, updating my will, establishing power of attorney, setting up financial support for the kids. The questions in my mind never stopped. Will I live to see the birth of my son? Hear his first words? Watch his first steps? The thoughts were like a constant wave crashing on every waking moment. Then my defenses would kick and fight their way to conscious thought and I could briefly regain my composure and summon up courage to fight and face my fear—the fear of living!

Adversity is one of life's character builders. My whole life had taught me this. When I was a teenager, my football coach disliked me but could not leave me on the bench because I was too good a player. I could tackle anybody and when I hit someone, it hurt. In sailing, I had to contend with being in the shadow of America's greatest sailor, my dad. In skiing, the coach resented the fact that I played football, which prevented me from attending preseason ski practice with the rest of the team. Luckily for me, I was good enough to become a Class A racer. When I realized the coach was not going to give me the chance to try out for the Nationals, I turned professional. After I abandoned my skiing career, co-workers tried to make my life miserable. Then the AVM came along and made everything but survival seem irrelevant to the big picture called life.

When I was with my friends, I confided the news that I was very ill, or so the doctors said. That was my denial speaking, my refusal to accept facts. My friends saw an active, healthy man with no outward signs of illness. When I looked in the mirror, I saw the same thing. It was difficult to comprehend the seriousness of my illness when the only thing I suffered from was migraine headaches! I sought strength and comfort in several places. Sue provided strength. She never wavered in her devotion and dedication to our relationship. Sure and steady, she stayed on course, although all the while her responsibilities were growing. She was pregnant, taking care of Shannon, running a successful travel agency and somehow managing to spend time with me while immersing herself in knowledge about my disease.

We spent most of December waiting for the doctors to review my lab test, MRI film and angiogram and anticipating the results from the conference on AVMs taking place at Mass General. The world's experts on neurovascular disorders were studying my case for the entire two weeks. On December 8th we celebrated Shannon's birthday but the celebration was lost on me. I wondered whether I would celebrate her next birthday or be around to see my son when he was born. Time and time again I reminded myself to be strong and courageous. But more time was spent thinking rather than doing, and my dark thoughts robbed me of precious moments.

To stay occupied, I went skiing—an activity that wasn't really on the doctor's "to do" list for me, but when did I ever listen to anyone? Riding the chairlift with friends made the days bearable. Skiing distracted me from looking inward, from searching my soul for reasons. When I skied at Waterville Valley Resort, N.H., that December, I took more risks than usual. The thought of getting hurt on the ski hill was not a consideration. I skied as much as I could; for all I knew, I was never going to ski again.

During this time, my relationship with Sue started to change. I did not want her to be too dependent on me and I began to say things like, "Do not depend on me! I will not live to be 40." Sue would respond, "Don't talk like that." As ambitious and materialistic as I was, I was losing the ability to satisfy those needs! How in God's name could I put my life on hold and support my family? Where was money to afford the cure going to come from?

On the Wednesday before Christmas, Sue and I had an opportunity to forget all our problems. Our long-time friend John Cremmen came over for dinner. Although John and I went back to elementary school, he had not heard of my illness. I did not want to ruin our time together and decided not to say anything. We spent a wonderful evening of dining and drinking and telling stories and lies. Sue and I let it all go and enjoyed a break from the darkness.

Christmas day came and went. I remember having Christmas at home in Wayland but could not tell you what I got for Christmas or what anyone else received. I cannot even remember what I gave Sue. Shannon was not aware of the seriousness of my condition and it was too early to confront her with my illness. Dinner was tense and low-key. The doctors had not told me what the cure was and I wanted to believe that the situation was manageable. The date for my next consultation with Dr. Crowell was scheduled for the day after Christmas.

Chapter 3

Sue, my father and I were quiet on the drive to Mass General Hospital on the morning of the 26th. I was hoping I would wake up from this nightmare. We parked in the garage and walked over to the Ambulatory Care Center. Julie, Dr. Crowell's secretary, a truly wonderful and upbeat young lady, invited the three of us into the office where Dr. Crowell introduced himself to my father and Sue. Dr. Darryl Gress was also there—he reminded me of an intelligent and highly educated Henry Winkler. This is not a putdown; it's just that he looks like the Fonz. Although I didn't know it then, a bond with these two doctors was about to develop—an affectionate bond filled with love.

Dr. Crowell began explaining to Sue and my Dad what an AVM is and talked about the results of the studies in the Netherlands. I wanted to believe that the angiogram had indicated a false alarm and we could all go home. Fat chance! At that moment, Dr. Crowell was calmly pulling up the films of the angiogram and I could hear him say "the AVM is the size of a lemon" and "there is an aneurysm within the AVM." An aneurysm is a bubble on an artery. Over a person's life span, the artery begins to look like a balloon that has been blown up too much. The veins in the AVM stretch and blood weeps through. The intense pain in my head was the result of blood leaking into my brain.

Then Dr. Crowell casually started talking about a second, smaller AVM that also might contain an aneurysm. Both doctors indicated that there were signs of hemorrhaging within the two separate lobes of the brain—a rarity among rarities. All this became a complete overload for me and I started to have an out-of-body experience. My eyes searched the room for the person they were talking about while my heart sought a comforting face. Instead, all I saw was horror, fear and disbelief on the faces of Sue and my father. My brain shut down; denial took over. I heard words coming out of the doctors' mouths but did not comprehend their meaning.

The news was like being hit with a bomb. Instead of having one problem, I had four: two AVMs and two aneurysms that were weeping blood into my brain. Regaining my health was going to be a long haul. The subject turned to probabilities and it seemed like a high-stakes game where the stakes were my life. Dr. Crowell ran the probabilities that I would die and the odds kept getting worse. The long and short of this consultation was that I would most certainly have a major hemorrhage at some time over the next two years. The outcome would cause my death. Both doctors agreed that would be the most merciful outcome. If I survived, I would be a vegetable.

Sue was sitting up straight, listening intently, looking stoic but sweating. She held my hand and sweat dripped between the two of us, leaving a mark on my thigh. I heard her whisper, "How the hell are we ever going to get through this!" I was in shock and could not speak. The only question I could think of was "What are my options?" The doctors laid them out for me: (a) surgical incision, (b) something called a proton beam or, in laymen's terms, nuke it, and (c) a new procedure called intravascular neuroradial surgery. Surgical incision would remove the AVM/aneurysm by removing part of the skull, moving the folds of the brain, and cutting and cauterizing the veins, vessels and arteries until the AVM could be removed and disposed of in the lab. Someone asked about the probability of success using this procedure. Dr. Crowell explained that all surgery carries risk. Brain surgery is the riskiest of any surgery, with a high probability the patient will incur neurological deficits. The neurological losses could be up to 50-percent loss of peripheral vision on the right side in both eyes. Neurological blindness is different from blindness. In simple terms, the eyes see but the brain does not know what it is seeing as it can no longer decode the images. If the surgery were successful, however, the risk of hemorrhage would be eliminated by 98 percent.

It was hard to understand all that Dr. Crowell told us that day. He described the blindness by using the face of a clock. Vision would be lost between 12 o'clock and 6 o'clock, the top-right quadrant first and possibly the bottom-right quadrant. I might keep some peripheral vision but it is difficult to predict exact results when dealing with the brain. The deficits, Dr. Crowell went on to say, may not be limited to vision and could include speech difficulties, as well as memory and other minor neurological deficits. As I was to learn, the "other minor" deficits are the most devastating. The risk of neurological deficits was 100 percent. How severe would the deficits be? Neither Dr. Crowell nor Dr. Gress was willing to be quoted.

Mentally distraught, I felt that Santa had left me a terrible Christmas gift. If this was fate, God had a nasty streak in him. If God wanted me dead, why did it have to be like that—not just one part of my brain in serious trouble but two! At the time, I thought there would be only one operation, but in two places. Was I naive, stupid or in shock? Actually, all three applied.

After discussing the operation on the left occipital lobe, our attention was brought to the smaller AVM located in the right temple. This area of the brain is the region that controls motor skills. Tampering with this region can mean paralysis and, at that point, death looked better to me. Dr. Crowell explained that the AVM in the temple was easier to get to because it was smaller and not as deep in the brain. However, he felt it posed a greater risk to me than the larger AVM. In fact, both doctors believed that the larger one might not be operable at all. The AVM in the temple was an easier target and, if surgery was my choice, they felt it best to remove this one first.

The second option was the radiation treatment, called proton beam or gamma knife by some physicians. The conversation became technical and I started daydreaming about Sue's father. A brilliant pathologist, Dr. Howard had recorded the highest scores ever in the medical board examinations. I was sure he could help me understand all that I was being told. Unfortunately, he had died in 1977. My mind drifted back to what the doctors were saying. During the proton beam treatment, the doctor screws your head into a device called a halo. Then, with another device too scientific for me to explain, he focuses a beam on a precise location in the brain and nukes it. What happens if the cell tissue is radiated to the point where the antibodies in the cells of the body freak out and multiply? If all goes well, the vessels, arteries and cells scar and multiply to thicken the walls of the vein and prevent a rupture or hemorrhage, similar to the way calluses form on your hands from hard work. The doctors kept talking about the many variables. This procedure scared me—it was so imprecise! Besides, I had never heard anyone refer to radiation as a precise science. Not only that, the success rate was around 40 percent and it would take two years before we could tell if it had worked. On top of all this, the proton beam treatment would require more angiograms, which put this option off the scale. Neither my father, Sue, nor myself asked any further questions about this option and it was never discussed again.

The third option, intravascular neuroradial surgery, was a new field. The doctor enters the brain from two different arterial systems, the femoral and coratid arteries, and places catheters on each side of the AVM to block the arteries with a glue similar to Superglue, stopping the blood flow into the AVM. One catheter delivers the glue; the second is a safety catheter to catch the glue if it doesn't adhere. If the glue passes through the AVM and is not caught as it leaves, the patient dies. The result, in theory, is that the AVM shrinks when the flow of blood is reduced or stopped. This option was tied to the first option, because once the AVM became smaller, surgery would be possible, reducing brain damage by reducing the surgery area. We didn't discuss this procedure very much because we felt it was not an option.

When Dr. Crowell asked me to choose the treatment for the first AVM, I asked what he would do in my shoes. He replied that because he was a surgeon, he required the use of his hands.

Surgery in this area of the brain could cause some paralysis, which would prevent him from doing what he most wanted to do— surgery and playing the piano. In my case, all three procedures were options. I chose the first option—surgery. It was risky but held out a high probability of success without too many deficits, or so I thought.

Choosing a date to operate on my temple was next and the doctors decided that January 28th would be the first opportunity to assemble the team. However, there was a big problem with the date. I had planned to take my annual ski trip to Whistler, British Columbia, and enjoy some heli-skiing. When I asked Dr. Crowell how active I could be before my surgery, he said, "Do not do anything too strenuous." He recommended that I take it easy, enjoy my family and help Sue with her pregnancy. Not exactly the answer I was looking for.

Then I asked, "Is there anything magic about that date?"

He replied that approximately one month was necessary to assemble the surgical team and schedule an operating room. "Why?" he asked.

I replied that I would prefer to move the date ahead to February so that I could go heli-skiing in British Columbia. He responded, "Couldn't you pick something less strenuous or at least some place closer to Boston?"

It was the only time I laughed during the meeting. Sue smirked and my Dad shook his head in disbelief at my answer— No! I asked whether I would be able to ski after the operation. Skiing is my passion and if I wasn't going to ski again, I had to go to Whistler before the surgery. If the future held blindness, paralysis, or maybe death, I could not think of a better place to die than up on the glaciers at 10,000-feet, skiing in the virgin white snow. A place with a spectacular view across the beautiful Garibaldi Mountain range, with no signs of civilization. A much better option than on some sterile table in an operating room in the bowels of Mass General.

It seemed as if only an hour had elapsed, but we had talked for nearly three hours, a long time to spend with doctors on the day after Christmas. Together with the doctors, Sue and Dad coaxed me into the first operation. Although I wasn't focused on anything but heli-skiing, we set a date for the first operation, February 4, 1991, and we all agreed on the type of procedure. Slowly the fact that I was in very serious condition was sinking in. Why was I facing mortality at age 37? My wife was pregnant and I was in the prime of my life—it didn't seem fair.

We thanked the doctors and Dr. Crowell reminded me not to lift anything or strain myself, to take it easy and enjoy the next few weeks. "Yeah, right," I thought, "I'll just sit around and wait to die! This guy doesn't ski, he has no clue about the freedom and self-expression the sport holds." For the first time in my life, my mind became trapped in a dark place. No words could express my emotions, either to Sue or to my father. Disbelief filled my mind. Hundreds of questions came and went, adding to my confusion. Overwhelmed by fear, practical thoughts of setting priorities and dealing with family issues were pushed aside. My chest felt tight, my breathing was labored, and emotional pain took hold of my heart and soul. Tears drowned my eyes as we walked to the parking garage. I tried to hold back the sobbing, but it was hopeless. If only someone knew the answers to the future, if only someone or something could help me decide. Dad placed his hand on my shoulder and said, "Hang in there," then headed off to a business meeting in a taxi. Sue and I sat in our car in silence. What could we say? The issue was terrifying, but I could not hide from it. Holding hands, we drove home.

My Dad had once told me that the best way to solve a problem is to break the issue into the simplest terms and start to solve the problem from there. The issue was clear. I was going to have the AVMs removed surgically and would have to learn to live with any resulting deficits. Or, I would not live beyond 40—that was my harsh reality. The private person within me had to be the one I turned to in this crisis. That's where I went to deal with my fate. It became a lonely place filled with conflict between survival and death. At times the debate took place in the part of my body that was the cause of the crisis. My brain itself was a contradiction, holding both life and death in close quarters.

Someone was going to invade the most personal and private organ in my body—my brain, the human mind. They were going to mess with the most sophisticated living cellular mass known and no one knows a whole lot about what 60 percent of this organ does. For all the greatness that humans have accomplished, we can't come close to creating a machine that is as great as the human brain. Fill a huge warehouse with computers and they cannot duplicate 10 percent of the brain's capacity. My internal debate began to rationalize the decision I had made to schedule the surgery. I would have to undergo one surgery at a time; in fact, the doctors hadn't discussed the second AVM much, although they had indicated the probability of combining two of the three treatment options as a possible solution to eliminate the second AVM in the occipital lobe.

How quickly life can be shattered! Just three months ago I was on top of the world. Actually I felt blessed. I was the head of the department and making a lot of money, my wife was expecting our first son—the only namesake to carry the Fallon name for another generation. Sure, I had my troubles. I was the boss's son in a competitive business. Although some individuals ahead of me within the corporate structure wanted to discredit me, I was determined to work hard, thinking that would win them over. But the success I achieved in putting together big deals and earning big commissions only made them work harder to discredit me. Nepotism works both ways: It helps and it hurts. But by that time in my career I had outlasted all my enemies and the future was looking bright. In a short time, however, I had gone from king of the hill to death row.

The day after the doctor's meeting, I awoke hoping it was all a nightmare. I stayed up late talking to Dr. Karen, my sister, Pam, and my closest friends, telling them I was going to die or, worse to my way of thinking, become seriously handicapped. Although I did not want to face this reality, I had to. Everyone asked the same questions we had asked. They were kindly trying to minimize the impact and hold out hope that things would turn out all right. Their encouragement left me lost in a sea of emotion.

Everyone I talked to over the following weeks offered strength and support. I began to recognize the expression on their faces—mingled pity and disbelief. My world was collapsing and my usually optimistic outlook became sullen and empty. The good-natured Bill left me: I failed to see the humor in life anymore. The always-energetic Bill was dying: Despair and emptiness overwhelmed me. Loneliness crept into my being for the first time in my life.

Feeling totally isolated, I contemplated my past and future. I wondered how I had offended God. What had I done to earn this fate? I had not been an angel but I wasn't the devil either. Was it fate, the luck of the draw? My doctors said this birth defect was one of 250,000 cases known. Was my fate the fate of other Fallon men who had died a premature death? Throughout my life I had known about the early demise of my namesakes. Other William J. Fallons before me had met tragic ends. My great-grandfather William J. Fallon—businessman, philanthropist and sportsman—was a leather manufacturer born in 1895. During his lifetime he invented and held the patent for shoe welts, as well as for the machinery that made them. A welt is the part of a shoe that makes up the front half of the sole, allowing the soles to bend when you take a step. My great-grandfather's friends were famous men like Mayor Curly, Joe Timilty and Doc Kendall, all prominent Bostonians. William J. Fallon had five sons; all but one had their lives cut short in tragic fashion.

Joseph E. Fallon, the oldest of the sons, ran the family leather business. He was my father's father and died of pneumonia at the age of 26, leaving three children under the age of 8. Anna, my grandmother, never remarried. My father's uncle, Harry Fallon, died in a car crash on Commonwealth Avenue when he had a seizure at the wheel of his car and slammed into a light pole. He was only 31. His family reported that he had complained of feeling dizzy and a little ill that morning. Harry was the traveling secretary for the Boston Braves, had never married and at the time of his death was survived by only two of his four brothers. My father's brother, Joe Jr., died in the early 1960s from a cerebral blood clot, thought to have been caused from injuries he suffered while serving on the USS Thatcher for almost four years during World War II.

It was hard not to think about my family's history and wonder what part I played. I desperately wanted to live; I believed that there was a reason to life, a destiny to fulfill, and death was not part of the plan. Yet, every time I looked into the past, I saw death and, after speaking with the doctors, the near future probably held death as well. I was trapped and obsessed with this fact, but determined not to acknowledge the fact that I would die. Death could no longer be considered—it might increase the probability that it would happen. I would experience the unknown and ward off the dark Angel of Death, the fear of blindness, the fear of paralysis, the fear of diminished mental capacities—all the result of trying to save my life. I feared this double-edged sword, but clung to it like the last piece of floating wood from a shipwreck. Depression set in and I wasn't prepared to deal with it. Logic kept telling me that in the end I would be less than I was. All my pleasures would be out of reach: skiing, driving, sailing, hunting, shooting. The list grew and every time I realized there would be some other endeavor I would not be able to perform, I became more depressed. I was still unaware of the seriousness of the larger AVM in the back of my head. If I had known, it might have pushed me over the edge. Since the doctors had decided to tackle the smaller AVM first, all discussion revolved around that surgery. The operation on my temple was considered less risky.

As the days went by, I began cutting ties with my professional life. It was a huge blow to my ego to give up projects, clients, deals and responsibilities that had taken me 12 years to earn. Questions and phone calls rippled through our friends and family. The network of my personal relationships hummed with the news of my disease. The business community whispered about my impending demise. One way or another, my little domain was coming to an end and I was powerless to do anything about it. There seemed no end to this nightmare.

Chapter 4

My upbringing created a need for acceptance through accomplishments, in sports and in business. If my father's motto of "Work to Live, Live to Work" worked for him, it could work for me too. But I came to realize that it all meant nothing—the years of climbing the ladder toward material things—hot cars, fast boats, piles of money and an ever-expanding client base. What did it all bring me? None of it could save me! Even my father, my idol, had little to say to me, as if he thought I was taking the easy way out—if only I would try harder, this would all end.

Sue and I talked about the future and I told her my will was in order. She would have power of attorney in order to make the disposition of my estate easier. We had often talked about our deaths and what we would do. I wanted a big party—a typical Irish wake with food, booze, and a good rock and roll band to play all my favorite songs. I asked Sue to do whatever she felt was appropriate at the gravesite.

"Sue, we have always stated our desires if one of us dies. You know what I want done and that's that. Don't go broke keeping me alive on some machine, either."

That was the last time we discussed it. Then we tackled the how, what and when of telling Shannon and decided it was better to discuss it openly, at the right time.

The day after the meeting with the doctors, we headed to Waterville Valley to spend the week skiing since Shannon was on Christmas vacation. Every trip to Waterville Valley is a reunion for me. Much of my time on snow has taken place there and many of my daydreams are filled with skiing. The resort is home to a fraternity of friends who travel there every weekend to ski and hang out. Robert Mann, Grover Daniels, Ross Hamlin, their respective wives, and Sue and myself are the heart and soul of the ski gang. We are a confederation, tied together to facilitate all of our recreational ski desires. Most of us have known each other for 25 years or more. All of us are world-class skiers and have taught, coached or competed as amateurs and professionals. Our passion is to ski any time, any place. Skiing is our vehicle of freedom. We endeavor to make it affordable and to recreate the magic the sport always gives us. These pals of ours and I all grew up in New England. Waterville Valley was and still is our home mountain. We are local legends and enjoy certain liberties when we ski there, like skiing closed trails with the ski patrol or getting employee rates in the café. The high-speed quad chairlift is our conference room where we talk about our problems, dreams and desires. Waterville Valley ski area is one of the best in New England and we use it to get in shape to ski in western Canada.

Sue was very pregnant by this time and had trouble with her balance because the baby was sitting on her sciatic nerve. The day after we arrived at Waterville Valley, she started bleeding. I came off the hill and rushed her to Laconia Lake Regional Hospital. The doctors told us that stress from the news of my illness could have caused the problem and decided to keep her in the hospital for the next three days. The gang kept me busy during the day while Shannon was at ski school, and Shannon and I entertained ourselves at night by visiting Mom in the hospital and eating out.

On the chairlift, I tried to explain to my friends the misfortune I was experiencing. The talk was heavy, as I explained the illness and its effect on me. In a way, this was war, and our discussions were helping me prepare for battle. To say my friends were supportive is a huge understatement. Their outpouring of compassion was overwhelming and formed a foundation of hope that I still fall back on today. They provided me with a distraction and shared my selfish desire to ski until I dropped. The doctors had said I would probably never ski again or, at best, I might ski but in a diminished capacity. I was crushed by the thought and hell-bent for skiing every possible minute.

The week became a pattern of jokes and tears on the chairlift followed by the rush of a pack of skiers bombing down the slopes, leaving behind deep grooves in the snow and less experienced skiers standing with their mouths wide open. My situation seemed to inspire all of our friends and I could see them putting their own lives into perspective. Bickering fell by the wayside and everyone seemed to have more fun as a family. The combination of how the week unfolded and the thought of skiing deep untracked snow in western Canada kept me going through the holidays.

Years ago I had the good fortune to discover a ski area in British Columbia called Whistler/Blackcomb, by far the finest ski resort in this hemisphere. Wayne Wong, a good friend and a great ski champion, had often spoken about heli-skiing in British Columbia and suggested we come out there to test it firsthand. This would be our gang's 10th annual Whistler heli-ski get-away and no brain surgery was going to keep me from going!

On New Year's Eve, I didn't feel as if I had much to celebrate so I stayed in our condo and enjoyed quality time with Shannon. After dinner that night, I stood alone and stared out the window watching the lights of the snow-grooming machines going up and down the slopes I had torn up all week. My thoughts revolved around the monster in my brain that had plunged my life into an abyss. Standing in this familiar place, I thought of Sue. She was my greatest gift and skiing had brought us together. If she hadn't been with me, I might have made another choice, one with more immediate fatal consequences.

My thoughts wandered to the well-wishers from all spheres of my life. It was hard to believe how many people's lives I had touched. If it weren't for this tragic turn of fate, I would never have realized it. The effort people put into contacting me touched me more than their words. That winter's night in the mountains stirred something deep inside me. I knew that some day my thanks and gratitude would reach every single person who took the time to wish me well—but first I had to survive.

The question of death was coming up often. When friends and relatives probed, my answer—"I don't know"—left me numb and empty. Time was becoming a blur. Shannon was back in school, and we made an extra effort to keep our daily routine normal. A smart 6-year-old is very perceptive, however, and the strain Sue and I were living under manifested itself in our behavior. I promised Sue that death was not an option. At times, however, it just didn't work; the pressure was too much. God, how I wished the nightmare would end!

The days of transition at work with the divestiture of responsibility became harder and harder. Giving up all that I worked so hard to create was a painful process. My clients and co-workers inevitably scheduled appointments or arranged property tours for dates I could not keep. I tried to come up with excuses for not being available, but could not hide the truth any longer. Everyone had to face the reality that this was an extended leave of absence with no return date scheduled. After spending several days tying up loose ends at the office, I emptied my desk and quietly left by the back stairs. The thought of having to say goodbye was more than I could bear, and I didn't want anyone to see me cry! As I walked down the staircase, tears ripped through me like a river in springtime. I was trembling and mumbling to myself, "Where am I going, where am I going?"

From January 10th on, I skied like there was no tomorrow. It was the only thing that kept me from losing my mind. Most people who have aneurysms, AVMs or tumors don't have much time to consider their misfortune. They have a seizure or hemorrhage and the next thing they know they are in the hospital. If it's a tumor, it is usually only a matter of two or three days before they are on the operating table, not much time to comprehend what is going to happen to them. Head trauma is the one injury that damages the spirit as well as the body. Most people incur brain trauma as the result of an accident; the person is quickly disabled and repaired shortly after the event. I was not that lucky—there was time to think about it. A sudden blow doesn't allow the patient to experience the psychological trauma, compared to someone who enters the hospital seemingly normal and healthy and, if he survives as I planned to, leaves with neurological impairments.

As I child, I used to think it would be glorious to be a soldier preparing to fight a battle. Now I know what it must be like lying in a foxhole waiting to be attacked. Or to be an inmate on death row waiting for the day of execution—no place to hide, no sanctuary to survive the inevitable. There is no glory in death, whether it comes in battle, retribution or illness. However death comes, it is a personal battle with a foe you can't see. The only weapon you have is your own spirit and courage. These weapons cannot be given; you have to conjure them up from within. These were the things I had to deal with, unlike the lucky ones who are the victims of quick deaths. They don't have enough time to think about their fate, to become really frightened. No time to plan for all the things that could go wrong and decide how to handle those situations for the well-being of your family and yourself, if you survive.

Every day I had to develop a strategy that allowed me to function mentally. Since deciding on surgery, denial fueled my belief that I could beat this, no sweat. My attitude, mixed with the ambiguity of the doctors about the deficits of surgery and the chances of survival, allowed me to minimize the truth. I was playing games with myself, hiding from reality. Deep down, I knew that this was for real, but I did not want to look at it. What defense did I have besides gut instinct? Do skills exist for this type of experience? The doctors had them, or so I trusted. But questions still remained. Was their diagnosis right? Should I seek other opinions? It boggles the mind when questions come at you faster than answers. I asked questions of any doctor or hospital technician who might have an answer. When that didn't satisfy me, I asked family and friends. Communicating my thoughts became one of the methods that gave me comfort.

I immersed myself in music; there was something soothing about it. The great rock-and-rollers, the blues guitarists and Bob Marley's music became important coping mechanisms. Marley's "Legend" album seemed most appropriate. The whole damn album hit all my emotions. I played it hundreds of times whenever fear overwhelmed me. The beautiful instrumentals of Eric Clapton and Stevie Ray Vaughn took my mind to faraway places where I could almost forget my fears and troubles. One of my fantasies is to play the guitar like either of those music legends. Listening to their music helped me sort out my feelings and deal with my emotions.

Weekends were the most fun. I skied with all my friends until exhaustion set in, then headed for the condo to take a nap. When I woke up, I would head to the ski-tuning room and go to work on my skis. I am very particular about my equipment. In New England the trails are icy and rocky because of the limited snowfall and conditions are generally hardpack snow, a result of the snowmaking equipment. The consistency of man-made snow is much denser than natural snow and ski conditions are fast. When you reach a certain ability level, equipment must be in top condition, which requires constant attention and hours of preparation on the bottoms and edges of your skis.

I ski a giant slalom style, fast and strong. Slower skiers who sometimes get in the way and force you to make quick decisions are a real problem. Usually the choice is to slip through a slot between the skier and the edge of the trail. This is a high-risk decision: If you fall, you will go into the woods and wrap yourself around a tree. At the speeds my friends and I ski, this means almost certain death. The combination of icy trails and high-speed skiing is a lethal combination. Trails seem to have become as crowded as city streets during rush hour, which has forced us onto the mountain earlier and off by 1:30 in the afternoon. It's normal for us to get in 20 or more runs during this time frame. Around 2 p.m. we pick up our children from the race program and we all ski the mountain for an hour or so, a great way of spending quality time with the kids.

I skied hard and fast trying to build up my strength for heli-skiing in Whistler, but I also knew that a well-conditioned heart in a well-conditioned body would make me strong enough to fight for my life. In the old days, my sister, Pam, a great skier in her own right, called it Bulgarian race training. Ski hard, play hard and party harder. And believe me, I did all three—why not, I had nothing to lose. December sped by like a Santa Ana wind and January wasn't any different. Skiing at Waterville Valley was becoming boring, the challenge was dwindling. But, as with any good addiction, I could not stop. Whether it was 90 degrees below zero or raining like a monsoon, nothing could keep me from skiing. All I could think about was that this was the last year I could ski for the rest of my life.

The departure date for Whistler was getting close. Robert Mann, Ross Hamlin, Ethan Thurman, Chris DuPont, Eric Prime and I were all going. Back home, we hired a nanny, Katherine, to help out around the house. This made it possible for Sue to stay in bed, the house could run in a somewhat normal fashion, and I was able to get ready for the big heli-trip.

Chapter 5

Deciding on which skis to take to Whistler/Blackcomb is always difficult. Conditions can be anything from 300cm of light powder to Sierra cement. That year Dynamic Skis had provided me with an all-terrain ski. I decided to take two pairs, one pair for my buddy Denis in Vancouver and one for me. I also packed the .olkl P9 GS 210cm skis designed for terminal velocity skiing. The skier usually will chicken out before the ski loses its stability—the reason for the expression "terminal velocity." The third pair was a shorter Dynamic GS ski in a 205cm length chosen especially to ski Sudan. At the very top of Blackcomb, there is a peak called Sudan with a vertical incline of about 45 to 50 degrees, a very tough trail to ski. It was named for Silvan Sudan, who has skied the impossible chutes and slides all over the world and was the first to ski this peak. He designated the trail the first double black diamond in North America.

Several years ago my friends and I went to Blackcomb with nothing but GS 210cm skis. One day we decided to take a look down Sudan. There were about 20 people staring down it trying to muster up the courage to step off the edge. Being somewhat of a show-off, I dropped in. Freefalling between each turn, I was getting tossed between the huge jagged moguls and the 50-degree pitch because of my stiff 210cm skis. The run was becoming a difficult task, but not an impossible one! Down I dropped at 32 feet per second, right jump turn, edges dig in, then jump, freefall and left turn. For more than 800 feet I arced my long boards and threw myself down the mountain. When I stopped at the bottom and looked back, out of breath and glad to be alive, all but one of my friends had followed me. With that run in mind, I decided to take the third pair of shorter GS skis.

Sue gave me one last lecture about not trying anything too crazy. She instructed me to give her regards to everyone and to come home in one piece. Then she made me to promise to come home! I promised, knowing that once I was at Whistler/Blackcomb, it was the mountain and me, and I did not care who won. Then she reminded me that the birth of our son was only two months away and that I was not only loved but very much needed. It was a moment of truth, a time when I deeply felt the love in our family and knew that my promise to come home must be kept.

The night before the trip, I lay awake, thinking about chest-deep snow, the pristine beauty of the alpine and three weeks of skiing. The anticipation of going out to British Columbia helped me forget the bad news from the doctors. I could hardly wait to rekindle ties with Denis and Shauna Vincent, and with Ken Hardy, the proprietor of Whistler Heliski. I had met Denis, a dentist in Vancouver, five years ago while we were both heli-skiing. Shauna and Sue are the two prettiest women in the world and they happen to be great skiers—the only women we invite to heli-ski with us. Denis and Shauna planned to meet my friend Ross and myself at the airport in Vancouver. Then the four of us would pile into Denis' new Pathfinder with a ton of ski gear and head north.

Next morning I kissed Sue good-bye, slipped into Shannon's room to whisper good-bye, and left for Logan airport. It takes three hours to fly to Salt Lake City, Utah, where I had to change planes and fly a couple of hours to Portland, Oregon, then fly another hour and a half to Vancouver. Add on time to get through customs and this makes for a long trip with lots of time to think. And thinking was a dangerous pastime for me. On the plane, words from my meeting with Dr. Crowell and from conversations with Dr. Karen flashed through my head. I tried to analyze all the information I had received about AVMs. I had learned how to fight for my life by staying busy, but the plane gave me idle time to think. The fact was that I looked the picture of health on the outside and was afflicted with a rare neurovascular disorder on the inside. I still had to accept that fact.

The unusual thing was the pain I felt in my soul. Hopelessness was prevalent in my thoughts. I had lost control of my life. I was holding a first-class ticket to a destination unknown. In order to live, I had to sacrifice neurological functions and activities. I finally escaped my anxiety by reliving a day Denis and I were treated to a special trip with Ken and the helicopter pilot, up in the alpine alone and at no expense. One day in 1989 Ken called near the end of a ski vacation at Whistler/Blackcomb and asked if I wanted to go bushwhacking, his expression for exploring the alpine. When I arrived at the Powder Hut, Denis was already there, along with a group of Japanese skiers. We all crowded onto a bus and Ken drove us to the heli-pad. I assumed we were skiing with the Japanese group and that I was the second guide.

When we arrived at the heli-pad and started unloading our gear, Ken asked Denis and I to stay seated. Confusion must have shown on our faces because he chuckled to himself as we drove away. We pulled into a logging depot where all we could see was a blue metal building and stacks of logs. Ken unloaded the skis and safety pack, then gestured for us to grab our gear and enter the metal building. Inside was a blue-and-white Baby Bell Jet Ranger. The pilot was opening the main doors of the building and asked us to push the chopper out onto the heli-pad. Then it dawned on Denis and me that we were being treated to a day up in the glacier with Ken and 18 inches of new snow on a clear blue day. I was in heaven! Denis and I were very proud because it meant Ken had confidence in our abilities and judgment.

The weather was perfect, the sky a crystal-clear blue, temperatures in the low 20s, which would keep the snow light and fluffy. Flying in the little Bell is very different from a 206 Bell. Most people know the 206 as a Huey from the Vietnam War. The Baby Bell is a smaller machine easily tossed by the wind. The little chopper climbed up the face of Blackcomb, then slowly turned left and headed northwest to an area called Rainbow, a rolling, mountainous region above the tree line. At the drop-off, the elevation is about 7,000 feet, an altitude easy to deal with since there is no difficulty breathing at that height. The flight in takes approximately 20 to 30 minutes flying at 150 knots, which translates to about 40 miles. The weather in British Columbia is a lot like New England's—it changes so rapidly it is wise to be vigilant and prepared. The plan is always the same: If the weather turns bad, park the chopper and build a snow cave to sit out the storm. The guide carries everything you need to stay in the outback for a short time. The guide's pack weighs about 40 pounds and contains a shovel, survival blankets, tools, saw, first aid kit, spare radio, some food, a little camping stove, avalanche test kit, rope, compass, socks and matches. Enough to keep you comfortable as long as you have some experience in survival in the woods.

Denis and I were pumped up with the thought of skiing the outback without several other people trying to be the first one to break tracks on a virgin slope. When we reached the Rainbow area, Ken instructed us that we would start skiing about 1,000 feet above the tree line and ski down to the trees. Once there, we would split up and ski down another 2,500 to 3,000 feet down to a clear-cut area. As the pilot descended to the peak Ken had picked out, the wind began to blow. We had dropped to about 20 feet from the landing area when a gust of wind hit the chopper and blew us off the peak. The helicopter pilots are experts: Most of them flew in Vietnam or in the bush in Alaska and the Northwest Territories. The pilot made one more pass at the drop-off with no success. Prudence dictated that we scratch this landing area.

Ken indicated to the pilot to land on a peak over to the right where it looked as if there was less wind. That was a comforting thought, but when we saw the landing area we looked at each other in disbelief. A landing zone is about 50 feet in diameter. This one was only 20 feet wide at the most. The helicopter skids would take up most of that space, leaving Denis, Ken and me only enough room to huddle together once we landed. If we moved a couple of feet either way, we would fall over the edge of the mountain or get chopped up by the rear rotor blade.

We knew the routine for getting out of the chopper: First the guide jumps out of the co-pilot's seat and opens the rear door for the skiers. Then he places the backpack in a location safe from the blades. We jump out, keeping our heads down, and huddle on our knees around the backpack until the guide removes the equipment from the basket attached to the skids. Someone is then responsible for closing the door and signaling the pilot that everyone is out and clear of the chopper's skids. Then the guide gives the pilot the thumbs-up signal and away he goes.

The three of us were alone. In the silence of the mountains, I could hear the sound of the transceivers we all wear in case we are buried by an avalanche. This device is a little larger than a pack of cigarettes and has an earpiece built into the on/off switch. The switch has three settings—one is on, two is transmit and three is receive. Peep, peep, peep—the faint sound is a reminder of the danger we faced. It's reassuring to know that the equipment can save your life, but disheartening to think about avalanches. We were going to ski below the tree line, however, where the risk of an avalanche is minimal. Ken quickly checked the snow pack to be extra sure and then gave us our instructions. He pointed us toward a snow-covered peak in the distance, telling us to ski in that direction for about 2,000 vertical feet, then go right for a couple of hundred feet, and then descend to around the 2,100-foot elevation.

"When you reach the clear-cut, you will see the helicopter has landed on a work road on the valley floor. Once there, you can ski down to the helicopter."

Ken skied off to the left and disappeared into the tree line. Denis and I looked at each other in disbelief. We could hardly believe he had left us alone up in the alpine—to be trusted alone is a major vote of confidence from Ken. As Ken disappeared, I let out a loud "Yeah!" and took off through the trees with Denis hot on my heels. The knee-deep snow was light as a feather and we cranked out short symmetrical turns. The pitch became steeper and we started using the trees as slalom gates. As we descended, the snow deepened and the snow wells around the trees were wide enough to bank turns around, the way a skateboarder banks turns on a half-pipe. It is awesome skiing in these conditions—your heart rate elevates, adrenaline starts pumping, excitement builds. You have a sense of weightlessness and the temptation to ski non-stop is overwhelming, but Ken had instructed us to make frequent stops to check our location.

In the middle of a deep cloud of snow, I heard Ken trying to make radio contact. The trees were closing in and I stopped with Denis right behind me. I keyed the microphone and returned Ken's call. He warned us to stay out of the snow wells because they could collapse and bury us alive. The other information he relayed was to watch out for the ravine because it was possible to collapse the snow pack and fall into a stream. Then he signed out. I didn't have the heart to tell him that we were about 200 feet farther down the mountain than he was and had just skied the ravine he was talking about. Our excitement had affected our judgement, which is easy to do, exactly what he was warning us about.

Denis took the lead and we started to work over to the right as instructed. After a hundred yards, Denis took a sharp turn left and continued to descend. His turns were perfect, kicking up a light spray of snow. Tracks in the snow were the only evidence of his presence. Before I realized how far we had descended, the trees ended and we found ourselves on the edge of the clear-cut. Ken was standing 300 feet to our left and the helicopter was another 1,000 feet lower, resting on a work road. In front of us were six-foot moguls about 10 to 15 feet apart all over the clear-cut, obviously tree stumps. It was a real temptation to ski up and down these bumps, over the edges and sides. The top half of the clear-cut was in the shade and the chopper sat another 200 feet down in the sun. The pilot radioed up saying that he could see all three of us. I called Ken and asked whether it was safe to ski over the bumps. He keyed his mike once, then took off. If you have worked with a radio, you know that means yes!

Denis and I took off toward the little chopper, going up the bumps and jumping off the backside. As I approached the shadow line, I heard the pilot say something over the radio but I could not distinguish his words. I crossed the shadow line and realized too late that the snow was heavy and wet from the sun. No sooner did I hit the sunlit area when my skis came to a sudden stop and I was tossed head over heels over the tips of my skis, doing a complete flip in the air. When I stopped tumbling, my goggles were full of snow and I could hear the pilot laughing on the radio. Apparently he knew we were going to crash when we hit the shadow line; the three of us suffered the same fate. The laugh was on us and we knew it. Once we had collected ourselves and skied the rest of the way down to the helicopter, we piled into the little bird and repeated the run four times.

Stirring from my daydreams, I saw we were flying over the mountains of Utah under the cumulus clouds that generate the world-famous Utah powder. My ski memories are filled with emotion that brings them back to life. I had three more hours of flying before arriving in Vancouver and wondered if I would ever experience that type of skiing again. The passion for the freedom and exhilaration I got from this sport was unique in my experience. I thought about the future and asked myself why. Why was I faced with losing my sight and health? I was a man full of ambition, courage and desires—why was my life coming apart?

Suddenly a recollection of an event eight years earlier leaped into my mind and a cold chill ran through me. In 1983 our receptionist at work, Jane Jacobs, asked me if I would give her a photocopy of my handprint so that her daughter could read my palm. Nancy, her daughter, told fortunes and read Tarot cards. After some prodding, I decided to humor Jane and gave her photocopies of my right and left palms. She sent them to Nancy, who lives in the Virgin Islands. A few months later, Jane informed me that Nancy had read the photocopies of my palm and was coming home to Boston for a visit and would like to read my palm over lunch.

The luncheon date arrived and I asked Sue to join us. I needed her encouragement! We walked over to the Café Rouge in the old Statler Hotel to meet Jane and Nancy. Once we placed our orders, I asked Nancy what she thought of my palm prints. She asked me to hold out my hands, palms up. The reading involved talking about my past, which was easy for her to know about. Then she mentioned that we would have a second child and since Sue was then pregnant with our first child, we asked if it was a boy. Nancy replied no, but that our second child would be a boy. She went on to say that I would have a tragedy in my life and a change in careers. This I found troubling and asked Nancy for specifics. All she would say was that I would have a tragedy in my family. It might be a relative or it might be me. She couldn't be more specific than that, but she felt that everything would turn out all right. I asked Nancy when this would happen. She replied, "Within your late 30s,"—at the time, seven years away. I was stilled dazed when the plane landed in Vancouver. The chill of my recollection had not worn off and I wondered whether Nancy's prediction was coming true.

Going through Canadian Customs is always a breeze, especially when you are carrying skis and declare Whistler/Blackcomb as your destination. Once through customs, I ran right into Ross, who had been there about an hour but had not seen Denis or Shauna. Not to my surprise, Denis was running a little late. When he finally arrived at the airport, I knew Sue had called him. The look in his eyes said it all. Later, when we saw Ken at Whistler Heliski, I realized Sue had spoken to him too. He was more guarded than Denis, but focused more attention than usual my way. Denis and Ken were two of my closest friends and the unspoken news between us strengthened our bond.

Denis and Shauna's brand-new black vehicle was a little small for the four of us. Ross and I had seven pairs of skis, three duffel bags and two pairs of boots between us. Denis and Shauna had an equal number of duffel bags and all the food for the three weeks. The packing job was an engineering marvel as skis and duffels were lashed onto the roof and the rest of the gear packed all around us. If we crashed, we would be saved by the luggage.

The road to Whistler is rough. In the early '70s, the road was a two-lane dirt road with hardly anything on the side of the road but wilderness. Since then, it has been upgraded to a four-lane highway with some short narrow sections. Every year the highway is either under construction or a portion of the road has been washed away by floods and slides. This year wasn't any different. We had to sit on the side of the road for a half-hour while rubble was bulldozed away from a slide. It began to rain about an hour out of Vancouver, normal for that region. The Northwest is a cold rainforest and when the warm Pacific trade winds blow in off the water and meet the cold arctic air, it rains. Every year Denis would say, "Too bad you didn't come two weeks ago. It snowed a bunch then." Usually we got a little of everything—rain, snow, fog, sleet—you name it, we ski it.

There are only two people in the world I know who will ski in any condition, no matter how wet and wild. My friend Robert Mann and occasionally Ross will tough out the bad weather, but when it gets really unbearable, it ends up being Robert and me. In the blizzard of 1978, it was blowing 40 mph, the snow was waist deep and heavy, and there was lightning and thunder all around. The only people skiing on Mt. Tecumseh at Waterville Valley that day were the ski patrol, Robert and I. It was so difficult to endure the elements that management decided to close the mountain and was looking for volunteers to sweep the trails before they closed the lifts. Naturally I volunteered. The visibility was less than 5 feet and Bill Cushing, head of the ski patrol, ordered us to rope ourselves together in pairs. If one skier fell, the other would know where to look for his partner.

As we drove closer to Whistler/Blackcomb, the weather forecast for the week did not look promising. Eventually the conversation got around to talking about my illness and I faced the usual barrage of questions. Denis, with his medical background, tried to minimize the risk of surgery. I could see the familiar look in his eyes—the look of pity or, as I called it, the "poor guy" look. A few weeks earlier, I had met a patient in the pre-admission lab area who was facing the amputation of his legs in order to stay alive. His heart was so weak that they couldn't operate on it. Amputating his legs would ease the stress on the heart. We talked about how tough it was going to be with no legs. When he got around to reciprocal questions and I responded with arteriovenous malformations, all he could say was, "Oh, I'm sorry." Shauna sensed my depression and said, "Hey, enough of that, we're here to cheer you up and have fun."

We pulled into the village at Whistler, met the real estate agent with the keys and got directions to the condo. We always get a place on the edge of the trail so we can ski in and ski out. Our motto is "Ski until you drop." The condo had a hot tub on the balcony looking across the village. The trail was about 50 feet to the left of our front door. The unit had three bedrooms, a big kitchen, living room and dining room. As the guys know, I tend to snore—the last to arrive would be the lucky one who had to share a room with me. With little wasted time, we unpacked and loaded up the kitchen with the supplies we had brought.

Robert Mann showed up a few hours later, and then Ethan Thurman, Eric Prime and Chris Dupont. We immediately sat down to party. The doctors had given me some pills to help prevent headaches—you should not drink while taking them. Yahoo! After one or two vodkas, I was in a partying mood. Most of the conversation revolved around our hope that the weather would clear up or get colder and turn the rain into snow. We connected with Ken about 9 o'clock that evening and had dinner at a new restaurant that he liked, a fancy place attached to the new five-star Le Chamois. We had a table for 10 and it did get a little rowdy when Ken's friend Tony the real estate entrepreneur arrived. He has more jokes than Rodney Dangerfield. Come to think about it, they were Rodney's jokes. We all drank too much wine and became a little boisterous, but it was all good fun. The evening was a release for me. For the first time in months, I was not constantly reminded of my illness. There was no barrage of questions, no poor-guy looks or expressions of sympathy. All but a few of the people there knew about my illness, and those who did were working hard at making me forget.

Chapter 6

The first day of skiing wasn't all that good. Rain had fallen during the night and low-level clouds socked in the helicopter. "No flying," was the word we got from Ken every morning for the next five days. Finally, on day six, we got a break in the weather—it was clear in the alpine and we were going to fly. We felt like a company of airborne rangers or the 10th Mountain Division getting ready for a firefight, full of energy and feeling strong. We checked over our gear, which included streamers for the skis—to find them in the snow in case we fell—and transceivers in case an avalanche buried us.

Our pilot, Tim, was a Kiwi who had flown thousands of hours in the bush, in the deserts of North Africa, and in the mountains of Canada. In the summer Tim and his helicopter fight fires, work for surveyors and timber companies, and log hundreds of hours flying in the most difficult conditions. Today's weather would challenge Tim at every landing zone (LZ) and every pickup. The winds were strong and the new snow made judging the LZs difficult. To make a safe landing spot, Tim might have to tamp the LZ with the skids of the chopper by lifting the helicopter up off the snow and then coming down several times. At our first LZ, Tim took a first pass and then settled the bird in for the dropoff. Unloading was quick and followed our safety instructions. Then Tim gently lifted the big chopper up above us, slid to the right and down the face of the peak. I looked down on the rotors as he swooped away, an awesome sight when added to the view from this 10,000-foot peak.

The wind was blowing hard and conditions looked tough, so Ken decided to dig a profile pit to check for avalanche conditions. He asked whether I wanted to go over the edge with him to dig the pit. As we skied over the edge, I recalled the advice of the doctors and wondered if what I was about to do was dangerous, then realized that just walking around was dangerous for me. A few hundred feet down the slope of the mountain, Ken stopped and took off his pack. He pulled out a collapsible shovel and started to dig. I felt I had to contribute to the effort and asked if I could dig for a while. Ken handed me the shovel and I happily started to heave snow out of the 3-foot-deep hole. When the hole was deep enough, I relinquished the shovel and watched as Ken carried out the tests. The objective is to measure the levels of crystal formation that make up the different levels of snow. The snow on the ground, or snow pack, is the result of snowstorms that fall over the winter. Each level of the snow pack is a distinct layer, so each level is measured and the temperature taken. Ken carefully read the data off to me and I made entries in his log. Then Ken scraped snow from the different layers and dropped it onto a special graph resembling a mirror with crisscross lines on it. He was looking for the layer with ice crystals that are sheered off or laying flat instead of standing upright. That layer is likely to slide and cause an avalanche. The deeper down the layer is, the greater the probability of an avalanche. Once the layers were identified, Ken decided the layer of instability was close to the surface, which meant the snow pack was fairly safe. The whole task took about 45 minutes. Then Ken turned to me and said, "Seeing how much you like to help, you can fill in the hole."

Ski conditions were less than ideal. The snow was wind-packed with a 1- to 2-inch crust over drier snow, but no one seemed to care—we were heli-skiing! Almost everyone took at least one major fall and it was beginning to look like a demolition derby on skis. After two runs, we considered another area where conditions with a different exposure might offer better skiing. Shutter glacier looked as bad, but we went in for a run anyway. The wind was blowing about 20 mph as we flew in close to the peak to get a sense of the wind direction. A gust caught the rotors and bounced us left with a sudden jerk, making everyone gasp. Tim made a second approach successfully. This was our final run—snow conditions were hazardous and everyone crashed and burned. It's a good thing we all enjoy adversity; otherwise I think everyone would have left after the first day of heli-skiing.

Early next morning, Ken called to say the weather report looked good—the temperature was dropping. We decided to head to Iago glacier, which has some steep pitches in its slides and chutes. At our level of ability, the steeper the better. There was broken cloud cover with plumes of cumulus-nimbus clouds and a backdrop the bright blue of an unpolluted atmosphere. I was carrying one of Ken's radios, an indication that I was going to have a special experience. If I was going to die by avalanche or hemorrhage, today was a good day for it.

We collected our gear and met Ken at the heli-pad where we split into two groups. My group went first and up to Iago glacier we went, looking for a suitable LZ. The chopper settled gently into the snow. First out of the helicopter, Ken grabbed the pack and placed it in the safe zone. Familiar with the routine, our group silently unloaded and huddled around the pack. Skis were emptied from the basket on the right skid; I closed and locked the side door. Ken pantomimed the all-clear signal to the pilot and, with a blast of prop washes, the chopper lifted and slid effortlessly over the edge of the peak. Whoop, whoop, whoop—the pitch of the rotors caught the air. Within minutes, the sight and sound of the helicopter disappeared; it was so quiet I could hear my transceiver peep.

This LZ was about 200 square feet with steep cliffs in front and a ridge descending right and left. Our first thought was to get off the peak and gravitate toward an area with more room and less danger. Ken checked each skier's transceiver to ensure all were functioning properly. Then he radioed Tim, who was picking up group two, and described the snow conditions and the approximate route of our descent. He looked off into the breathtaking view and casually remarked how tough it was to struggle through a day at work, then smiled and said, "Just kidding!" and he skied off with eight of his disciples hot on his heels.

The first pitch was steeper than anything we had skied so far. Exposure to the sun dictates the conditions and we were in and out of shadows all the way to the bottom. We skied about 1,500 to 2,000 vertical feet and stopped on top of a rolling ridge. It was steep, but not steeper than the toughest trail at Waterville Valley. Ken looked at me and gestured to go first. As the guides always go first, I wasn't sure whether I was getting a compliment for my abilities or being used as a guinea pig. The initial turns were easy, but as I descended the run, the snow started to get heavy and then I hit the crust. Have you ever seen the cartoon of ski tracks splitting around a tree, with one ski going on either side? That's what my feet started to do and I couldn't stop. Before I could pull my skis together, I experienced a split. Ouch! I did a radical face plant and cut my nose on the ice. When I turned around, the whole group was having a laugh on me. I wasn't about to tell them how bad conditions were and waited to see if someone could do better. What I didn't count on was that Ken had followed me, and he never falls. The rest of the gang followed him and skied the whole run without a hitch. Naturally my companions could not resist reminding me that the doctors had asked me to take it easy and avoid Class 10 falls.

As we waited to be lifted to the top of the next run, we looked up at the slides and chutes that emptied into the natural bowl forming Iago glacier. We were looking for a steep slide with good exposure to the sun and wind. We hoped this would give us more powder than crud and a stability to provide some safety. Johnny, Ken's partner, and the other group had taken a second route farther down the ridge of the peak and radioed to Ken that the snow was dry all the way down and that there were some "nice pitches." We decided to try it. In a matter of minutes, we made our way down the ridge and reached the point where our tracks split with Johnny's. The route around the rock outcropping required a traverse across a snow bridge. It must have been 100 feet deep under our feet, with an endless view down into a snow well the size of a football stadium. When we reached the other side, we slipped around the rocks and found ourselves looking down a run that fell away into thin air. This was the nice little pitch Johnny had radioed about: The drop was about 30 degrees and, as it rolled over the edge, looked as if it slanted to 40 degrees. Ken gestured for me to ski down the left side alone while he went around to a gentler pitch with the others to see if it was OK for me to descend on the steeper line. My abilities were about to be tested and the whole group would be watching from below. The thought of taking a major wipeout twice in one morning was not my idea of a good show. Ken had demonstrated a lot of confidence in me, and skiing well was my pay back to him. I visualized my first few turns, set up the rhythm in my mind and started to see myself floating down. The crackle of the radio interrupted my concentration and I heard Ken calling, "Ken to Bill, Ken to Bill." I keyed the mike and asked if it was safe to start my run.

"Yes," Ken responded. "Stay to the right and away from the rock face to the left, because the slope rolls away like a basketball and the last half is really steep."

I began my descent. My skis started to float just under the surface of the light snow, making the turns easier but causing me to accelerate. The run was rolling over steeper and steeper. I kept looking at the crest in front of me, straining to see the rest of the group standing at the bottom. The run was getting steeper by the second and I started to make sharp-radius turns to slow down my speed. An expanse of snow like a glacier creates an illusion. The snow-white domain tends to camouflage the vastness of your surroundings. The snow was getting deeper, making it hard to see the crest of the slope. When I reached the edge, I realized that the trail was increasing in vertical pitch. Between turns I could see the group standing 1,000 feet below me—looking very small. I was carrying too much speed. The grade of the slope was about 40 degrees and getting steeper. My heart jumped into my throat, my legs were burning and the temptation to stop was overwhelming. I tried to check my speed. It was so steep I was dropping 3 to 4 feet between turns. The sensation of a free fall with every turn is exhilarating and the gang at the bottom cheered and encouraged me to keep going. The snow was so deep that I was skiing in a cloud. I began hop-turning, descending 10 feet with every turn, gravity in control of my destiny.

The gang below waved and screamed with excitement. Suddenly I realized the snow around me was sliding down the hill with me! I was skiing in an avalanche, small but safe, and it was carrying me to the bottom. I got a high like no other high—yaaahoooo! Three more turns and then I flawlessly skied a wild radical run to the bottom. A smile, bigger than the glacier, was across my face and I was totally out of breath, exhausted but proud. When Ken and the others asked me what it was like, all I could say was, "Can I do it again?" With a big smile Ken agreed, but first we had to break for lunch.

The post-lunch landing sequence was the same—group one would go first. Group two would start one peak closer to the glacier in open terrain. The best snow was where my group landed, with a 2,000-foot shadow at the base of a sheer rock cliff. Ken was well aware of the difficulty of this slope and, in his own polite way, was testing us. It helps him discover our strengths and weaknesses and that, in turn, allows us to ski on more difficult pitches.

In the afternoon I was nervous, not because of the next run but because of my head. All morning I had been building up a good sweat and overheating. This can cause my migraines to develop and all morning I was on the edge of getting an aura. I could tell that Ken was constantly monitoring me. Ken knew me well enough to know that I planned to live a normal life and do the same things I had done prior to the diagnosis of my AVM. He knew my taste for risks and thrills for the sport we both loved.

He allowed me to dig the pit, carry a radio and ski the best runs first. I would have done the same for him. If this was a last hurrah, then let's do it in style, on the steep and deep.

There we were, standing about 10 yards to the left of my tracks from the earlier descent. We all felt the bond of sharing an adventure with friends. For the next run, we decided to pair up and leave figure eights for tracks, the ultimate way to leave your mark in the alpine. Denis and I paired up. I wanted him to go first, since it was easier for me to adjust my turns to him rather than the other way around. I also wanted the extreme left because there was a good chance it was steeper than my first run and I knew what to expect. Denis didn't. If he had to bail out, I wanted to know where he was. A collision on that trail could be fatal if it caused a slide.

A sweat broke out on my forehead. I was paranoid about getting the aura and tried to take a few deep breaths to ease my anxiety. I knew Denis was excited, but I don't think he or anyone but Ken had the faintest idea of the challenge ahead. I looked at Denis. He looked at me. We were focused and tuned into each other. Without a word, he pushed off and turned left, then right, then left again. Then I pushed off and turned in sequence with Denis. He started to accelerate with every turn and I could see he was beginning to comprehend the severity of the pitch. He tried to slow his speed with a few check turns, overemphasizing the weight in the turn. To lessen his apprehension, I let out a scream of exhilaration and shouted, "Keep turning, stay with it, hold on!" We were in synchronization and the plumes of snow coming off our skis shimmered with the reflection of the light on the snow crystals. I could see the colors of the rainbow reflected in the spray of snow from Denis' turns. As the snow got deeper and the hill steeper, our turns slowly evolved to hop-turns and we did them in perfect unison. This was turning into a great run, one of those moments in your life that remain vivid in your memory forever.

We had descended about halfway and made about 50 turns when my legs started to ache and burn, my chest tightened and my breathing became labored. If this wasn't exhaustion but something else, I frankly didn't care. If God wanted me, he could take me now. This was my Heaven. If I were to hemorrhage, it would be appropriate for it to happen out on the glacier. We were almost to the end of the run when I noticed my hands were touching the side of the mountain on every turn. It was as steep as you can ski before you step off the edge of the earth and free fall through space. Although we were tired, we had to stay in synchronization. With only a few turns left, I yelled, "Turn, turn, and turn once more!" At the bottom, our lungs were heaving, trying to replenish the oxygen sucked out of us by our workout. I had not taken a breath for the last 50 yards and I was aching from my chest to my toes. We had accomplished a soul experience and lived a dream! I had to keep my goggles on because I was crying tears of joy and sadness.

In the background I could hear the low drone of the chopper. As I looked up, Robert and Ross were just completing the run and the rest of the gang was about halfway down. Each pair was catching face shots on every turn and screaming with approval. They all came up to us saying the same thing. "Wow! Was that steep!" Everyone except Ross, who was short of breath and laboring hard to regain oxygen. We heard the thump, thump of the helicopter as it dropped down from above. Tim was in a steep dive, heading right at us. About 50 feet off the deck, he leveled out and streaked over our heads. Whoosh, the sound of air ripped through the glacier, then the whoop, whoop of the blades reverberated around the mountains. After a week of wet weather and poor heli-skiing, these few runs made the whole trip worthwhile. Ken was bombarded with a chorus of requests to take us back to the top. Ross was still slumped over his poles, struggling for breath, but he nodded his head in approval for another run.

We skied down the flats to meet the bird. Ross slowly made his way to the LZ. Upon his arrival, he announced that he was having trouble breathing and had a pain in his chest. Someone jested that he had been holding his breath from the crest of the trail to the bottom because the trail was so steep it scared him. Then Ross announced that he had a pain in his left arm. Ken became alarmed. Ross was complaining of symptoms common to heart attack victims. His color was gray and he was having difficulty breathing. Without hesitation, Ken decided Ross was going to the Whistler Hospital. We loaded him into the chopper and Tim radioed ahead to the hospital announcing that he was flying in a possible heart attack victim. Still excited about the run, the rest of us were not focused on the potential seriousness of Ross' condition. I tried to break the tension and joked about the possibility of his distress being an anxiety attack. Ross cracked a smile but it was short-lived. Both Ross' father and grandfather had died of heart attacks at an early age. Unbeknownst to us, that morning a skier who had suffered a heart attack on the ski slopes had died at the hospital.

The second group was informed that the helicopter was flying Ross to the hospital and advised them to take their time getting down. Johnny radioed Ken and said the route they were taking was very difficult because the snow was heavy. It would take them awhile to get to the landing area. Within 10 minutes, Tim radioed to tell us that Ross was at the hospital and that he was coming back to pick us up. The group discussed the situation and wished to ski that steep run one more time before heading to the hospital. Within minutes we heard the familiar sound of the chopper in the distance. With skis and poles piled neatly to one side, the group huddled over the pack, braced for the prop wash that creates a small tornado as Tim settled the big machine down. The whole pickup process only takes a minute, maybe two. You cannot afford to leave the helicopter sitting on the ground for long—fuel is too precious to waste.

Up on the peak, the steep and deep beckons us to her in a way that is a mystery. No one knows what he will face and that adds to the excitement. I wondered if this was it, the last chance to ski the steep and deep forever. Staring out at the beautiful wilderness, I became lost in the peaceful loneliness of the majestic tranquility and began to cry. Ken and Chris must have picked up on my sadness and tears and asked if I was OK. I could only nod. Not wanting to leave the peak, I wondered if Heaven looked as beautiful. Then the radio crackled with Ken calling, "Billy, are you on the way, come back."

"Yes," I responded.

I pulled myself together and reunited with the group. They were all peering over the edge looking for a line. Without hesitation, I went to the far left and called Denis over.

"Right on," he said, "you go first!"

Without a word, we stepped out into the challenge of the hill and fell into a dream-like world of silence. The gentle swish of the snow following our turns sounded like gentle waves in the surf. A feeling of weightless overcame me. I could hear and feel the excitement Denis was experiencing behind me—we were skiing as one. I fought the temptation to stop, fearing that this would be the last opportunity to leave synchronized figure eights in the snow. Was this my last run on the glacier forever? Tears flowed down my cheeks. My goggles started to fog up. I closed my eyes and let the feeling of floating take over. The cold snow hit my face between turns, melting and running down my neck. I was lost in emotion and the freedom of the sport I love.

There was no excitement left in me after the run was over. The rest of the group was overjoyed from two awesome runs in deep powder on the steep vertical, but I was slipping into self-pity. Robert skied over and tried to cheer me up and Ken started to tell jokes. They all were happy and cheerful; I was sullen and withdrawn. I should have been smiling from ear to ear, but all I could think of was that the doctors had cautioned me that I might never ski again.

Tim informed us he was landing in two minute; we scrambled around to our positions for the pickup. Soon we were loaded and flying to the heli-pad above the Rendezvous Restaurant at the top of Blackcomb. The helicopter wobbled as the wind buffeted us on our descent to the top of the Jersey Cream Express Lift. Our next task was to ski all the way from the top of Blackcomb to our condo and then to the hospital to see Ross; we had just 10 minutes before visiting hours were over. It was possible to make it, but we would have to ski nonstop at full speed. Luckily, speed skiing is something we all enjoy because it pits our ability against the mountain.

Someone yelled, "Race ya!" and we were off like a stampede of buffalo at an average speed of 40 mph. Within minutes we were at the condo and grabbed Ross' wallet and some clothes. With little time to spare, we arrived at the hospital at the base of the mountain. We found Ross sitting on a gurney with a bunch of electrodes on his chest. The monitors and the IV bottle reminded me of what I might be doing in seven days. I told Ross that he had things mixed up—I was supposed to be the one in the hospital. It got a little smile out of his worried face. All of us wondered whether Ross was in serious peril or suffering from an anxiety attack. To our relief, we received a call from Ross later that evening informing us that he had experienced some kind of digestive spasm.

The best memories of the trip were of the ultimate steep and deep day of heli-skiing. Before we parted company, the whole gang went out to dinner. Jokes, wisecracks and good wishes were showered upon me in an attempt to lift my spirits. My farewell to friends and to the sport I loved brought on melancholy. Fear slowly began to well up in my soul. It was difficult to breathe—as if I had an elephant transferring his weight onto my chest. The whimsical thought of calling home to ask for a stay of execution so I could fulfill my wish to have a memorable week of ultimate powder skiing was tempting. One goal I had expected to achieve on this trip was to accumulate enough verticals to reach the 1,000,000 vertical feet club. Some of us were close and had over 800,000 vertical feet.

When Denis, Shauna and I left for Vancouver, there was a foot of new snow and it was still coming down. Driving was slow and difficult but Denis was determined to fulfill his promise to Sue—that I would be on the plane home on the designated day. I was hoping the highway to Vancouver would be impassable. Shauna sensed the conflict that raged within me and did her best to divert my thoughts.

We arrived in Vancouver and stayed overnight at a friend's condo. My flight home was scheduled for the afternoon of the following day, so I called Sue to inform her of my pending departure. On the drive to Vancouver, I had the feeling that Shauna and Denis had something on their minds. As I talked to Sue, I had the same nagging feeling. After 10 minutes on the phone, I asked if there was something wrong. She paused long enough for me to know something was up—the date for my surgery had been delayed a week. I thought my prayers had been answered! The impulse to get in the car and drive back to Whistler/Blackcomb was powerful, but I could hear the strain in Sue's voice as she said that the decision to stay another week was mine.

My wife was eight months pregnant. I had left her alone with Shannon and indulged myself enough. It was time to go home and face the music. Denis and Shauna had known about the delay and promised Sue not to inform me. I assured them that the next week, or should I say my last week, would be spent with Sue and Shannon. The reason it was hard to go straight home was that I no longer had any place to run. Being a husband and father meant sharing my fears and apprehensions with my family. I could delay no longer.

Shauna and Denis gave me a book, "Way of the Peaceful Warrior," by Dan Millman. According to the back cover, the book is based on the story of Millman, a world-champion athlete who is led toward a final confrontation that will deliver or destroy him. On the inside cover, Shauna wrote, "The winds of change are blowing, as though to test your spirit. May you find strength in knowing that we are very close at heart. Feel the wonder of life and remember the call of the glacier. With all our love, Shauna and Denis."

The flight to Portland was uneventful. I was occupied with my thoughts and wondered whether there was a Heaven. Was there an afterlife or would my soul wander the earth distressed and alone? Would I meet friends and relatives? Would my grandmother scold me for my impure thoughts and would my grandfather be disappointed in the ways of the '60s? Ghost stories came to mind—would my soul haunt my family because of my untimely death?

In Portland I had to either move fast to catch the next plane or remain in Portland for hours. Soon after takeoff, stories of near-death experiences ran through my head. Some people say that the spirit leaves the body and can look down on its own body. Then it floats through the air into darkness, where there is a far-away light at the end of a dark tunnel. The deceased person feels compelled to go to the light and on the way meets a loved one who leads him forward with soothing talk, encouraging him to accept the light. Some people have claimed they were about to see the face of God when they were suddenly revived by the doctors, only to find themselves back in the hospital.

Would I recognize the light? What if I resisted and clung to life? How would I know whether the light was the Light of God or the lights over the operating table? This was not the first time I had thought about this. In one of my conversations with Dr. Karen, I asked her to describe the lights in the operating room so that I could distinguish between them and the Light of God. She had laughed and said she would be there to lead me to the right light.

The book helped occupy my thoughts and I read for the first hour on the plane. The words on the pages were easy to read but difficult to comprehend. It was a vain effort to deflect my thoughts from my impending ordeal. I found myself daydreaming and trying to imagine the unimaginable. When it became impossible to focus on the book, I resumed my 1,000-mile gaze out into the heavens and imagined myself skiing through the clouds, like a free spirit without cares or worries.

In Boston, my brother was waiting to give me a ride home to Wayland. John looked healthy and happy, a barometer of the status of things on the home front. For the brief time that I was away, they were not constantly reminded of their anguish whenever they looked at me. In a strange way, my trip had been a relief to all of us. John said Sue was incredibly strong, and I replied, "She is my hero!" Sue had mustered up a strength so strong that we called her Gibraltar.

John, Pam, Mom and Dad all went out of their way to be with me during this dark period. But Sue was the one who walked through the days and nights with me.

Tangled in my mind were thoughts of how the prospect of death was forcing me to leave her with two children and a big mortgage. The death of a friend, a loved one, a husband or a child can be devastating to the ones left behind. In my case, anticipation of the loss placed a huge emotional burden on my family. Slowly I began to identify with Sue's pain and stress. She was eight months pregnant, looking after Shannon and the house, running a travel agency, all the while knowing her husband was facing two life-threatening surgeries. Fear and anxiety overwhelmed both of us.

Chapter 7

By the time I reached home, Shannon was asleep in her room and Sue was dozing in front of the TV, looking tranquil and at ease. I tried to sneak in and leave her undisturbed, but she woke up. I gave her a kiss and told her about the exciting days on the glacier. Then we talked about Shannon and considered what to tell her. Shannon knew I was sick and that there was something very wrong. We decided to address the issue during one of our usual dinner conversations, when TV or the radio did not distract her.

Next day I decided to pay a visit to Mom and Dad. There were problems I had to address with Dad and this was the best opportunity. We were planning a weekend trip to Waterville Valley, Monday was full, and I checked into the hospital on Tuesday. When I arrived at the house, Dad was still in his robe working the phones and Mom was at church praying for me, which was just as well. Mom wouldn't be able to remain composed during the conversation. I poured myself a cup of coffee and waited patiently for my chance to talk straight with Dad. When we finally sat down together, I told him I didn't know how I was going to manage everything. How would I pay my bills and fulfill my obligations? I wasn't sure whether Blue Cross/Blue Shield would cover my medical expenses. The stress on my father was obvious. Here was his grown son back at his feet as vulnerable as a young child. Although my Dad is supportive and filled with love for me, he has trouble showing it. As we talked, he assured me that his real estate company would take care of my bills. The company had a long-term disability policy and would place a claim as a means of meeting my financial responsibilities. The accounting office would be assigned to pay my bills and keep a record of payments. Sue would have power of attorney to cash any checks issued in my name.

I felt more secure after setting up the account, knowing that my bills would be covered, but I didn't like it. For the past 12 years I had been self-sufficient, earning my money the hard way. When you are paid on a performance basis, you tend to feel that you truly earn your money. You don't have that same feeling of accomplishment when you receive disability payments. But there was no other way to pay my bills—I would have to tolerate this insult to my pride. My ego was as big as my father's; I had been raised to succeed him. I drew strength from his ego in order to survive the sharks at work and in the world, but in the back of my mind I had always questioned myself about my accomplishments: Were they real or a result of being the boss's son?

I waited until Mom came home from church and gave her a hug and a kiss. The strain on her was all too evident. My Mom is a very emotional and loving lady who has suffered from depression from time to time. It is important for me to be strong for her. I noticed the time and excused myself because Shannon had to be picked up from school at 1:30. I thanked Dad for his help and support, told him I loved him and headed out the door.

I arrived at the bus stop on time and Shannon came tumbling out with a smile on her face. She gave me a big hug and a kiss and announced how glad she was to have me home. We drove up our road and bumped into the mailman leaving our house. He had brought letters and cards from friends and family who had heard about my illness. Reading them brought tears to my eyes. It was hard to hide them from Shannon and she asked why I was crying. It was time to have that talk with her—it would not wait for the dinner table. It took me a while to regain my composure because I had just read a thoughtful note from Senator Kennedy. I turned to Shannon and asked if she knew that Daddy was sick. She acknowledged she did, but added that she didn't know what was wrong. We talked openly and frankly. I told her that Daddy was born with too many veins in his head and that these veins caused headaches. She quickly said that she remembered the headaches. Then she asked a painful question, "Daddy, are you going to die?"

There she was, 6 years old, a beautiful blue-eyed little girl with blonde hair, asking if her Daddy was going to die. I took a deep breath and promised her, "No, not if I can help it! The doctors are going to operate on me to fix the bad veins in my brain," I explained. "The first operation will be on my right temple and the second on the back of my head. The first operation is easy and for now we should only worry about that one. "

Then Shannon said, "But Daddy, I'm afraid!" As best I could, I mustered up a big smile, gave her a strong hug and told her Daddy was going to be all right. I asked her to be a good girl and to help Mommy. She tried to be as mature as she knew how and said she loved me.

"I love you too, Shannon, and it is that love that will help me get better." I was astonished at the level of comprehension Shannon displayed. We spent the rest of the afternoon playing and horsing around the house. It was a bonus day, one I would have missed if I had selfishly stayed for another week of skiing.

That night in bed I felt dazed by all the details that needed to be addressed, details that normal people handle when they are in their '60s and '70s. I was 37—not the time of life to grant powers of attorney, prepare wills and discuss funeral arrangements. Especially when I felt so normal and healthy! It was extremely difficult to think about funeral arrangements, so I put that off. Sue and I planned to see our lawyer about the power of attorney on Monday. Tomorrow, Friday, we were headed to Waterville Valley for the last few days of skiing that year and maybe for the rest of my life.

As we drove north on I-93, I slipped in and out of tears every time I drove by a familiar landmark on the way to Waterville Valley, thinking of all the things I enjoyed. I tried to be strong for Shannon, but the closer we got to the north country, the faster memories flashed by. I have lived on the fast and exciting side of life. I have sailed the entire eastern seaboard many times, skied the highest peaks in the country, and scuba dived around sunken sailing ships. After a hurricane, I saved people in my 17-foot powerboat. I sailed through a whole gale while crossing the Gulf Stream 120 miles off the coast of South Carolina. Powerful accomplishments, but I felt cheated. This challenge was too large for me to beat. I could not see the opponent and had to trust others to do battle for me.

For now I had to stay in the moment and enjoy the few days I had left with Shannon and Sue, my sweet Sue. How she was holding up under this kind of pressure while eight months pregnant was amazing. I drew great emotional strength from Sue and showed her my weakest side. Sue was the one who had to deal with my emotional breakdowns. It was a confusing time and the stress was intense. I remembered a line from a Clint Eastwood movie, "The Outlaw Josie Wales." After Josie rescues an old Indian, Chief Dan George, he asks him how he is able to tolerate all the abuse from the bad characters in town. The old man uttered three words that to this day I repeat in an attempt to cope with all my problems. We Indians must "endeavor to persevere." Comforting words, I must endeavor to persevere!

As we reached our exit and drove the last 12 miles to the valley, I looked only as far as tomorrow and hoped for a good day of skiing. The more I skied prior to surgery, the better physical condition I would be in, which would improve my chances of surviving the surgery. I started to worry about my unborn son— would he inherit my birth defect? I could not handle the thought that he or Shannon might have to face the same ordeal. The doctors assured me, however, that there was no evidence to confirm that possibility. It sounded as if they were not 100 percent sure of their answer! After all, I was the 1 percent of the population with this AVM defect.

I skied from 8 o'clock in the morning to 3 in the afternoon each day. The skiing was good and I skied fast and hard, like a test pilot pushing the envelope, trying to defy gravity. I had nothing to lose. On Sunday, our skiing friends and I decided I should shave a message into my hair before surgery. After a passionate discussion, everyone agreed that I should find a barber to shave an arrow in my hair and the word "Up" next to it. I spent the last afternoon at Waterville Valley cleaning my skis and sharpening the edges. Although the probability of skiing again was pretty slim, I could not face that reality. Working on the skis gave me some comfort.

Sue suggested that we head home early on Sunday because the weather was bad and driving was going to be tough. There was little difficulty driving home, however, and the ride went by quickly. Sue and I were deep in conversation and Shannon was under the headphones of her Walkman. I told Sue I loved her and let her know I was scared. I had not asked the doctors about the specifics of the surgery and it was the unknown that I now feared. Dr. Crowell had given me a cursory overview of the procedure but failed to give me any real details. It was probably for the best—if I had fully comprehended the surgery I probably would not have had the courage to walk into Mass General.

When we got home I called Chuck Bass, owner of Rococo's salon, and asked if he would do the honors and cut my hair. I said I wanted to shave a message into my hair like some of the kids were doing. He laughed, probably thinking I would not do anything that outrageous. "Meet me at the shop on Tuesday early, say eight o'clock," he said.
I replied, "Be there on time."

Monday came and went so fast, I hardly remember any of it. That morning I had arranged to meet our attorney at my company's office to sign the power of attorney over to Sue. We reviewed my will with Sue so that she understood the intent. I gave her instructions to let me die if I did not do well in surgery and told her not to spend all our money keeping me alive on machines. We also spoke about being an organ donor and I left the decision up to her. I was nearing the day my life would change forever! My memory of what Sue and I did on Monday night is vivid in some areas, in others it is gray and fuzzy. Mainly we held each other tightly, swore our love for each other many times over, and both of us prayed for things to be different.

Chapter 8

Tuesday morning I awoke early, grabbed a travel mug, filled it with coffee and set out for Rococo's. Chuck, the owner, was making coffee in the back and we had the place to ourselves. He seemed nervous, so I struck up a conversation about the Red Sox and the recent trades they had announced. Chuck knew his baseball and relaxed a little. Still, he seemed stiff and I did not want him to cause any damage to my skull. I joked about being under the knife later, here I was just under the blade. He laughed and then I shared a moment of truth with him. I said I was ready mentally to face my fate and that he was helping instill some humor into a situation where there was little. At that, Chuck realized the importance of his task and we both smirked, thinking about the doctors laughing at what he was about to do.

Within a half-hour I had the word "UP" shaved into the right side of my head and a large arrow pointing to the location of the AVM. Chuck refused payment, saying payment would be my safe recovery from the operation. I reminded Chuck to think of a new expression for the second surgery. It would have to be pretty good to top this one and we needed both our heads to think of one. This was the beginning of a journey that would change my life and I was determined to do it with grace and humor. Walking out of Rococo's, I pledged that I would cherish every minute I was alive.

I was instructed to be at the hospital by 10 a.m., and it was already 8:30. When I returned to the house, Sue was on the phone to friends. She was trying to act normal but stress was evident in her stiff expression. While Sue dealt with the phones, I looked for a camera to take a picture of my haircut. Sue laughed when she stood back to look at my head. We smiled, hugged and kissed. Optimism was my best weapon. This was war and I wanted to win! I mustered up enough clarity and concentration to pack my bag for the hospital. In went pajamas and sweatpants for comfort and to avoid hospital gowns. Then in went the CD player along with my CDs. Sue ended the last phone call by hanging up on a solicitor trying to sell me life insurance, took a couple of pictures of my new look, and then it was off to the hospital.

As we stepped out the front door, Sue and I knew we were hours away from the beginning of a journey and neither one of us knew where it would take us. We held hands walking to the car. It was a beautiful February day, crystal-blue sky, crisp temperatures, a bright sun shining—oh, how I love winter. The snow and cold make me feel alive. I thought about skiing untracked powder and wondered if I would ever do it again. In the car, my mind was whirling like a tornado. It was hard to decipher recent thoughts, conversations and events. Both Susie and I had slept little last night and I started to feel empty, out of gas. November, when all of this craziness started, seemed ages ago. Time was up, the party was over, and reality hit me in the face. Back with my family after surgery, I would be different mentally, physically and spiritually. And no one could tell me just how different I would be. In all my conversations with the doctors, we always talked about recovery in time frames of six to nine months for each operation, maybe longer. Optimistically, I thought the whole ordeal would last one year.

During the ride to the hospital Sue and I were silent, holding hands. I cried, but my solid soldier sat next to me, steady and sure. Sue held fast to her inner strength, transferred to me through the touch of her hand, giving me courage to face the unknown. She knew her husband was almost certainly going to die or else be disabled, probably for life. She refused to think about the worst in order to stay healthy emotionally for Shannon and our expected child. Sue parked the car in the garage. I took a couple of deep breaths to regain my composure, looked at Sue and told her I loved her. We kissed and both of us stated that we would "endeavor to persevere." Then we fell into a long kiss and loving embrace. It was time to gather the courage that people thought I had and enter the hospital. Walking through the entrance, I felt cold and alone. For a moment, I felt like running back out the door, jumping into the car and driving away. "Please God," I muttered, "let me walk out that door someday soon."

The corridors were crowded with medical personnel, patients and their families. I felt invisible or as if I was in another dimension. We arrived at the admittance office, late as usual. The receptionist handed me a list, asking me to sign it and be seated. I was now officially part of the bureaucracy of the hospital, another faceless patient for the administrators to process. The surgeons and their assistants were the only ones who treated me as an individual, perhaps because they understood how critical my condition was. While we sat there, I joked with Sue that she should play 2222 in the lottery because it was February 22, I had two AVMs, and I was on the 22nd floor. The admittance nurse began reviewing a mountain of forms: admission forms, indemnity forms for the release of liability and surgical consent forms. After explaining all the risks and variables of the surgery, she asked me to sign the documents. As she handed me a pen, I thought, "What choice do I have?" Wishful thinking was not going to help me, but there was always the hope that a doctor would walk up to me and say, "Bill, there has been an awful mistake—you are OK. You will not need this surgery."

Sue and I went up to my room overlooking the Charles River. Flowers and good luck cards from co-workers and friends were everywhere. I was not in the room for more than a few minutes when Barbara Dunderdale, the head floor nurse, came in with her friendly smile to start reviewing procedures on the floor. Not long after, another nurse, Ann Geary, came in to introduce herself and start the first IV. Then Dr. Karen, who I called the Angel of Mercy, arrived to check on me. I kidded her about taking time from her orthopedic duties to visit with a "neuro" case. She replied that she was there to make sure I walked to the right light.

By 3 o'clock Dad arrived and the phone started to ring with calls from my sister, Pam, and her husband, Kevin, along with a dozen or so family members and friends, all wishing me luck. Nurses were coming in for routine medical data, checking my blood pressure, hooking up intravenous needles, and taking fluid counts while a lab technician started taking more blood than I thought necessary. The hours flew by and soon the ladies from the kitchen were asking me to fill out the order forms for the evening meal—which felt like my Last Supper. The hospital has the system worked out so that medical personnel are not hovering around you when the fine gourmet hospital cuisine arrives. Sue was given a dinner tray as well. Visiting hours were nearly over when Mom and my brother, John, arrived, accompanied by Monsignor MacNamara, who was visiting at the request of my Dad.

When the Monsignor walked into my room, I was confronted with a dilemma. I had not gone to church or confession in years. In the situation I was in, I didn't want to offend anyone, least of all God. The Monsignor was a very cool man from an old Boston family of "good Irish Catholic stock." Well respected, he was the past head of the Catholic Charities. I asked John and my folks to leave the room with Sue so that the Monsignor and I could talk. He asked when I last went to confession. Not a regular churchgoer, I was honest and told him about 10 years ago, maybe more. I didn't think I should lie, considering what lay ahead. I like to cover all my bases!

The Monsignor asked whether I was afraid and I said yes, very scared! Rambling, I told him that I was basically a good person and had not violated any serious sins. I was faithful to my wife, not a killer or a thief, maybe swore a little more than usual recently, but overall a good person. I told him I believed in Jesus and a higher power in the universe. I went on to say that I had faith in my will and spirit. I did not know in what condition I would survive, but I knew I would not die. I told him my spirit had the strength, determination and good moral character to triumph over adversity. And I had been praying for courage. I knew the strength of the spirit was a matter of believing in something bigger in the universe. He said that power was God and that we should pray to him. Then he took my confession and we said some prayers. Whenever I lost the words, the Monsignor refreshed my memory. When you grow up as a Catholic, you pretty much have the words engraved in your mind. I used to think that I would never feel religious, but it's better to be safe than sorry! From that day on, I felt strong emotions for Monsignor MacNamara. There is a quality about him that I like very much. I label it a feeling of safety. As he prayed, an acceptance came over me for the first time. The doctors had stated my condition as life or death—I couldn't lose sight of that fact. Whatever Monsignor MacNamara had to offer, I would take. From a practical viewpoint, his prayers would most likely be heard over mine.

My dinner was good but cold and I didn't eat much. My nerves were jumpy. Had I done something to offend God? The Monsignor had said no to that question. Did I believe in God? Frantic thoughts raced through my mind like a whirlwind. Confused and scared, I didn't want anyone to know it. I had to be brave—any weakness would invite failure and death. Inside I was a mess! I was too naive to realize how traumatic and profound this ordeal was going to be, especially on my family.

As I sat there on my bed engrossed in my thoughts, the first doctor came in to see me: Dr. Desanctis, a top-notch cardiologist. He was overseeing the big picture of my medical health and wanted to reassure me that the surgery was going to be a piece of cake. I liked Dr. Desanctis very much. He was a large man, over 6 feet tall, with a gentle smile and soothing manner. I thanked him for coming in and, as I did, another doctor entered, one I had not met before. He was in his 30s, with a slender build and brown wavy hair, wearing a white coat and dungarees. His nametag introduced him as "Schumacher, Jim, neurosurgeon." He breezed in with a self-confident smile, introduced himself as a resident under Dr. Crowell, and explained that he was assisting with my surgery. The conversation started with small talk and some past medical history. Soon I was asking him where he came from. He had noticed the ski poster on the wall that my sister had sent and remarked that he was from Idaho and also a skier. I made him promise to go skiing with me sometime when this ordeal was over. I promised to give him some skis if I made it. Then I asked him the one question I had neglected to ask, perhaps out of fear, but up until then I had felt that ignorance was bliss: "What are they going to do to me?"

Chapter 9

As the hour for my surgery grew near, I felt a need to know exactly what was going to be done to me. Dr. Schumacher explained the initial incision, and I realized that it was not going to be the small hole I had envisioned—I would be left with a large horseshoe-shaped scar over my right ear. The surgeons would cut the skullcap off, bore holes into my skull, break the skull into four pieces and remove the sections to expose the brain. Then, with microscopic instruments, they would carefully cut and cauterize all the veins, arteries and vessels that led to the AVM until it was completely excised from the brain. When that was accomplished and the AVM removed, they would wire the bone fragments into place, pull the skullcap back and close me up. Obviously this was a brief and layman's description of the surgery, but I got a clear picture. The surgery would take about six to eight hours. When I asked if there were any surprises or problems I would face after the surgery, Dr. Schumacher soothed my nerves and said the only repercussion would be a headache like no other hangover I had ever had. My instinct told me to trust him. The thought of putting up with a major headache was so straightforward that I felt more at ease. The mystery of my operation was out in the open. Dr. Schumacher finished his visit with more words of comfort and said he would see me bright and early in the morning. I realized that all these brilliant surgeons, with the exception of Dr. Crowell, the most critical member of the surgical team, were younger than me, not by one or two years but by five or more. I wasn't a kid anymore; I was close to 40 but felt like a teenager.

When Dad, Mom and John had left and Dr. Karen had gone to check on her patients, the nurses left Sue and me alone for the night. The night nurse showed us how to pull out the convert-a-bed from the couch and Sue started getting ready for bed. She was very pregnant with Flash and had problems with bleeding; her obstetrician had told her to spend the last month of her pregnancy in bed. Sue is a petite woman standing 5 feet tall and weighing 100 pounds dripping wet. She is very athletic and in good shape. With the present adversity in our lives, she proved her unwavering strength. Her strength gave me strength and we supported each other. It was too frightening to go through this alone. Sue was the reason I had to fight and live. Without Sue, I would not have subjected myself to the horrors or results of brain surgery.

I told Sue that if something happened to me, to listen to my Bob Marley's "Legend" CD. The words to "Is This Love" made me think of my wife and best friend. If I died, "No Woman No Cry" expressed how I wanted Sue to think about me. "Get Up Stand Up" encouraged me to be brave and strong and "Redemption Song" gave me hope against terrible odds. I wrote a note to my love, signed it, and decided to give it to her on the way to the operating room.

Sue, I love you. If anything happens to me, promise me you'll tell the children about me. Don't let them forget that I loved them very, very much. Please name the baby after me, he'll be the only namesake left for the Fallon clan. I feel a great sadness that I may never know him and that he may grow up without a father. Remember my request for an Irish wake. My favorite CD helped soothe me—please listen and try to understand how I feel.

Goodbye, your husband and love,

Bill

Lying in bed looking at my beautiful wife, I was afraid. Afraid of the unknown! Afraid of death and of what might lie on the other side of life. I remembered Sue's father. Sue and I were with him the day he died and I'll never forget our last conversation. In intensive care on a respirator, he could not talk so I told him about our wishes and dreams. He listened and then wrote a message to me on a notepad, "Will you take care of Sue?" And I said, "Yes, until the day I die!" That was a promise I intended to keep, but how could I now! All the legal documents and powers of attorney were transferred so that Sue would have financial resources at her discretion for herself and the kids, if necessary. But I knew her dad had meant more than watching out for her material well-being. My soul was in turmoil over the difficulty all this was going to cause my wife and children. I finally slipped into a restless sleep, but morning seemed to arrive moments after my last conscious thought. The night nurse gently woke me around 5 a.m. and handed me a bottle of sterile soap to wash my hair.

I went into the shower and washed my hair several times as instructed. Infection is a danger in brain surgery and I washed my hair again to be extra careful. When I emerged from the shower, Sue was awake; John, Dad, Mom and Dr. Karen were there. It was getting close to the time I had to head to the pre-op room. If I was nervous, I did not recognize it, but the tension in the room was overpowering. You could part it the way the bow of a schooner knifes through a wave as it plows through the sea. I had a sudden compulsion to leave my mark and decided to plaster Mass General with the Dynamic Ski stickers in my wallet. I stood up on my bed and stuck one on the curtain track.

A gurney was wheeled into my room by an orderly named Darren. My voyage through the unknown was to begin. I kissed Mom and Sue, then shook Dad's hand and whispered that I loved him and that if anything happened to me, to please take care of Sue and the kids. John got a big hug and all of us except Mom headed to the surgical floor. It was very tense and Darren broke the tension by asking whether a white man or a black man had cut the arrow and the word "UP" into my hair. When I told him my barber was a white guy, he laughed and said a white guy could not have possibly cut my hair. His teasing broke the tension in my entourage. All along the route, I plastered Dynamic Ski stickers on anything within reach. The halls began to narrow and more gurneys were converging on the floor where the operating rooms wait in the deep recesses of the hospital. One more corridor, one more set of double doors, a left, and then, wham, I was wheeled into a large dimly lit room. The walls on either side were lined with gurneys, some with patients, others empty. This was it; I shuddered and twisted on the gurney. I heard Darren tell Sue and the others that they could go no farther. I waved goodbye.

Dr. Karen was beside me now and, sensing my anxiety, went to find a nurse for some medication. Lying there, I watched the medical staff hustle from one doorway to another. They had smiles on their faces and a demeanor that had a sexual connotation. It was like watching Hawkeye and BJ on the TV show "M.A.S.H.," but this was real. Soon Dr. Karen returned and said she had to go on her rounds. She gave me a hug and said not to worry—she would be there when I woke up. As a nurse stuck me with a needle, I prayed to see my children grow up and to grow old gracefully with Sue. That was my last conscious thought. For the next 24 hours I remember nothing—zip, nada, blackness, lights out, and any other word that describes a state of suspended animation.

* * * * *

Out of the blackness of my subconscious mind I thought I could hear voices and then, like dawn slowly lighting up the day, I heard a familiar voice; Dr. Karen was telling me I was going to be OK and not to talk. The darkness turned to gray, the gray became a dim light growing in intensity to a bright light—as if I were stepping into the sunlight after being in the dark for a long time. There was a deep pain in my skull and the light hurt my eyes—but all of this told me I was alive!

A surgeon asked me how I felt. I did not answer his question but asked him what time it was. He replied that it was well past 10 p.m. I responded by saying, "I guess I missed lunch." He laughed and continued asking dumb questions.

"What is your name?"

Faintly, I responded, "Bill, and I guess a beer is out of the question."

The doctor laughed. "Who is the president?"

"Bush as in shrubs," I answered.

Then he took both my hands and asked me to squeeze his hands. After I passed that test, he proceeded to tickle my feet and I gave a dry hoarse giggle. The doctor asked me again how I was feeling. I told him I had the worst hangover ever! As the anesthetic wore off, my head ached as if a mule had kicked it. My jaw felt broken on the right side. I was shivering uncontrollably and my teeth began to chatter. The doctors and nurses scurried around for blankets.

I was moved to the recovery room, feeling violated in body and spirit. Dr. Karen came by to comfort me, but the pain was so great all she could do was hold my hand. She left just as the nurses started to put inflatable tubes connected to a compressor on my legs. Every few minutes the tubes inflated and deflated. They were similar to the inflatable casts that the ski patrol uses on an accident victim. Curious about the purpose of these bizarre contraptions, I was informed that they prevent blood from clotting in the legs.

"Why would that happen?" I asked.

The nurse mentioned low heart rates and blood clots. Apparently, my heart rate had been lowered to around 38 to 41 beats per minute.

Then I asked, "Why am I so cold?"

The nurse explained that the doctors had lowered my body temperature to about 45 degrees to minimize the rate at which brain cells die. The effect is similar to what happens to drowning victims who fall through the ice. Sometimes, as much as an hour later, the victim is revived with normal brain function. The doctors use the same theory when performing brain surgery.

The boots annoyed me because of the sound of the pump and the hiss of air escaping through the release valve. They were cumbersome and restricting and I sensed I would have to wear them for several days. I slipped back into unconsciousness and woke up in the intensive care unit (ICU). There the nurses gingerly transferred me from the gurney to a bed. I recall a nurse laying an electric blanket on me and, for the first time since I regained consciousness, I felt warm. I felt like curling up and falling asleep but the boots prevented me from rolling over and sleeping on my stomach, the only way I can sleep. Finally, I fell back into the abyss of semiconsciousness and slept.

I awoke to the gentle touch of Sue holding my hand, crying with joy that I was well and alive. We didn't say anything—just having her beside me was comforting. I fell asleep again and woke up to see Dad standing over me, saying how proud he was and how much he admired my bravery. I thanked him but did not think I was brave but, rather, dumb for going through with the surgery. I was cold and hurting, the pain in my head was growing in intensity, and I wanted to know what had happened to my jaw. The boots were constantly inflating and deflating. I tried to bribe or trick any doctor, nurse or orderly to remove them, but no one listened. The family all visited with me one at a time in accordance with the regulations. After three days, Dr. Gress, director of the ICU, felt I was out of danger and ordered that I could move to my room. What a relief! That meant all the monitors would be removed and, I hoped, the boots. When the orderly came and the nurses piled the compressor and wires onto my bed, I realized the boots were to remain on my legs awhile longer.

I had not seen myself in a mirror, but with the head dressing the surgeon had wrapped around my head, I felt like Lawrence of Arabia. The pain in my jaw and in the right side of my head was intense, so intense that I often used my hand to put pressure on the left jaw in an attempt to distract my mind from the pain elsewhere in my head. When Dr. Schumacher visited my room, I asked why my jaw felt broken. Apparently, on the way in to my brain, the doctor had to sever all the muscles that control the face and jaw. He went on to explain how the doctor pulled all the muscles up and re-attached them to my skull so that there would not be a huge dent in the side of my head. He used the tissue from my jaw and face muscles to fill in the depression where there used to be bone. I asked him if I had a steel plate where the skull was removed.

"No," he said. "We drilled little holes around the outside edge of the skull and bone fragments were removed. Then we wired the skull fragments back into their original location."

It sounded complicated, but I understood why my jaw hurt so much. Soon the orderly showed up and I was transferred to the gurney for the ride up to my room. I wondered if I was going to see Dynamic Ski stickers everywhere. Once in my room, I checked the curtain track for the sticker and, sure enough, it was still there. I knew I was safe and alive in my room with Sue, Dad and Mom. Phenobarbital was prescribed and made me feel heavily sedated. I seemed to move slower, talk slower, even think slower. As the days went by, I found it difficult to stay awake. The doctors had told me that the brain would want to sleep an unusual amount of time, which is the way it heals itself, but I was struggling to stay awake. It was so much of a problem that the doctors reduced the dosage. After that I still felt drowsy but did not have to struggle to keep my eyes open.

Slowly the multiple IVs were removed and, best of all, the boots were taken off. I was liberated from all the detriments to mobility and was soon allowed to stand up. I must have been in denial of my deficits because I was alive and, according to the doctors, recovering faster than expected. My pride had not yet been assaulted. My ego was intact; I felt invincible for having survived the first surgery. When I tried to sit up, however, I experienced dizziness. On day five, the doctors removed the bandages from my head, lifting them off the way you remove a hat. The look on Sue's face was sobering. The incision was about 10 inches long, forming an inverted horseshoe shape over my right ear. When I looked in the mirror, I saw that the doctor had shaved only half my head. On the left side I had a full head of hair; on the right side, my head was shaved clean and had a huge bulge. I think Dr. Schumacher had looked at my haircut in the operating room, laughed and, somewhat of a prankster himself, had only shaved half my head. The incision had been stapled closed with about 50 staples. I looked like a character from a Mad Max movie.

After the bandages came off, I was allowed visitors. When they first arrived, everyone entered my room tentatively. The door was to the left of the bed, and as they came in, they would not know what to expect. With their first glance, they were surprised to see me looking so normal. Because the left side of my head still had a full head of hair, visitors first thought my surgery had been delayed or that the incision was not that bad. But when they walked to my right or directly in front of me, they were horrified when they saw the actual incision. The reaction of first-time visitors was unmistakable shock. When Sue first brought Shannon to visit, she entered the room very tentatively. When she finally reached a position to view my scar, she was so frightened she backed right to the wall and wouldn't come close to my bed. After a half-hour, however, she calmed down and warmed up to me. Sue and I decided to keep the flow of well-wishers and phone calls to a minimum. There are some side effects from my surgery that no one tells you about, like eating—the muscles on the right side of my head had been severed. Or sensitivity to sound, light and movement—too much of any of these and I had difficulty dealing with them.

Dad brought one of my co-workers to the hospital to reassure him that I was well and would be back at work in no time. But just the opposite happened. I will never forget the look I got from Dad. We realized then that I might have to have extended time off to get through this ordeal. That meant at the tender age of 37, my career was on hold—just as I was starting to hit the big leagues, making mega deals with mega commissions, the kind of deals that are the result of years of developing relationships and cultivating clients. You simply cannot take yourself out of the business mainstream for a few years and pick up where you left off. After a few minutes, both Dad and my co-worker excused themselves and left. I closed my eyes and cried!

On day six after surgery, I was allowed to take a shower, with the help of Barbara Dunderdale. She held my hand so that I did not fall over and whack my head. The whole time I showered, I teased her and kept inviting her to join me; however, she declined my invitation. It felt wonderful to be clean and shaved. I was able to stand on my own, but my balance was shaky. The nurses brought a walker so that I could take short walks to the nurses' station and back to my room by myself. In a few days I did not need the walker and could walk short distances without it.

As the days went by, I became more alert and the pain became tolerable. As I improved, I became a prankster and especially enjoyed freaking out other patients. One of my favorite jokes was the Frankenstein act. I was fortunate enough to stay on the 22nd floor at Ellison, a floor for VIPs and not the traditional location for neuro patients. There was a wealthy Venezuelan patient on the floor at the time with at least 15 family members who visited constantly. Usually they walked the corridors or sat in the waiting room by the elevators. The hospital rooms were nice, but small. The patient's whole family could not fit all at the same time, so they rotated in and out of the room. One day, when I felt especially perky, I heard a group arrive and decided to freak them out.

I got out of bed and headed down the side corridor to intercept them. I really did not know what kind of joke I was going to play; I just wanted to see how strangers would react to the horrendous sight of my right temple. Family and friends were prepared to see an ugly scar on my head—total strangers were not.

As I reached the corner of the hallway, I stiffened my legs and thrust out my arms like Frankenstein's monster and proceeded around the corridor. At the same time, the group of Venezuelans walked by! They were startled into silence by my demeanor and hurried along, not knowing what to think.

As the week went by, I played with this routine frequently. On one occasion Sue and I were walking down the corridor when the Venezuelans came through the double doors. I stiffened up, shoved my arms out straight and bulged out my eyes. Sue grabbed me by the arm, spun me around and hurried me in the opposite direction, laughing uncontrollably. Once back in the room, she hugged me, laughing and crying. Through her hysterics she was saying, "You're back, you're back, my Bill is back."

That night Barbara came into my room and stared at me like a mother looking at a child who has misbehaved. She explained that the floor was a critical floor for certain patients and informed me that I was upsetting some of the visitors with my Frankenstein act. In response, I asked her if my Quasimodo impersonation was out of the question. And then, just like a little boy who has been bad, I started to crack and said, "Death has been staring me in the face. You people told me I was going to die and there is only a 40 percent probability that I will survive the cure. I need to laugh." Then Barbara gave me a hug and talked about the hopeful side of the situation.

My thoughts turned to my next goal. I had reached my first goal and survived brain surgery. I was not foolish enough to think that I had incurred no deficits, but I had survived. As I lay there trying to focus on the next step, Sue walked into the room; she was now almost nine months pregnant. Seeing her helped me decide—my next goal was to be present for the birth of William Joseph Fallon Jr., a name that carries the weight of my great-grandfather, great uncle, and great-second cousin. I had reservations giving him that name; one being the fact that the only William Joseph Fallon to date whom had lived a full life was his great-great-grandfather. My great-uncle, William Fallon, was a flamboyant guy who owned a Duesenburgh, which he had bought from a German General, Herman Goering, prior to World War II. His best friend had been Babe Ruth. On Christmas Eve, he and the Babe were known to go out and buy all the newspapers from the paperboys so that they would have money to celebrate a good Christmas. Bill was a dapper, handsome man with a pencil-thin mustache and a flair for dating the famous women of his time; his wife Louise was faithful throughout her life. Their only son, William J. Fallon, died as an infant. Bill drank himself to death in his 50s.

We decided our son's formal name would be William Joseph Fallon and that, in time, we would come up with a nickname. As we sat there, Sue remarked how the baby was constantly moving and at times seemed to be running in her womb. That reminded me of the cartoon character the "Flash" and it dawned on me! We could nickname him Flash. Flash Fallon had a good sound to it and Sue liked it too. When the grandparents-to-be heard the name Flash, they thought we were joking. Before long, however, everyone was referring to the baby as Flash. His birth became my focal point. I focused on getting strong enough to be able to be with Sue for his birth. In order to do, that I had to improve within two weeks or else still be in the hospital for the predicted date of birth.

The bright side of my days occurred when the doctors made their rounds. Dr. Schumacher and I were a lot alike. He understood my active life outdoors and the thrill of life on the edge. He said that my attitude had the whole neuro department enamored of me. Due to the nature of their field of expertise, the department had few successes. Many of their patients had gone through car windshields and would wake up cursing because they were paralyzed. According to the doctors, the majority of their patients do not appreciate them for saving their lives. Dr. Schumacher said that many head trauma patients are the result of drinking-related accidents or domestic disputes. When these patients regain consciousness, they try to impose their anger for their neurological deficits on the doctors instead of on themselves.

There is another reason for a patient to direct anger in the direction of the doctors: denial. Denial is a powerful tool that the brain manifests in an attempt to deal with deficits. I too was in denial. I refused to be denied my dreams, aspirations and ambitions. I refused to acknowledge that the worst was yet to come. I stilled believe I would recover quickly and get the second surgery over with. So far I had not realized any of the defects of surgery. And I planned on skiing within a year.

Chapter 10

One of the first things I wanted to do was get my head shaved. I felt like a freak with a normal haircut on one side and the shaved side looking as if someone had installed an industrial-size zipper in it. The whole right side of my head had no feeling: Pain, yes! Sensation, no. At times I felt relaxed and at peace, yet at the same time I was experiencing powerful emotions. I realized that all the materialism in the world would not get me through this experience. For the first time since I quit skiing full time, I was beginning to understand where inner peace lives. Whenever I meet people who have had a near-death experience, they know the sensation. An eerie peace falls over you and a warmth rushes through your veins. The day I was discharged from the hospital, I got a taste of this inner tranquillity. I had stared down the Angel of Death and earned a second chance at life.

Going home became a beginning, not an end. I had months to go before I would be strong enough to face the challenge of the second operation. Sue showed up as Dr. Shumacher was leaving my room and he joked about getting her to the maternity floor soon—she looked ready to explode. Sue quipped back that Mass General had no maternity ward. He laughed—what did he know, he was only a brain surgeon. Then the driver called the room to say he was waiting at the emergency room entrance. It was time to go and who should bring my wheelchair but Darren.

"Say, so how you feeling, man?" He asked.

"Great, I'm going home, bro!"

Darren slapped me five and gave me the handshake. Looking at my hairdo and zipper-like incision, he remarked that I have good taste in barbers, although we agreed the last haircut was better. I told him to be around to see the haircut for surgery number two. We both laughed as I suggested he see my barber.

I was headed home and couldn't wait to get there. On the way down to the car I could not help but see the reaction of anyone who noticed my head. This must be what it feels like to be retarded or crippled. I suddenly got the notion that I could use my scar and haircut to amuse myself with people's reactions. This dawned on me when I got to the car and the driver did not see my right side. As he walked around the car to open the door, he got his first look at my head and hesitated just enough for me to see his stunned look. He quickly recovered and proceeded with his duties. Once Sue and I were in the car and headed home, he asked the question, "What was it—a tumor?"

"No," I replied, "an AVM."

As we headed along the Mass Pike, I sensed the world was different. Everything seemed to be moving faster. I felt overwhelmed. Some scientists have studied sensory deprivation; I was experiencing sensory overload. The cars hustling by made me dizzy, so I tried not to look out the window. I turned on the radio in the back seat but had to turn it off—the sound hurt my head. My senses of sight and sound had been affected in some way. When we turned off the highway onto Route 20, we asked the driver to swing by the drugstore to get my prescriptions filled. Since the pharmacist knew of my plight and I wanted him to see my scar, I went in with Sue.

The ladies who had worked at the drugstore for years were on duty. When I walked in the door, they gasped at the sight of my scar. The pharmacist was happy to see me up and about and greeted me with a big smile and firm handshake. He voiced his pleasure at the success of the first operation. On the way out, I walked by one elderly lady who was unable to suppress her shock.

She was so jolted I almost had to turn and keep her from knocking over one of the displays.

When we finally arrived home, I began to relax. It was a warm March day and I wanted to sit outside for a few minutes to feel the warmth of the sun. A slight wind was gently blowing around my head and everything seemed magnified, almost surrealistic. It was a good day to be alive and home, safe from the sterility of the hospital. That afternoon I decided to change my lifestyle. At 37, I was in good shape but that was only due to my pre-operative skiing. I was told that my heart rate and the successful results from surgery were partly due to my good physical condition. If this were the case, I had to do something to be strong for the second operation. My stamina was nonexistent and fatigue came easily, almost unnaturally. I determined to eat the proper foods and eliminate sodas and snack foods. And I also determined to walk every day, even if it was only around the yard at first.

I tried to walk around the side lawn, a small area approximately 20 feet by 40 feet. It was exhausting to walk that short distance. I finally comprehended the words of the doctors and realized that recovery was going to be a long and difficult process. My physical fitness goal was to walk to the end of the driveway. On the next day, I made my attempt to walk the 100 feet to the end of the driveway. When I got there, I realized that it was 50 feet too far. I turned around to head back to the house and actually thought I might not make it back. I had to sit on one of the boulders along the driveway to regain my strength. What a shock to my ego that experience was! A sobering reality crept through my consciousness—one of the penalties for the intrusion into my brain was fatigue.

My next goal was to lose the 10 pounds I had gained eating pancakes every morning in the hospital. This was going to be a difficult task considering I was only able to walk very slowly for about 50 feet before I needed to rest. The two goals were codependent and I pledged to start right then and there. I wanted to be strong enough to be with Sue when Flash was born.

The baby was almost two weeks overdue and Sue looked like the Goodyear blimp. Enough attention had been paid to me, now it was time to help Sue. We planned to have Elaine, Sue's mother, come and stay with us when Flash was born. I was obviously unable to take care of Sue and Shannon but, as misfortune would have it, Elaine fell down on a patch of slick ice and broke her hip. My mother was off to Davos, Switzerland, for her annual sabbatical and Pam had her hands full in Oregon with her two children. That left Sue's oldest sister, Linda, or my brother, John, to help us.

The job fell to Linda and we worked out a game plan. On the March 15th weekend, Linda arrived with her family. Ron, her husband, a lawyer who specializes in medical cases, was amazed at the extent of my surgery. Ron is a smart man with a heart of pure gold even though he puts a hard crust over his emotions. He had some very touching things to say during their visit and I developed a whole new respect and appreciation for his friendship.

Since the doctors did not want me to drive, we agreed that John, who lived in nearby Waltham, would carry a beeper and drive us to Lawrence General Hospital, 50 minutes away. When Sue went into labor, we would beep John and he would rush Sue to the hospital. Linda would bring me later as the baby's birth drew closer. It was not possible for me to stay with her throughout all her labor. I simply did not have the strength.

During my first few weeks at home, I felt like an exhibit. Every day friends came by to check me out. Their eyes showed pity and, when they saw my scar, horror. The phone rang constantly with inquiries from relatives and co-workers. Concerns for my health from clients especially touched me. My days were filled with visitors; it was a real morale booster to see people so concerned about my well-being. On the other hand, I paid a price for those visits and Sue had to control the flow of well-wishers.

Busy days fatigued me or else I became easily irritated. Too much activity confused me and I experienced radical mood swings. Pain topped off the whole package and made me a difficult patient. I was distressed at my inability to cope with everyday things. The sounds of kids playing tag or too many people talking at once were difficult to contend with. Depression was slowly creeping into my personality and my moods made things difficult for Sue.

My whole personality had changed. I was able to maintain my equilibrium with others but I would let out my rage when I was alone with Sue, and sometimes directed it at her. She was going through the changes that pregnancy brings to the body and mind and still she was supportive. Sue's strength came from within; she had an ability to deal with the problem, one step at a time. She never became overwhelmed with the big picture; rather, she woke up each day and dealt with both Shannon and me. There were times when she would start to cry and then, as if something deep down inside slapped her, she would straighten up, turn off her emotions, bite her upper lip and fight off the demons. She told me she believed in karma and that if we believed in the best, only the best would happen. There was both good and bad associated with this strategy: The good was the hope, the bad was the internal damage Sue was suffering. I kept thinking that there must be a purpose for the tragedy, but that did not stop me from wondering whether I had offended God. If this operation was taking this great a toll, the "big one" was too frightening to consider. I tried to forget about going through surgery again and concentrated on growing stronger. I hoped the baby would wait long enough so I could walk from the Lawrence General Hospital parking lot to the maternity ward.

* * * * *

Spring was in the air and William J. Fallon Jr. was taking his sweet time about arriving. Sue looked as if she had swallowed a huge beach ball. Then two weeks past her due date, Sue went into labor. John arrived in a panic, eager to drive Sue to the hospital before he would have to deliver the child himself. Sue was waiting for him in the driveway, calm and sedate. Linda was calm and excited, and Shannon, not really aware of the events unfolding around her, went to school. We all had agreed beforehand that when the nurses determined Sue was about an hour away from delivering the baby, John would call us and Linda and I would drive up to the hospital. As planned, we went into action and Sue was on her way.

Around one in the afternoon, Linda and I got in the car to drive to the hospital. I was heavily sedated from my anti-seizure medication. When we arrived, the emergency entrance lot was full. We had to park across the street and down the hill. This left me with a 200-yard uphill journey. I don't think Linda realized that the walk in could have killed me. I had to walk slowly and paused for a rest at least twice. Linda looked at me and asked if I was all right. I responded that the doctors had warned me not to strain myself. At that we both broke into laughter as we huffed and puffed our way up the hill.

On the maternity floor, we walked into a hailstorm of fathers and relatives of at least five women in various stages of labor. All the commotion and noise were hard for me to cope with. We found Sue and John just as Sue was being moved to the delivery room. Linda went in first and helped transfer Sue to the new table. Things were starting to happen fast and the nurse had not seen me. John was sent to the waiting room and I was invited into the delivery room. As I walked into the room, the nurse looked at my scar, then turned to Linda and said, "If he falls down, you catch him. I don't do tops, I only do bottoms."

What a wild scene it was with all the different accents of women wailing in pain, some swearing at their husbands or the nurses. Visitors and family were gawking at the newborn babies in the incubator room. At least three other women were in the same stage of labor as Sue. It was almost a comical scene, as the nurse ran from room to room checking each mother to determine who would be first to deliver. Sue was calm except when hit with a labor pain. Then she would say she could not go through with it. I tried to comfort her but all she could say was, "I don't think I can deliver a 10-pound baby." My response was not compassionate. I told her, "If I can go through brain surgery, you can deliver a 10-pound baby."

There was not enough help on the maternity floor and my son was not waiting for anyone. His head started to emerge when the nurse and doctor were not present. The nurse came back with Dr. Grossman in tow just in time to catch my son. It was a special moment for both Sue and me as we had not been sure I would be able to witness the birth of William J. Fallon Jr. Like all mothers, Sue had forgotten the pain and was admiring her son. I was happy and sad, joyous and fearful. Perhaps I would never see this beautiful 10_-pound blue-eyed, blonde baby boy grow up. I might never see him ski or play catch with him or relive my youth through my son, like thousands of fathers before me. I was beginning to feel an unfamiliar emotional pain—a pain of separation from my children mixed with the sadness that my son and I might never know each other. I remember times when my father played baseball with me or watched me play football from the sidelines. Would I be cheated of those precious moments? At the same time, I felt happy about future possibilities. I hoped to be able to concentrate on the future and start taking each day one at a time—to forget about the tomorrows and live for today.

Our son was whisked off to the nursery for a closer inspection, only to be returned in a few minutes wrapped in a blanket. The nurse was filling out forms for the birth certificate and asked what his name was.

"William J. Fallon Jr.—also known as Flash," I added.

Sue cried out, "Don't put that on his birth certificate!"

"Why not?" I asked.

"If you put that on his birth certificate, you have to put it on every formal document like his license or passport."

Eventually I agreed with Sue, but he was already being referred to as the Flash. The nurses put Flash Fallon on his I.D. tag and on his bassinet in the nursery. The nickname was a hit with the hospital staff and visitors to the nursery. My son was a celebrity 30 minutes after he was born. What an auspicious beginning for a child born into so many uncertainties. I was very tired by that time and it was evident that I was ready to head home. Flash was born around 3:15 in the afternoon and it was now almost 5 p.m.—time to let mother and child rest. John had already gone to Boston to boast of his aid in the birth of his nephew. Linda and I said goodbye to Sue and then made a brief stop at the nursery to check on Flash. He was quiet and asleep. We could overhear the other visitors commenting on how big he was compared to the five or six other babies. It made me proud to be his father, to hear strangers comment Flash on his good looks, size and especially his nickname.

Chapter 11

Flash and Sue came home a few days later and Linda stayed for another week to help us get accustomed to the new addition to our family. Each day I would wake up, shower and shave, dress and attempt to walk to the end of the driveway. After three weeks, I decided to go beyond the driveway. As I started walking down the road, it was not as tiring as I had thought, so I kept going. About half a mile along, I felt tired and turned around. After several steps, I became exhausted. I stopped to catch my breath, worried that I might not make it back unassisted. After a rest on a neighbor's lawn, I was able to continue as if my batteries has been recharged, although I had to rest several times. It is an odd experience to go from being an extreme skier to someone hardly able to walk a half mile within one month's time.

I had concluded that my life was to consist of a series of small goals. Each goal was an objective that had to be attempted as an athlete trains for a contest. So far I had won all the contests. My next goal was to be well enough to go to Florida with Sue, Shannon and Flash, where I could rest and get stronger before the second surgery. We decided to fly to Florida during the first week of April, only a week away. I looked forward to the stay at my folk's winter retreat. It was a little house on the ocean in a town called Golden Beach, a one-mile strip of land sandwiched between the intercoastal waterway and the Atlantic Ocean. When I was a little boy, we spent two weeks every spring at Golden Beach. Every spring for as far back as I can remember, we would fish and swim, take long walks on the beach and watch the foreign vacationers. I remember digging for sand fleas and using

Bill, the youngest competitor on the Chevy Pro freestyle Tour, performing a Spread Eagle to an Iron Cross above Sun Valley.

Above: The 75th Anniversary Race of the Wianno Senior Fleet – Bill rounds the leward mark and went on to win the race.

Below: In the same race, John Fallon sets the spinnaker, Bill is at the helm and Sue trims the sheets.

February 1991, before surgury, Bill and friends leave perfect powder tracks.

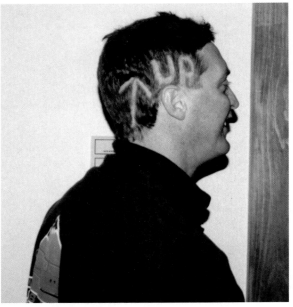

Hospital check-in with instructions for the doctors.

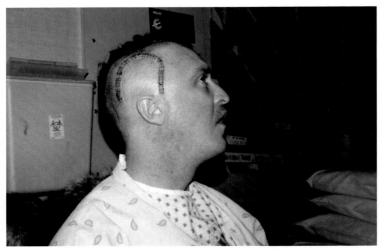

Bill displays 53 staples holding his skull together.

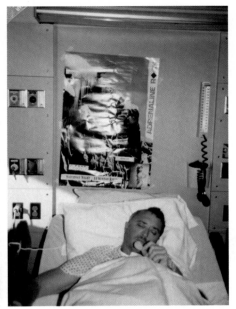

Left: Back in bed after the first surgury.

Below: A reminder of Operation #2.

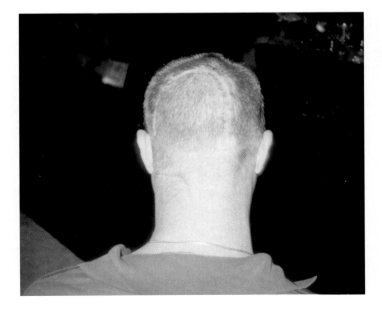

Bill feeds
"Flash Fallon"

Shannon dashes
for the beach in
Spring of 1991

Bill's Dream Team—Flash, Shannon, and Sue in 1994 (left to right).

Left: Before Bill's Black Belt Test (l to r) Bill Fallon, Satoru Takamiyagi, Walter Mattson, Toshio Higa, and Shigaru Takamiyagi in 1995.

Bill and best friends, Sue Fallon and backcountry mentor Ken Hardy.

Triumph and Tragedy— The day Bill had a nervous breakdown heliskiing in Sun Valley.

Bill and friends set Whistler heli-ski records with the most runs in one day, 21, and 72,000 vertical feet.

Bill returns to winning form at Mount Hood during the summer of 1998

them for bait when we surf-cast for bonita. Florida was a perfect prescription for my recovery.

The day before we planned to leave, I had an appointment at Dr. Crowell's office to have the staples in my head removed. When I reached his office, I saw a young woman about 25 years old in the waiting room. Her mother was holding her hand and they were talking in hushed tones. I always noticed patients in the waiting room and, if they look troubled, usually struck up a conversation. In my typical fashion, I asked her which doctor she was seeing and, as I anticipated, she said Dr. Crowell.

Then I asked, "Tumor or AVM/aneurysm?"

"AVM," she said shyly.

"Where?" I asked.

She pointed to her right temple.

"What kind of treatment are you going to have?"

She shook her head and said she didn't know. I started to tell her that Dr. Crowell is the best and that she should follow his recommendation. Just at that moment Julie, Dr. Crowell's secretary, entered the waiting room and motioned for the girl to follow her. About half an hour later, the young lady and her mom left the office and it was time for me to see a resident to remove the hardware from my head. Dr. Jill Wong was in the exam room with a device that looked like a pair of pliers. Noticing my worried look, she assured me that the procedure was as painless as the surgery. I laughed nervously but in no time was free of the ugly staples and on my way home. I told Julie I would be in Florida and wrote down the phone number where we could be reached. I left the hospital, not to return until I was ready for round two.

On the way out, I ran into the young lady and her mother, found out her name was Jane and asked what she was going to do about her AVM. Jane had decided to do nothing. Shocked, I asked, "Why?" She repeated that she was not going to do anything and walked away. I pursued her to the garage and asked what Dr. Crowell had recommended. It turned out to be surgery.

Thinking it was fear that made her decide not to do anything, I showed her my scars and told her about my surgery and how it looked horrible but was not as bad as it sounds. Although she tried to avoid me, her mother encouraged her to listen to what I was saying. The reason Jane gave for not having the surgery was hard to believe: She did not want to do anything because she did not want to cut off her beautiful, long brunette hair. Something so simple, yet so vain, was the reason for not trying to saving her life. Apparently she only had minor headaches as symptoms and was in so much denial that she refused to believe she was in serious danger. When we reached the garage, I gave Jane my business card and wrote down my home number in case she wanted to talk to someone about her condition. On the way home, I could not rationalize how Jane could be so cavalier about her AVM. On the other hand, I could sympathize with her denial because I had experienced it myself. Months later I learned that Jane was a patient who had consulted doctors about her head-aches for more than a year and still refused to accept the reality of her condition. Two years later I was told that Jane had died of a hemorrhage.

At home we set out about the business of packing for a long stay at Golden Beach. The trip to Florida was a welcome respite from the frantic activities at the house. The outpouring of con-cern and goodwill that I received from all directions overwhelmed me. I needed to get away from all the well-wishers who often stopped by to see how I was. The phones were constantly ring-ing and prevented me from getting the sleep the doctors said I needed. On a sunny Monday morning, we were picked up by the airport limo and whisked off to the airport. I had anticipated a difficult flight with a baby and a little girl. As it turned out, Flash slept and Shannon behaved like a princess.

During the four-hour flight, I pondered the bureaucratic pa-perwork that Sue and I had to submit to Social Security as re-quired by my catastrophic disability insurance. It was a dehu-manizing process—I was no longer an individual but a number.

Instead of feeling the self-worth of supporting myself and my family, I had to open my life to the insurance company and the government. The insurance company had specified a 90-day limit as one of the requirements for qualifying on the disability insurance. I had qualified medically as the insurance company used that period to contact my doctors and review the medical records. The insurance policy required me to apply for Social Security benefits for the children and myself, but there was some question as to the effective date of payments so that they would coincide with my insurance payments. It was an involved process of filling out forms in triplicate and submitting them to all parties. At times I felt like a ghost in a room full of people who were talking about me. Until I qualified for disability insurance, my employer supported us. We received our first insurance and Social Security checks, retroactive to February, the week we left for Golden Beach. I was very fortunate to have the proper insurance protection or I would never have been able to afford the cure.

It was invigorating to feel the warm southern air blowing on my shaved head and to smell the salt of the Gulf Stream. The weather was tropical with enough humidity to convince you to wear nothing but a bathing suit. We lugged our bags upstairs and set up the crib for the Flash. In a short time, we were settled in and down at the cabana just in time to watch the foreign tourists walk up the beach from hotel row. The sun was still fairly high in the sky and I was grateful for its healing rays. I felt warm on the outside and inside, sitting there with my family in the Florida sun.

It did not take us long to get settled into the routine of breakfast on the lawn with the kids, two cups of coffee, and a handful of pills for me. Around 9 a.m., we moved the kids to the cabana, built sandcastles on the beach and swam in the surf. When 12 o'clock rolled around, we ate a light lunch in the shade, usually sandwiches and lemonade. After lunch we lathered up a second coat of sun block on the adults and kids. Flash was always in the shade or covered from head to toe. We spent the afternoon sun-bathing or walking the beach searching for some of the prettiest shells found anywhere in the world. We collected miniature conch shells, nautilus shells, sand dollars and turkey wings—the variety compelled us to keep every shell we found. And sometimes we took a trip to the mall. The one constant for me was sleep. Every day, without fail—no matter where I was—I would lay down and sleep for at least two and sometimes three or four hours. It seemed as if I slept 14 to 16 hours of every day.

The weeks in Florida were quiet and peaceful with no stress or controversy to aggravate me. While the pressures of my job were well out of my reach, I could not shake the anxiety of my uncertain future. Often when I walked the beach, I wondered if I could return to work or play baseball with Flash. Would I see Shannon graduate from college and marry? Confusion over these and similar issues made it difficult to keep from breaking down. I would simply have to learn that the future could not be contemplated.

Shannon was getting restless with the mundane lifestyle we were leading so we decided to take her to Seaworld for a day of fun. We saw all the exhibits and caught the shows at each tank. The killer whale show was awesome and Shannon's eyes were wide with excitement. At the end of the killer whale act, a group of seals displayed their abilities. At the end of the show, a seal named Sophia was doing her thing when the trainer asked if there was any child in the audience who wanted to meet Sophia. As it turned out, Shannon was picked to get a kiss from Sophia. She hurried down to the spot the trainer directed her to, and then Sophia jumped into the tank and bolted over to Shannon. When she reached the platform in front of Shannon, she slipped up to Shannon and gave her a kiss on the lips. For the rest of our trip, Shannon was in heaven over the attention she had received at Seaworld and let everyone know that she had a new friend there.

Our time in Florida was coming to an end. We had spent about six weeks in the sun and were getting itchy to return home.

It was May, and as Florida was getting a little too hot and humid for everyone's comfort, we made plans to leave. My strength was coming back and I had to start preparing myself for the second operation. I was in a hurry to get on with it. The reason: I hoped to ski that winter. I honestly thought I would recover in six months and be able to return to work and the slopes by February, or March at the latest.

The time we spent in Florida was not all wine and roses. There was not a minute of any day that the memory of the first operation did not cause physical and emotional stress and it was impossible not to think about the next operation. It was hard to face every day and be pleasant to my friends, family and children. It was easy to lash out in anger. I think part of the reason we strike out in anger at our loved ones is that we want them to feel our pain. Most of the time I forced myself to be agreeable to my family. It was a time to give the kids wonderful memories of their father. Memories were all I could give them that would last forever. That thought helped me laugh and play with them. I showed them as much love as I could because the joy of that love would last in their minds. I spent the last full day in Florida just like the first day, on the beach, deep in thought, lost in dreams of days past and wondering about days to come. Surrounded by my family, I felt the healing power of the bright sun.

Chapter 12

Our home, a small cape, was nestled on a granite knoll on a hill in Wayland. We lived in one of the oldest towns in New England, rich with history of revolutionaries and patriots. The familiar smells of our house assaulted my senses and its warmth soothed my soul. At the same time, I felt a slight anxiety about any unknown conditions I might find in the house. There was no mail to mull through and the newspapers were missing from the driveway. The weather was warm with very little humidity—the time of year to prepare the toys of summer for a season of power boating and yachting. Descending from sound sailing stock and sons of a sailing legend, John and I inherited the duty of defending our honor on the racecourse in Dad's pride, the Marna. We did not stay long at home, but soon headed down to the Cape to the family retreat.

The Marna is a 28-foot gaff-rigged sloop with a shoal draft keel and a deep-water centerboard. She is simply the most beautiful craft afloat in the world with the lines of a fair maiden and the strength of a blue whale. The Marna is without exception the winningest sailboat in America—not because of John or me, but because of my father. He is the most recognized sailor in yachts today and has raced in everything from the America's Cup to the Admiral's Cup in Cowes, England.

My father was the only American to win a silver medal in the prestigious Admiral's Cup during most of the '70s and early '80s. The boat was a 56-foot cutter called Yankee Girl and won all five races, including the infamous Fastnet Rock race. Dad's accomplishments have placed him in the winner's circle in races from the Olympic trial in 5.5 meters to match racing the big J boats, Endeavor and Shamrock II. It is our legacy to race in any kind of sailboat and to excel. The summer of '91 was no exception and it was John's turn to race for the Scudder Cup. For more than 40 years we have competed for this coveted trophy over three weekends—six race regattas held at alternating ports on Cape Cod. This year the races were held at Edgartown on Martha's Vineyard, Hyannis and Bass River. It was John's turn to campaign the boat and I was reduced to a support role, unable to crew for him.

John had chosen Stu Roche, Jacquie Colella and Scott Degrasse as his crew for the Scudder Cup Championship, which was to be raced in July. He planned to enter a few June races to warm up and tune up the Marna. The first race was the Max Crosbie Memorial trophy and the crew of the Marna was chafing at the bit. The second major warm-up race was the Fourth of July race. These two races often turn out poor performances from our crew and, in typical fashion, they did not win but did gain valuable experience. It is a daunting task to fill Dad's shoes in the world of sailing and even more difficult to win as he did.

In the '60s, my father had found a beautiful old stucco house sitting high on a hill. It overlooked a little saltwater pond in front and a freshwater pond to the north of the property line. Originally the land in front of the house was a fairway on the first public golf course in the East. A section of the house goes back to 1918, when it was a hunting lodge. The tiled livingroom floor has drains in key places so hunters could clean ducks and geese in the house and wash away the innards. Two huge fireplaces with iron arms for holding cooking pots stand at each end of the living room. The house overlooks the saltwater harbor and bays that stretch out to Nantucket Sound. High on the 14 acres there is a level spot on the point that sits between the freshwater pond and the saltwater bay. The views in all directions are breathtaking and the area is invisible from any other vantage point. Since the house is always full of family, friends and guests, as well as children, I found it difficult to cope with the noise and activity. Often I would take a chair and place it out on the point, where I could watch the boats and the activities at the house from afar. A gentle breeze kept me cool and free of the pesky bugs that come with the warm summer days.

The freshwater pond has two great swans that reside in its waters as well as great blue herons, white egrets, geese and a host of songbirds. Adjacent to the saltwater bay are more geese, some ducks, a couple hundred seagulls and, occasionally, flocks of migratory birds. The most impressive feathered inhabitants of the neighborhood were two pair of osprey. Early morning and late afternoon are the best times to watch the birds feed. The great swans gracefully duck their heads into the bottom of the pond for algae. Egrets and herons walk the shoreline stabbing at minnows swimming between their long slender legs.

However, there is nothing more impressive than to see an osprey dive from 100 feet up, with its wings folded in, and hit the water at tremendous speed to catch a fish. The bird stays completely submerged for a full three to five seconds before its head surfaces. Then its wings come out of the water reaching for the sky, straining to catch the air and pull its body out of the water. The fish is often heavier than the bird and it is a Herculean feat for the osprey to get airborne. Once in the air, the bird must align the fish headfirst with one talon in front of the other, otherwise the bird's aerodynamics will fail and it will crash into the sea. Slowly the feathered hunter circles around and around, straining to gain altitude. Reaching a thermal, the osprey soars and rests while rising in the tepid air and then starts the lumbering flight home to the nest with a feast for its young.

Sometimes a huge snapping turtle would surface and snap at prey in the pond. Songbirds swooped in the air to catch bugs. At times I wondered if heaven would be as serene and as beautiful. The time I spent on the point was both restful and cerebral, often so tranquil that I would fall asleep for hours on end. The point became my sanctuary and everyone respected my need to be alone.

Although all my family helped and supported me, they could not understand the loneliness of my situation. I was the one who had to confront my mortality and that is something no one can help you prepare for. Sitting at the point offered me the tranquility to sort out and prioritize the issues that a dying man has to face. Some call it soul searching, others call it introspection. I began to analyze my life, relive events of the past and assess the meaning of my existence. Time became irrelevant and I stopped wearing a watch. The hot sun warmed me right to the marrow as I lay in the lounge chair, warming not only my body but also my soul. It reassured me that I was alive. The uncontrollable shivering I had experienced after surgery was still fresh in my mind and I associated that feeling with death.

On the Fourth of July, Dennis and Shauna Vincent, our friends from my heli-skiing trip, came for a visit. By the time they arrived, we were all well rested and ready to entertain friends. Their visit would be a perfect complement to my big Fourth of July show. I have always loved fireworks and we had a formidable arsenal. There were four delivery systems for the fireworks. The first one consisted of a trash barrel full of firecrackers and kerosene with a one-quarter-inch grate wired over the open trash barrel. Placed through the grate were more than 1,000 bottle rockets with whistles or reports. I made a cloth wick for a fuse and placed the trash barrel on some plywood sheets. The next three systems were plywood sheets with the mortar tube launchers screwed onto plywood. The launch platforms were rafts and the plywood would protect the rafts from sparks.

On the day of the Fourth, John and I moved the rafts to moorings in the middle of the bay. Each platform had a different sequence of shells and the shell types varied from red carnations to palms and orbiters and sonic booms. Red is the hardest color to make when you work with gunpowder. We had about 50 mortar shots laid out on the plywood sheets. All we had to do was touch off each mortar shell fuse to have a continuous rain of fireworks. If we set one off every minute, we would have hours of display. The trashcan of firecrackers would last somewhere between 10 and 20 minutes. Total all that up and the Fourth of July celebration would run almost two hours. I was confident that this would be John's and my finest pyrotechnic accomplishment. We had positioned three rafts with sets of fireworks; all we had to do was set off one raft and then move to the next raft using our small power boat as our base of safety. A perfect plan if all went well— if not, we could always jump into the harbor.

That afternoon John and the boys were racing the Marna in the Fourth of July race as a warm-up to the Scudder Cup in three weeks. It was a windy day of about 20 knots with a crisp clear blue sky and southwesterly winds. The Vincents, Sue and I towed the sailboat and crew out to the starting line and set them free. They were off to the races and we were headed to Dead Neck for the day. I napped while Sue, Dennis and Shauna gossiped the day away. That afternoon was slow and easy for me and allowed me to save energy to put on the fireworks display that night. Around 4:30 we hoisted anchor and sped out to Can Three to watch the Wianno Senior fleet finish the race. It is exciting to see 20 or so boats beating to windward, racing to be first across the line. On that afternoon Holly Edmonds was in the lead with Alan McDonough second, followed by at least two boat lengths by John. Their positions did not change and they ended the race in that order.

It was time for the whole gang to get showered and dressed for the evening's festivities and fireworks. The grill was roaring with hot coals glowing white and the chicken was soaking in barbecue sauce. After dinner, John, Dennis, our friend Herbie and I quietly slipped down to the dock with the arsenal and placed all the delivery systems onto floats. When we had fastened the plywood sheets down on the floats, we towed the three rafts out to separate moorings. We were set up and all we had to do was turn the sun off; it was only 8 p.m. and darkness didn't fall until

9. The sky was black without the moon but the clarity of the heavens and the stars above was beautiful. Almost no wind—a perfect night for a fireworks display.

There were several boats from North Bay loaded with spectators and at least 30 people had gathered on the pond's various docks. I tried to set the fireworks off in an order that would let me see them as well. A sharp pain zapped my head. Bending over to light the fuses was too much, so I let Herbie take my place. I drifted away to watch Herbie's silhouette dance in the smoke and sparks of more glorious explosions of brilliance. The Coast Guard came to investigate the noise and tried to navigate the unmarked channel into the little pond. Fortunately, they did not have a clue about how to get in and finally turned off their engines to watch like everyone else.

It was an excellent show and I was proud of myself for having pulled the whole thing together with John's help. As the night was nearing an end and the display had lasted about an hour longer than we had anticipated, the three of us decided to let everything else go off for the finale. John, Herbie and I each fired up a flare and started to light the fireworks designated as our responsibility. The crowd was laughing and screaming with joy and enthusiasm over the display. Three hours after we started, the last floral shell and boomer went off and the crowd cheered their approval.

We decided to abandon the rafts and clean up in the morning. It had been a big night and I needed to sleep—my head was aching. No one tried to convince me to stay up and party till the wee hours of the morning as we had in years past. That was how I knew I was not myself, it was obvious I had paid a physical price for the brain surgery. I did not want to admit that I was different. In a way, I was on the outside looking in; I could be involved at one time and invisible at another. A strange existence, where you are treated as if you are Humpty Dumpty, as fragile as an egg, but bigger than a compact car. But it had been one of the better Fourth of Julys and, I hoped, not my last. If it was, I sure went out with one hell of a bang.

The weeks leading up to my second operation were heavenly; everything seemed to be irrelevant. I was not pressured or pushed, people let me flow through the day as if I were a meandering river. I did, however, have problems coping when things were not running right. On several occasions during the Vincents' stay, I experienced moments of irrational behavior. Fortunately, Dennis is a doctor and understood my problems. His compassion and forgiveness were a blessing. As soon as Dennis and Shauna pulled out of the driveway to head home to British Columbia, I disappeared over the hill to the point where I could resume my soul searching, ponder past events and take a look into the near future.

Days passed and before I knew it, the first race of the Scudder Cup was only a few days away. John had assembled his crew and the boat was ready. The first regatta is in Edgartown on Martha's Vineyard, where sailing ships have anchored for hundreds of years. The first race was on a Friday: Winds were light at about 8 knots out of the southwest and the seas were calm with a 1-foot swell. Thirty Wianno Seniors were jockeying for position on the starting line. BANG! The preparatory gun roared over Cowes Bay. At 10 minutes before the start, the graceful boats with their big gaff-rigged mainsails glistened white in the sun. The boats sliced the water with their distinctive Hereshoff bows as they surfed down the waves with a powerful surge. Each skipper was watching the traffic pattern develop while searching for the best position to take the start. Eight minutes to go until the starting gun and thousands of pounds of teak, mahogany and Dacron positioned themselves. Some boats practice the timing and positioning they wish to have at the precise moment the starting gun goes off. Others luff their sails, analyzing the wind to see which way the shifts are going.

BANG! The five-minute warning gun echoed through the fleet. The tactics of starting require a special talent for judging time, space and distance. As a little boy, I had the honor of sailing many times with my father and Donny MacNamara, two of the finest sailors to sail under the American flag. One thing I had learned was their method of determining the favored end of the starting line, which involves a series of gyrations and wind direction calculations that mathematically identify the favored end. On the first race, John had used some of that famed sailing legacy to time the start brilliantly. Don Law, a talented and accomplished sailor, was shut out trying to barge in illegally. John had closed the door and luffed Don up. If you are at the right spot but a little late with your timing, it gives you the chance to slip around the committee boat and get clear air to the right side of the course. This happened to be the tactically correct thing to do on this day and the two boats that knew it were John and Don, the first and second boats to win position. Sailboat racing is a game of geometry, an attempt to find the shortest route between several points under the constraints of sail and wind. The one who is most efficient at this task is usually the winner.

John was on top of his form and ended the first weekend of races with a first and second place, giving him the best score for the weekend. He had won the Edgartown regatta and taken a solid lead in the series. Don Law finished with a first and a third, putting him in second place. He was in hot pursuit of John and the Scudder Cup Championship. In the sailing world this was significant because John was the namesake of the one man who had won this coveted prize 11 times. It would also be the first time in 75 years that the trophy had been won first by a father and then by a son. Dad had retired the Scudder Cup three times and had two championship series on a fourth. He only needed one more victorious season to retire the trophy for a fourth time. It is clearly the most impressive sailing record standing in America and John and I tried to live up to our father's legendary status.

The challenge was to be Hyannis and it was soon upon us. That day was a spectacular picture of white sails and multi-colored spinnakers billowing in the wind and sailboats headed in all directions. Of the three regattas, Hyannis is the biggest, with up to 20 different fleets sailing on eight to 10 racecourses. All the Wianno boats sail to Hyannis in the morning; it is a memorable scene watching these boats sail. If you close your eyes, you can almost imagine being back in the 1800s.

The day was what we call a blow, with winds gusting up to 20 knots, and white foam topping the waves with whitecaps. On a day like that, the wind starts off steady at 10 to 12 knots, then gradually, over the day, accelerates up to 20 to 30 knots. The marine weather forecast indicated steady strong winds out of the southwest, 20 to 25 knots—a day when the Fallon boat is un-beatable. There was no need to tow the Marna out. All John had to do was cast off the mooring line to feel the power of the wind. Within moments the Marna was mingling with the rest of the Wianno fleet.

My crew of beauties was sitting on the transom of my 70-mile-an-hour Formula, the CunaMara. It was a sight to behold: Sue, Cindy Degrasse and John's girlfriend—two blonde bomb-shells in bikinis, one a gorgeous brunette. I was in heaven as we paraded around the starting line. All the male chauvinists on the racecourse drooled over my crew. Most of them spent more time straining to get a good look at the girls instead of concentrating on the starting sequence. BOOM! roared the starting gun, indi-cating 10 minutes to the start. Just then, Senator Kennedy's blue schooner silently slipped past us 20 feet to leeward. He was alone with Doug, his captain; Teddy looked resplendent sitting at the helm in a special chair to support his back. As he passed, he noticed the girls and altered course to get a better look, standing up and straining to see who they were. He knew the boat, but the ladies were a different matter. He barked a dozen orders to Doug in coming about, a task that normally takes six to seven men. That, in itself, is a major accomplishment for two people, a trib-ute to their abilities. When he approached us on the second pass, he hailed, "Hello, Bill, I like your crew! May I come aboard?"

"Good day to you, Senator. I can manage the boat with my present crew, thank you!" I responded.

"I'm sure you can, Bill, give my best to your father," and off into the horizon he sailed.

BOOM! The five-minute warning rumbled in the distance. The Marna was at the committee boat end of the line trying to time the start and position to have a clear wind and freedom to tack. At the one-minute mark, I lost sight of John and strained to see the sail numbers on the boats around him. In a race of this size, boats of all colors mingle and it is easy to mistake one boat for another. Thirty seconds to the start—there was a traffic jam at the committee boat end. Some boats were early and sped on to the buoy end; others luffed their sails in an attempt to slow their speed. Everywhere confusion reigned with skippers shouting rules and regulations to each other, weaving in and out of traffic.

Ten seconds to go! The wind increased, knocking boats down with powerful gusts. Waves were bobbing the boats like corks in a pool full of kids. Nine, eight, seven, out John emerged from behind a blue Senior. From our vantage point down the line from the committee boat, it looked as if he was early. Six, five, four, ran the clock. Three seconds to go and John had a slot 10 yards from the end of the line with clear air and plenty of ocean in front of him. One boom resonated—the black powder cannon sounding the start of the race.

John was the third boat across the starting line and, more importantly, had a free wind and room to navigate in his bid to win the third race of the series. When the gun started the race, the winds were a strong 20 to 25 knots, the seas were 3—maybe 4—feet tall and building. It was going to be a tough physical day with fast-paced action and possible injuries or damage. When the boats reached the first mark, there were three boats well ahead of the rest of the fleet. John was in third, Karl Anderson second, and the Tracys—the local favorites—were in first. The Marna rounded the mark with its spinnaker pole up and the Mac Pacs ready to pop the spinnaker. WHOOP! flapped the sail as it filled with wind and the bow surged ahead of the waves. It would be a parade from here on in, with the Marna taking third place.

Sunday rolled around quickly and soon we were out to the starting line again. This time conditions were calm with light south winds at 5 knots. The contrast from Saturday to Sunday was dramatic—little or no swells, light and inconsistent winds. These conditions can be the most stressful and nerve-wracking. The crew work on this day had to be flawless. In some instances, the light-air days demand as much care as the windy days. The boat that makes the least mistakes will be the winner. The start is crucial and, if the boys are to do well, they have to be in a good position with clear air ahead. Several times the race committee attempted to start the race and several times too many boats were over the line early and the recall signal sounded. Finally, on the fourth attempt, the majority of boats were on the line and not over early. The few that were would be hailed by the committee boat and would have to turn around to restart the race. On that particular day the boys had woken up late, a bit cranky from their celebration the night before. Overconfidence and cocky attitudes can be the downfall of any young sailor. The sea has a way of teaching those who try to master her who is the mightier; she can be as placid as a reflecting pool or as violent as a tornado. The crew of the Marna was going to learn a lesson from Mother Nature and the sea.

At the first windward mark, the lead boats all rounded in such a mass of confusion, with sea lawyers screaming rules at one another, that it was difficult to determine which boat was in the lead. The wind shifted radically and the lead changed hands several times. John was in the lead once minute and last the next. It was a frustrating day; the wind's velocity ranged from zero to 5 knots. At the halfway point, the race had taken almost two hours, with an hour and a half to go before the time limit expired and the race would be abandoned. No boat would be awarded any points for the series. I hoped the race would not count, then prayed it would count, depending on the position John was in. At the last mark before the long windward leg to the finish line, the Marna was in fifth place. A respectable placing that would not hurt John's results when averaged out over the series. Just as they reached the halfway point to the finish line, the wind changed direction by 180 degrees. That meant the wind was coming from behind and the whole fleet was riding the puffs down on the lead boats. It was agonizing to watch as the Marna sat helplessly in a wind hole while 25 sailboats sailed up to it before they would all be in the same wind. When the fleet caught up to John, they easily took his winds and about seven boats passed him before he obtained enough momentum to stave off the rest of the fleet.

John had lost ground to several boats. He was in 14th place— the result of the winds, not his ability. It would even up the results between the top four boats; John had slipped to third in the standings. The weekend was not the success that Edgartown was, but kept John in the running for the coveted Scudder Cup.

Chapter 13

The end of July was approaching and I spent hours on end at my private spot on the point—a self-imposed exile. Before, every minute of every day was important. Post-surgery, it was easier to ignore the hour of the day or the week of the month, to be free of responsibilities. The natural beauty of the point and the sweet warbling of the songbirds saved me as I pondered my health, trying to assess the damage and imagine what would happen next. The weeks before I faced my next challenge were flying by. I had an appointment with Dr. Crowell on August 7th, two days after the Scudder Cup series. At the meeting, I would listen to the doctors' recommendation for dealing with the large AVM in the left occipital lobe of my brain.

The Friday before the Wianno regatta marked the end of a milestone I had set for myself. The present endeavor was the Scudder Cup and after the last race was sailed, I would set a new goal. Around 4 p.m. on Friday, John rumbled into the Ponderosa. He was nervous, with good reason. The standings between John, Karl Anderson and Don Law were close. Historically it has come down to the sixth and final race before any one of the best four boats could win. Race five was only 18 hours away. The crew was trickling in, and the atmosphere in the house was convivial as preparations for a feast got underway. Scott helped cousin Jackie and me fold and pack the spinnakers and John polished the bottom of the Marna to a shine.

Dinner was ready, hot on the table. In a surge of humanity, the whole gang gathered around the 14-foot oak dining room table with thrones at the ends and benches on the sides. The scene was almost medieval, the epitome of an Irish clan gathering to celebrate a festive holiday in this huge room with fireplaces at either end. The noise and commotion were almost more than I could process and I felt pain and anxiety building inside me. At one point, it was so distressful that I went onto the porch until everyone had filled their plates and taken a seat.

At the dinner table, Dad espoused the virtues of the competition while offering his wisdom and tactics for the last two races. In his own way he was trying to help, but from John's perspective, it only added pressure. John had scored impressively in the first four races with a first, two thirds, and a 14th. The point spread was less than four points between the top three leaders and anything could happen. I offered little advice, knowing the effect it would have on my brother. I did not want to add to his stress level.

As is the custom, John reviewed "The Eldridge" to determine the direction and velocity of the tidal currents. This publication has guided New Englanders for generations, indicating the tides and currents that have wrecked many sailors on the tricky shoals of Nantucket Sound. That day it indicated a westerly current travelling at 1.8 knots until 4 p.m., then shifting to the east initially with less than a knot of current. At approximately 5 p.m., the current would head east at a strong 2 knots. That information may not seem important to the non-sailor, but to an experienced one, it meant winning or losing. The tidal currents around Wianno are very strong and local knowledge is critical in determining tactics. Dad was trying to give John the benefit of his 35 years of knowledge of these currents. To escape after dinner, John headed out to Joe's Twin Villa, a local watering hole where the skippers and crews assembled. Next morning the effects of the evening showed on John and the crew.

On Saturday, the sky was blue with a slight scattering of high clouds. Sue and I were set to tow John out to the starting line while Mom and Dad watched from their boat. For some inexplicable reason, John was held up, probably experiencing a combination of nerves and a hangover. This meant the Marna was late getting to the starting line, which did not allow time to study the wind shifts or determine the favored end of the line. When they finally got their act together, the first gun had fired; they had about seven minutes to the start.

As Jack had predicted, the right side of the course was the favored side to defend. Traditionally, under these conditions, the first boat at the committee boat side of the line takes a substantial advantage. All that needed to be done from there was to tack to the right side of the course and be the first boat to take a tack to the west. If you had boat speed and implemented good covering tactics, the race could be won in the first five minutes after the start. Today that person was not John. Due to his late arrival and poor mental condition, he was in a terrible place for the start. The lead boat was Karl Anderson, some other Hyannis Port boats were behind him, and the other lead boat in the series was Don Law in ninth. I could tell it was going to be a long afternoon. Sue and I knew Jack had been right in his assessment of the race the night before but John had not taken his advice.

John was in bad air and decided to tack to the left side of the course. His positioning went from bad to worse. I could not stand to watch John blow the race after prematurely celebrating his first-place standing in the Scudder Cup, so Sue suggested we run over to Baxter's up the coast for some fried clams. We turned the boat east and hit the throttles of the CunaMara. The big 454 horsepower twin Mercruisers roared with the acceleration as we powered up toward Hyannis. The service at Baxter's is fast. In less than an hour and a half, we had eaten and were westbound toward Wianno. When we arrived at the starting line, 1_ miles off the beach from the Wianno club, the race was about three-quarters of the way through. At the end of the race, John had finished ninth. A lucky break—when the scores were totaled up through the five races, he had only dropped a few points into second place. Don Law was in first and Karl Anderson was back in fifth.

One more race and the results would be final; John could still win the coveted prize with a strong finish on Sunday. If he was not careful, however, he would have the dubious honor of giving away the cup to a good time on the town. Someone must have prevailed on him to stay in Saturday night, because he and the crew prepared the chutes and reviewed the tide books after dinner. When those chores were completed, the whole gang rented a movie. My head felt like a soccer ball after the World Cup, and I headed to the crow's nest for a long night's sleep. Sue woke me up late Sunday morning—it was obvious to her that I was pushing it past my limits.

On the way down the path to the dock, I could not help thinking that this might be the last time I would use my boat or stand on the dock. The anxiety was like no other pain I had felt before. I had to think of something else and stay active, or I would lose it. I don't remember much about Sunday's race because I was lost in that secret internal world everyone has deep within consciousness. I was filled with the notion that everything I did was my last act: the last boat ride or the last time to see someone I loved. Anything I did until the day of surgery might be my last act ever.

The fate of my brother's sailing career was on the line, the last Sunday of the Fredrick A. Scudder memorial trophy—the Wianno Senior Class championship. The day was a little cloudy with light southerly winds at 8 to 10 knots. The current would run to the east, strong all afternoon. A racing day for tactics and wind slants, steady winds with slants of 5 degrees and no more. These brief instances were the key ingredients for a victory on a southerly wind. If you can position your boat on the course to capitalize on these little wind shifts, you can add valuable boat lengths between yourself and the competition.

Sue and I decided it was too stressful to watch the entire race, so we went to the windward mark in the CunaMara, anchored a safe distance away from it and snoozed. Since I was fatigued, a nap would do me some good and Sue could catch up on her lost sleep too. Even with help, the kids were a bundle and exhausted us with their youthful energy. When Sue and I woke up from a well-earned nap, it was after 4 p.m. and the last boats in the fleet were rounding the final mark, heading to the finish. The usual yelling and swearing from the racecourse had woken us from our sleep. The crew work on the mark rounding is an exciting moment in the race when the sails are jibbed and spinnakers set for the 1-mile run to the finish. If this ballet of movements is choreographed and executed well, you can move up in the standings. If not, there is usually a lot of yelling orders and reciting rule infractions accompanied by denials from the offenders. I had no idea where John was positioned in the fleet. As the last of the fleet headed downwind, we weighed anchor and cranked up the big engines to blast our way to the finish line. On the way, we would try to find John.

Within minutes we were positioned near the finish line, along with the usual retinue of spectators anxious to see who would win the race and the coveted trophy. In the lead was Lew Gunn, then a white chute—which could be John—and then Holly Edmonds. I could distinguish Holly Edmonds and Lew Gunn from the colors of their spinnakers. Since several boats in the fleet have white spinnakers, whoever was in fourth was a guess, but it appeared to be Karl Anderson. If John was the second-place boat and Karl Anderson was in fourth, it could be a great day in the Fallon home, for John would be the first son of a Scudder Cup champion to win the cup. As the lead boats drew closer to the finish Sue and I could clearly see the sail numbers of the top four. It was still too close to call and a luffing match developed between the fourth- and fifth-place boats. I hoped the fifth-place boat overtake the fourth-place boat—that would give John a little breathing room in the scoring. Then we saw that John was in first or second place. It was also apparent that the two leaders would have to jibe for the finish or they would not reach the finish line. This is the crucial point in the race where a good or bad jibe can mean the difference between first and second place.

No sooner had I said that to Sue than the two leaders started to make their moves and jibe for the line. John was second and Lew Gunn first, but they were very close. People were shouting and screaming from the spectator's fleet. It was a great way to finish a series that had been very close from race to race. One minute it looked like John was in first, the next minute it was Lew Gunn. Horns started to blare from the spectator's fleet and excitement was at a fever pitch. The race for third, fourth and fifth also was important, but the excitement of the two lead boats was overwhelming. To win, John had to place in the top five and put two places between himself and Karl Anderson. The race for first and second was down to a matter of yards and appeared to be a dead-even race.

Seconds passed. It was down to a matter of feet and the winner would be decided. The horns of 20 spectator boats blasting away were so loud I could hardly hear the cannon shot signaling that the winner had crossed the line. I did not need to! From my vantage point, I could see that the white-hulled boat slipped across the line 2 feet behind the blue-hulled Wianno. John had redeemed himself and sailed the best race of his life, only to lose the race by the surge Lew Gunn got from a wave. The real winner overall was not to be decided until Holly Edmonds passed Karl Anderson on their jibe to the finish, putting him three boats behind John.

John had won his first Scudder Cup championship and received the traditional toss over the side. It was a great day for John. It was also the end of the milestones I had set for myself before I submitted myself to the doctors for the real race for my life. It had been five months since my operation and I was getting impatient. On Tuesday, Dr. Crowell would review my options and determine a date to enter the hospital.

When we reached the house, we found Dad waiting for the results on the dock. He had decided not to watch the race and had no idea how John had finished. When he heard the news, he had a smile and a hug for his youngest son, congratulating him sincerely. The gratification he received from John's victory would last a long time. A legacy had been perpetuated and a Fallon had earned the right to place his name on the trophy for the 10th time, something no other family or individual had come close to accomplishing. I am not aware of an individual or a family dominating a fleet as much as my father has. John had the potential of perpetuating the legacy. The next day, The Boston Globe ran an article about the race and the sailing world knew that there was a new Fallon name being uttered in the back rooms of the Wianno Senior fleet.

In my heart I knew the day was coming for me to face my toughest challenge. As it drew near, I was becoming stronger physically. At the same time my apprehension grew—I was terrified. The consequences of my ordeal so far were not as bad as everything had sounded at the beginning. Even though I had taken a beating physically, emotionally I felt I was holding up. I kept telling myself that if the second operation was anything like the first and if I recovered as well as I had after the first, I should be back on my feet in six to nine months. I honestly started to think I would be able to ski again by March 1992.

Some of my friends felt I should wait a year before I endured the second operation. I could not stand the thought of living with that kind of uncertainty. The argument for surgery as soon as possible was strong. In contrast, some of the physicians believed time to recover and letting technology advance was the other side of the coin. I did not think time was in my best interest. A salesman and an athlete, I always took big risks. The danger and excitement of any challenge were alluring. In a deal, you have to work toward the close, pushing all the time. In heli-skiing, you are at risk every second you're out there. It doesn't matter whether you are standing on top of a steep chute or flying to the top of the next peak. You are in constant danger and do not have time to be afraid. In my present condition, I had nothing but time to think about the risks. I could not bear it any longer.

Monday night was a long slow night. I lay in bed staring at the ceiling, wondering what the doctors would say. I hoped that they would walk into the room with the news, "Bill, we have a new technique to cure your AVM. All you need is a series of shots over the next three weeks." The next day, Sue and I took Shannon to camp, left Flash with our nanny and drove slowly to Mass General.

Chapter 14

Sue and I arrived first. Dad arrived shortly after 10 a.m. and Dr. Crowell came in right behind him. My nerves were on fire; my feet felt like moving—I wanted to pace the floor like a caged tiger. Sue grabbed my hand to reassure me I was not alone in this nightmare. The shirt under my suit jacket was wet under my arms and down my back from sweat. Just as we reached the threshold of Dr. Crowell's office, Dr. Gress and Dr. Desanctis walked in through the back door of the office. The doctor had an escape route—I had none! Dr. Gress was strong and confident. He helped me read between the lines of medical jargon, took time to explain procedures and conveyed the seriousness of my plight without scaring me to death.

Dr. Crowell began by explaining that the first AVM had been a small, entangled bundle of veins located in the brain with an aneurysm inside that had shown indications of hemorrhaging; in many ways, more dangerous and life threatening than the one in the occipital lobe. However, the larger AVM involved a more serious operation. If they were to try to remove it, its size and location would cause some deficits. It depended on how much the tumor could first be shrunk. This was the first time I had been told I might not be suitable for surgery!

The conversation turned to the options for reducing the size of the malformation. One procedure, the photon beam or gamma knife, was not a viable option due to the size of my AVM. The second was called cerebral immobilization. Dr. Crowell explained the procedure as similar to the angiogram, but the catheters are inserted in the femoral and carotid arteries. I interrupted him to ask where they insert the catheters and how long a session takes.

"The catheters enter the arteries in the groin and serpentine up through the vascular network until one catheter is located on one end of the malformation and one is at the other side. In essence, they are a delivery and receiver setup," he explained.

"A sender of what?" I asked.

"The deliverer releases glue into the holes that are located where a capillary did not form," he replied.

"What is a capillary?" I asked.

"They are the vascular equivalent of a mixing box; the capillary reduces the rate of blood flow and is the valve between the arteries and veins. Without them, the veins will eventually burst. If the glue holds, the flow of blood will be reduced and, in turn, the malformation should shrink."

"What kind of glue is it?" I asked.

"It's acrylic glue, somewhat like Crazy Glue," he said. Dr. Crowell then explained that it was an experimental procedure and that the glue might cause cancer at a later date! "Wonderful," I thought, "I'm a guinea pig who will either be dead from this strange birth defect or dead from cancer at some later date from the glue." The whole thing sucked and my mood grew worse.

"What is the other catheter for?" I asked.

"It's to catch the glue if it doesn't adhere to the holes," explained Dr. Crowell.

"What happens if the catheter doesn't catch the glue?" I wanted to know.

"You suffer a stroke and probably die," were his words.

"How long does this procedure last?"

"Seven or eight hours," he said.

"How many times will you do the procedure?" I asked.

Dr. Crowell replied, "We do not know, if it works the first time we may do it four, five, six, maybe a dozen times."

"Is there any pain associated with the procedure?" I asked.

"We are very good with medication. It will be painless. The immobilization will be performed as many times as we can until we shrink the AVM enough to reduce the risk of surgery."

"So this will not eliminate the need for an operation?" I asked.

"No, if this treatment does not shrink the AVM, we may not be able to operate at all. The AVM in the occipital lobe is too large to operate without causing major deficits," explained Dr. Crowell.

"What are the probabilities of death?" I asked.

"In all surgery, death is a possible result, but I believe you will survive with the deficits we have talked about. There is a 100-percent chance of these deficits occurring. However, the degree of deficits depends on how much we can shrink the malformation. The end result will be a loss of about 50 percent of peripheral vision and a number of other deficits."

I wondered if he meant both eyes or one eye?

"What are the other deficits?" I asked.

"There will be no other major deficits but many small neurological functions will be lost," he said.

"What are the major deficits?" This seemed to me to be an important question.

"Walking, talking, seeing and motor skills are the major functions; we do not know which minor functions will be affected, although some cognizant abilities will be impaired. It's the major functions we concern ourselves with," said Dr. Crowell.

"What determines the extent of the deficits?" I asked.

Dr. Crowell replied, "It depends on how much brain tissue we damage or remove during surgery, and I cannot say until we attempt the immobilization."

I felt detached from reality as I listened to the good doctor; it was as if I was not in the room. I could see his mouth moving, but I could not hear the words. Then I heard his voice clearly as I came out of my daydreaming.

"Because you are a 'go for it' kind of guy, we are going to first immobilize the AVM as many times as we can. We will move you to your room and observe you for a couple of hours. Then we will send you home for a week and bring you in again to immobilize the AVM a second time. We will do this until we cannot shrink the AVM anymore. Then we will schedule surgery for the next day and surgically incise the malformation.

"How will I feel after the immobilization?" I asked.

"There is a good chance you will have a headache for a while," said Dr. Crowell.

"Tell me about the surgery," I probed.

"Well, we will go in at the back of the head in the general region of the occipital lobe, remove the skull, and start to cut and suture each vein, artery and vessel until the malformation is removed. Then we will send it to be biopsied at the lab. When the malformation is eliminated, we will perform a post-surgery angiogram to confirm that all the malformation has been removed. Then we will close you up and move you to the neuro-intensive care unit for observation."

"How long will I be in intensive care?" I asked.

"It depends on how slowly we bring you back," he explained.

"Where am I going?" I asked myself. I asked Dr. Crowell what he meant.

"We will keep you down for a day or two to monitor your vital signs and to be sure all the hundreds of vessels and veins are sutured completely. We can observe you for any hemorrhaging. By keeping you under anesthesia, we can quickly re-enter the brain to stop any bleeding before too much damage occurs," he explained.

All of this really frightened me, but I tried not to show it. I pondered the meaning of "bring you back." Back from where? Sue asked a few poignant questions, Dad inquired about the risk, and the doctor explained that the percentage of risk was dependent on the type of surgery. Clearly brain surgery has the greatest risk of all surgery, but the risks were greater if we did nothing. I listened to the dialogue and realized that I had a greater chance to live through brain surgery than without it. There were a hundred things to ask, but I was still thinking of the words "bring you back." Was I going someplace? Where would I be? Would I know where I was? Would I remember anything or have any conscious thought? I was paralyzed by fear. A hundred times before, I had called Dr. Karen with questions and now I could not muster the courage to ask any of them. I did not know what to think, but I was sure being told what to do. I had to undergo this surgery or die.

The doctors had done a compassionate job of coaching me into the surgery and it was time to determine the schedule. I found myself agreeing to anything they asked. My subconscious was making the decisions my conscious was too afraid to handle. I was trying to act calm and brave while deep down I wanted to cry my eyes out. I wanted to parachute out of an airplane or bungee jump from the Golden Gate Bridge. I wanted to challenge death in any way other than brain surgery or a cerebral hemorrhage. Let me run with the bulls in Palermo, Italy, or fight communist insurgents in South America—anything but the doctor's scalpel.

It would have been cowardly and selfish not to say yes to the surgery. I felt Sue's gentle touch on my hand. She was repeating a question Dr. Crowell had asked me.

"Do you want to be an autologic donor again?"

"How much will you need?" I asked.

"Two, like the last time," he answered.

"Should I do one today?"

"Yes. I'll call them and arrange an appointment," he replied.

Dad was consulting with Dr. Desanctis in hushed tones and Sue was quizzing Dr. Gress. I was thinking of a zillion images and desires, all dealing with the question: "What will life be after the operation?" Was this the only way to deal with this genetic deficit that left me so powerless? When the doctor asked if a date near the end of August was acceptable, I reluctantly answered, "Yes."

"Julie will call you with a date and time to come in for the first angioplasty. In the meantime, she will set you up with an appointment at the blood center."

Dr. Crowell grabbed my shoulder and reassured me with a light pat on the back.

"You will do alright, you have a lot going for you. Spend the next few weeks taking it easy, enjoy your family, spend some time with that new son of yours, and we will see you at the end of the month."

"Thank you," I said.

I followed Sue, Dad, Dr. Gress and Dr. Desanctis out of the office. As we passed Julie, she informed me that the blood bank was waiting for me and that she would call us by Friday with a date to be admitted. I excused myself from my three companions and meandered toward the blood bank. My movements felt awkward, as if I were an animated cartoon character.

When I arrived at the donor center, I introduced myself as an autologic donor and was subjected to the first of thousands of blood samples and blood counts that the hematology department required. In the donor area I obliged one of the technicians, took a relaxed posture on a vacant table, and rolled up my sleeve. I knew the routine and cooperated reluctantly. I lay there imagining the next few weeks and the unpleasantness ahead of me. I was told the angioplasty was similar to the angiogram but longer in duration. Over the next 40 minutes, I lay there despondent, lamenting over the events of the morning and wondering what else could go wrong in my life. After a while, Sue arrived to pick me up and drive home. I asked her if I could drive the Porsche—I felt the need for speed, some impetuous selfish act to purge my deep despair by driving that red rocket home at maximum velocity. One hundred sixty miles an hour sounded like enough speed to travel through time. I was going to be irresponsible and drive home as if I were racing in the Grand Prix of Monaco.

Sue and I walked quietly to the parking garage where my bright red Porsche sat pristine and clean, shining in the glare of the sunlight filtering in. I instructed Sue to buckle up because I was going to be foolish and drive fast. I wasn't worried about being busted for speeding because I had the makings of a great story to talk my way out of any encounter with the law. We got into the car and buckled up. Sue looked into what must have been the eyes of a terrified man and asked that I try not to kill us both on the way home. I had nothing to lose; she, on the other hand, was the picture of health, the mother of my children and the love of my life. I assured her the last thing I wanted to do was harm her. With that declaration, I turned the key to hear the awesome purr of a finely tuned, German-engineered racecar. I glanced at her with a devilish gleam in my eye. She smiled and off we went.

We were going to revert to the foolish days of my teen-age years and race home on the Mass Pike, fast, real fast. I hit the tollbooth at the Brighton exit coming off Storrow Drive at about 60 mph, decelerating to almost a stop. The coins flew out the sunroof with a hook shot and, as the tollgate raised, in seconds we were above 70 and closing in on 90 mph. It was a sunny day with a light-to-moderate traffic and a dry road. When one of these cars gets to around 90 mph, the characteristics change—the car feels as if it is sucking up the road. At 110 mph, the noise from the open sunroof becomes deafening. As you go under an overpass, the air explodes in your ears. The slightest movement of the steering wheel and the car reacts like a cat. The engine starts to take on the whining sound you hear when you watch the Indy 500 or the Grand Prix.

At 130 mph, your heart is in your throat and the white dotted line becomes a solid line. When we approached an overpass, it appeared that we were going to fly right over the top. My heart was racing and the adrenaline was pumping hard—a sensation I had not felt in a long time. All of my nerve endings were tingling and I felt alive. I glanced over to look at Sue, and she was loving it. Yes, she was scared, but in her eyes you could see the adrenaline rush she was getting. In a matter of minutes we had reached the Weston tollbooth. I downshifted through all the gears, rolled up to the money basket and tossed out a couple of quarters as I glided through the gate.

Back in November, around the time I was diagnosed, I was accepted into the Weston Golf Club and had been playing the game as often as I could. You can always see a couple of different types of hawks soaring on the thermals rising from the fairways. I asked Sue if she would like to play 18 holes of golf to counteract the effects of the morning at the hospital. With adrenaline still rushing through her veins, Sue said, "Golf? Sure!" Late that afternoon we headed back to the Cape to be with the kids.

Chapter 15

On Sunday, the day before I checked into the hospital for the angioplasty, I went for a sail on the Marna to be alone doing something I loved. Sailing the Marna on a sunny day on North Bay or Nantucket Sound is very cerebral and peaceful. There was a typical breeze, powerful and steady, like a reliable friend who had come to say hello. Answering the call, I pointed the Marna hard to the wind and sat on the rail. The sails bellowed, the boat healed my spirit, and I laughed out loud, a continuous belly laugh that shook my soul and raised my hopes. I had not laughed a good laugh for months. Alone on the sea, my soul was free. Sailing away from shore, I felt like I could leave everything behind and disappear over the horizon. Dark thoughts tried to break my serenity, but my mind held fast, focused on the sails, blue sky and cool water. My body basked in the warmth of the sun as sailors have done for centuries. It penetrated deep into my body and soul with a power and force that rejuvenated me spiritually. I derived a sense of comfort and tranquility from its rays. This must be what it is like to bask in the light of God. I soaked up the life-giving rays as if I were a sponge.

The day was coming to an end as I reached the Wreck Shoal and came about for the long run home and the sanctuary of our little harbor. I tied the helm down with the lines from the running back stay and went forward to set the spinnaker. When it was up and full of air, I unlashed the helm and set a course for the breakwater. I had tears in my eyes but could not cry. The wind spoke to me as it pushed my boat back toward home; it seemed to say, steer the course, hold tight and have faith.

Sailors have a sense to follow their gut feelings. I had this sense; my father and his great sailing mates had taught it to me. I have used this instinct in skiing, in hunting and in business. Now the real test was before me. "I must not lose faith," I thought, then I said it out loud, "I must not lose faith!" I shouted it again to reassure myself and the sound of my voice was met with a gust of wind that accelerated the boat's speed. I settled back and gazed in wonder at the beauty of the Sound. When I finally reached Dam Pond and put the boat away, I felt as if I were doing it for the last time.

I hoped the scrutiny I had been under would soon end. For almost eight months my vigilant wife and family had watched over me as if my every step would bring disaster. But all the watching and waiting was coming to an end. It was time to begin the process again. When preparing for the first surgery, I had packed a CD player, CDs, books and a change of clothes. This time I need not concern myself with those peripherals since I was only going in for the day—and possibly the night—for the first angioplasty. Early Monday morning, off we went to Boston.

Sue and I arrived at Mass General and signed all the waivers and releases of liability. The stack of consent forms was at least 3 inches thick and I was directed to read them carefully. When I asked the admitting officer why there were so many consent forms, she informed me that the procedure was still experimental. In addition to the inherent risk involved in the angioplasty, there was the issue of the carcinogenic acrylic glue that they planned to use to occlude the arteries. Either way the risk of dying was the end result; if the AVM/aneurysms did not kill me, the cure would. As I pressed for more information, I was informed that everything they were going to use on me did not have enough research data for the FDA to approve its use.

After signing the mountain of release forms, Sue and I headed up to Ellison 22 where we were greeted by Anne Geary and Barbara Dunderdale, my Angels of Mercy, who were well aware of my status. They helped me relax, informed me of the routine and made sure I did not eat that night. As soon as they left my room, Dr. Crowell and Dr. John-Pyle Spellman (JPS) arrived to explain the procedure to me. JPS was the best neuro-radial surgeon in the country. In fact, he had spent three years learning the procedure in Russia from the doctor who had developed the method. The proper name for this is intravascular neuro-radial surgery— what a mouthful!

JPS was in his mid-40s, a short, round-faced man with glasses and a little baldness up top. He was soft spoken and polite, always attentive to the emotions of the patient. I sat quietly as, once again, he described the procedure and the risks. He informed me that the procedure was similar to an angiogram except that they placed two catheters into the femoral and carotid arteries, the superhighways to the brain. As he finished the brief lesson on intravascular neuro-radial surgery, he asked if I had any questions.

"Why do you need to go through two arteries instead of one?"

"The first catheter releases the glue into the hole," he answered.

"What hole?" I asked.

"The hole where there are no capillaries to reduce the flow of blood from the artery into the vein," he said.

"How many times will you occlude the AVM?"

"As many times as we can, until the flow of blood into the AVM is reduced sufficiently to reduce the size of the malformation. If we are successful in stopping the flow of blood into the malformation, we may reduce its size and, at the same time, reduce the area of brain tissue we damage. This will minimize the deficits," he explained.

Then I said, "The second catheter is located on the other end or the exit artery from the malformation. This catheter is supposed to catch the glue if it does not adhere to the holes. What happens if the second catheter does not catch the glue?"

JPS responded, "The result is a stroke and most likely death."

I could not win this struggle. All the cures for me were extreme, experimental and could kill me, or, at a minimum, disable me for the rest of my life. I thought, then asked, "Why do you have to use a substance that may be cancer-causing and unapproved by the FDA?"

"The FDA approval process is a long and expensive ordeal that is used only when the return on investment is warranted and the approved drugs can benefit many patients, not a few. The fact of the matter is that you are a member of an exclusive club of patients. The cost outweighs the benefits. In addition, the technologies are advancing in this field so fast that tomorrow there may be something else to use that is not cancerous," he said.

Well, that made sense, but it did not make me feel better. "What will I feel like after the glue is released?"

"Once the catheters are in the right location, we will use a little sodium nitrate to replicate the effect of occluding the arteries. The drug will duplicate the effects of removing the flow of blood to the brain and, if everything goes black, we will stop and not go any further. If nothing happens, we will continue to occlude the holes until we can't do anymore," he said.

I was afraid now. This was the first time anyone had indicated that I might go totally blind. "How long will this procedure take?"

"Usually seven or eight hours, sometimes less and sometimes more," he answered.

Oh God! I never imagined any of this and I was too naive to ask before. The fight for survival was much more involved and uncomfortable than I could have imagined. I was beginning to think the less I knew, the better off I was.

I asked the inevitable question: "After the test of the sodium nitrite, what happens then?"

"Well, if all goes well and your vision and other functions are working, we will proceed with the glue," he said.

I thought to myself, "If all goes well, what else could go wrong?"

I asked, "When you finally occlude the arteries, what will that feel like? Is there any pain?"

"Yes," he replied, "there is some pain but it lasts only a few seconds, then it will pass."

"What kind of pain is it?" was my next question.

"Some patients have described it as a hot or burning sensation," he explained.

"Well, that does not seem too bad," I thought. "What time are we going to do this?" I asked.

"Tomorrow morning around seven-thirty, is that all right with you?" JPS asked.

"Yeah," I mumbled and we shook hands.

Sue and I were left alone. I felt as if I were on a sinking ship where I was the one passenger on the boat who could not fit into the life raft and had to swim in shark-infested waters. I was going in for some major brain sculpturing and would suffer battle damage of major proportions. Over the next few hours, Sue and I talked about the process and how I had started to feel that I was not able to endure all of this poking and prodding. I was afraid of the intrusion into my brain. I was also fearful of the complications that every doctor had outlined. The enormous risk associated with each treatment was more terrifying than the surgery. At least in surgery I would not be aware of any problems or deficits until I woke up—that's if I woke up.

Soon our conversation turned to issues we philosophized over in our college days—the Vietnam war, civil rights, free love, experimentation with drugs, the anti-establishment movement. We were skirting the real issue—the reality of my death. I had to talk to Sue about my wishes for the disposal of my remains and how to mourn my passing. I believed the fateful day was coming soon. I did not believe I would die during the angioplasty treatments, but I knew that once past that hurdle, surgery and death might only be a week or even days away. I did not want to think of or discuss these issues, but I had to or I would never make peace with my life. I told Sue that if anything happened to me, she should use my trust to pay off the mortgage and spend the rest on herself and the kids. I would make sure that any of my inheritance from my parents went to her and the kids. I did not have any life insurance policies because I had never liked the industry or the people in it.

I had to be strong and confident and maintain a positive outlook. A positive frame of mind was the only way I knew to fight an unseen foe or combat depression. Yes, I was waging war of sorts—the ultimate battle that takes will power, courage and, most of all, confidence. The tug of war in my emotions was constant and relentless. Whenever my depression or fear began to threaten my confidence, Sue lifted my spirits. She labored most of the day and night to maintain a positive attitude and ward off the demons that tried to overpower me from within.

As the night lingered on, we reminisced about years gone by, recalling the six months we spent traveling the United Stated and Canada, living out of my van. The train trips across the continent and backpacking were some of our best memories. In our 36 years of life, we were fortunate to be able to do things that many people would never have the opportunity to do. There were hundreds of reasons for us to consider our good fortune, there were also hundreds of reasons to lament our potentially lost aspirations. It was inevitable for us to return to the harsh realities of my predicament and talk about my wishes if I were left a vegetable or in a coma. I did not want Sue to incur the expensive responsibility of using all our funds to maintain my life if I were incapacitated. I told her to let me die if that were the case. I could not endure the thought of her standing a vigil while I slowly withered away on life support systems.

The evening hours were passing quickly and soon the night nurse came in to help us make up the convertible bed so that Sue could stay. Sue always falls asleep between 9 and 10 p.m. This trait was so prevalent that you can set your watch by it. That night was a little different, however, and we stayed up until midnight talking about the future and how things might change. Sometime in the late evening, Sue fell asleep and I lay there staring at the ceiling.

Early in the morning, I slipped out of my room to go to the waiting room on the east side overlooking Boston Harbor and Logan airport. The sunrise was a kaleidoscope of colors against a pale blue sky. It was a beautiful sight and reinforced my will to continue to fight the odds. Quietly, I returned to my room to avoid the wrath of the nurses. I also did not want Sue to worry about my whereabouts. If she woke up and found my bed empty, she might have thought I had gotten cold feet and split. I stealthily entered the bathroom and took a shower and shaved to feel clean and refreshed. If I were to lie on a cold sterile table stark naked, I might as well smell clean for the 10 or 12 people standing over me. When I emerged from the bathroom, Sue was up and the nurse came in to tell me my ride would be in by 8 a.m. It was now quarter of eight and I was starting to get a little nervous. In walked Barbara with a handful of Phenobarbital and two little yellow pills I had not seen before. When I asked her what they were, she said they were Valium.

Chapter 16

At precisely 8 a.m., the gurney arrived to take me to the second floor, the radiology floor. In the center of the operating room was a surgical table surrounded by several large X-ray machines. Suspended from the ceiling was a big screen for viewing X-rays. My gurney was maneuvered adjacent to the table and I was asked to slide over to it and lie on my back. My first sensation was of cold steel, but the table soon absorbed my body heat and I was covered with a white sheet. The table felt about 1 foot too narrow and my arms kept sliding off and dangling in the air. A technician then placed supports on the table for my arms and tied them to the table with sterile gauze. A nurse helped me squirm around on the table as X-ray machines were positioned to focus on my head from every possible angle. The room was full of people, about 12 doctors, nurses and technicians busily hustling about moving equipment and instruments into position.

In walked JPS, Dr. Crowell and three other doctors I had not met. JPS introduced everyone and reassured me that they were going to take good care of me. The three doctors were all from the neurology and radiology departments. I was introduced to Dr. Lotfi Hacein-bey, who was JPS's right-hand man, and Dr. Pasquale. These doctors would have the delicate job of working the catheters. The other doctor was the anesthesiologist. As he inserted an IV into my arm, he explained that he was giving me morphine and Valium to make me comfortable. The next thing I knew the sheet covering my body was pulled off and there I was, fully exposed to a dozen men and women. I was embarrassed, to say the least, but the speedball medication was starting to take effect and it did not seem to matter. Dr. Hacein-bey, a compassionate man, placed a cloth over my genitals and a heavy lead protective shield on my chest. If I survived all this X-ray exposure, I would probably glow in the dark for weeks.

I began to lose consciousness of my body from the waist down. I was told of each injection in my groin to neutralize the nerve ending before each incision. I felt a little moisture on my right leg and then on my left—blood from the incision in order to get at the two arteries in my legs. It was really weird to feel the blood trickling down my crotch but not to have any sensation from the manipulation of the catheters as they were inserted into my arteries. All the time this was going on, Dr. Hacein-bey and I were conversing about my ugly feet and then about my family. He was aware that I was a little uptight and tried to ease my tension. The combination of morphine and Valium was taking effect and my limbs felt as if they were held down by heavy lead weights. I had absolutely no sensation from the waist down, and I did not care about anything at all.

Dr. Hacein-bey was busily working the catheters and occasionally glanced over at the monitor. I could see for myself the location of the first catheter as it slithered its way through my vascular system. I was aware that the catheter was within my body, but felt no sensation. The delivering catheter was in place. It seemed like several hours had passed before Dr. Hacein-bey began to insert the second catheter, the catcher catheter. I felt a little popping sensation behind my ears as the catheters entered my brain. The constant "*ssst ssst ssst*" sound of the catheters as they snaked through me was unsettling. Every so often Dr. Hacein-bey would tap out the oxygen bubbles that were forming in my blood.

JPS asked if I was ready for the sodium nitrate test, and I replied, "Ready when you are." At that, he gave me a reassuring pat on the leg and disappeared into the control room. Within a few minutes I heard JPS over a PA system telling me that they were going to release a little sodium nitrate into the areas where no capillaries existed to control the blood pressure from the arteries to the veins. I was told that I would feel a warm sensation in the back of my left eye, but that it would subside very quickly. It felt as if someone had touched the back of my left eyeball with a burning cigarette. The pain jolted me as the intense but precisely located burning sensation started at a low level of intensity, peaked quickly and then faded as fast as it arrived. Then JPS asked what I could or could not see. Dr. Hacein-bey held up his hands and asked me to tell him how many fingers he was holding up. I replied, "Ten," and they all exclaimed, "Great! Now we will start to glue the holes." I did not feel anything until JPS announced over the microphone that he was about to occlude what he called the feeder artery.

He started a countdown that reminded me of NASA and as he reached zero, I experienced a sharp, jabbing sensation of pain. It was as if someone had pinched me real hard at the center of my brain. It was a brief but jolting pain that lasted only seconds but felt like minutes. It was weird as the artery or vein collapsed, because I could feel it run along the artery in the back of my left eye to the back of my head as the flow was cut off. It was slow at first, but then a steady pressure developed within the center of my brain.

I thought the gluing took only a few minutes, but I realized later that from the time the procedure began until the time they started to glue me lasted about three hours, and the actual gluing took at least another hour. Then the anesthesiologist slipped me a mickey and I awoke sometime later to find Dr. Pasquale and Dr. Hacein-bey applying a great deal of pressure to the arteries on either side of my groin. They placed sandbags on my legs and it took almost 30 minutes for the femoral artery to clot enough for the sandbags to be removed. Then I was wheeled off to a room somewhere on the second floor to allow the drugs to slowly wear off. The sensation in my head was unbearable. It felt as if my brain was swelling up to the point where my head would explode. I hoped when I woke up the intense pain would be gone and succumbed to the desire for sleep. When I woke up, JPS and Sue were standing over me and discussing the angioplasty.

To my dismay, I had a major-league headache on the level of one of my migraines, a pressure pain spread out on the left side of my head. I described it to JPS and said it felt as if the pressure was going to pop my eye out of its socket. He stated that in a week the pain would go away, referring to the upcoming operation. I was amazed when he told Sue and I that I could get up and go home in an hour. I could not comprehend the fact that after such a traumatic invasion of my brain I could go home. The doctors gave me a bottle of Percocets to ward off some of the pain while I waited to be glued again. "Oh, joy," I thought to myself as I staggered toward the door, "I can hardly wait for the next session." That night, after we left the hospital, Sue drove us to the Cape, back to tranquility where I could sit undisturbed out on the point.

* * * * *

The events of the following seven days are blurred and hazy. The days were typical warm August days with steady southerly winds. The first signs of the changing season were appearing on the pond: The white swans had returned, and the great blue herons and snow egrets had headed south. The warm air seemed to fade earlier in the afternoon and the ocean started to cool. I sat out on the point in a lounge chair, sleeping through my pain. The discomfort and pressure were relentless and unending. The only weapons at my disposal were sleep and Percocet, which only relieved the pain temporarily.

As the week passed, I was able to move around, but my headache made it difficult to get motivated for anything more active than working on my suntan. I did have some visitors, but I could not sit and discuss anything because the subject always dealt with events in the future. I began to joke about being disabled for life, but Sue found some of my humor macabre. The best way to snap me out of it was to bring Flash into my world and the day seemed a little less dark.

As the day to be admitted for the next angioplasty grew near, I thought of several messages to shave into my hair: "X marks the spot," "Fragile," "Handle with care," and "#2." When I recalled that Dr. Crowell had referred to me as a "Go for it kind of guy," that made my decision easy—I would ask Chuck to shave the words "Go 4 it" into my hair. As the big day was drawing closer, I called Chuck to make an appointment. He suggested that I come in early on Tuesday—my admittance day—five days away. Since I still had to donate a liter of blood, Sue and I drove home to Wayland the next morning to stay the night before I went to the hospital blood bank. We left the kids at the Cape with our nanny.

Whether I survived or died, this would be the last time Sue and I would be alone together. I needed to be alone with her, since I would never be the same person after this night. I needed to be with her and hold her, possibly for the last time. To think I would lose her for an eternity made me want to become a part of her. That night I could not let go of her. I needed to feel her warmth and tenderness, to feel her heart beating against mine. I had to have her all to myself, there was not enough time to share her with anyone, not even our children. I did not want that night to end. I might never again feel the softness of Sue's skin or recognize the sweet smell of her presence. My fate was cheating me of her companionship. My love for Sue was so deep that I was going to risk life and neurological deficits to stay with her for as long as I could. I was willing to trade a few years of good health for a lifetime of disability to be with Sue, the most precious thing in my life.

As a matter of fact, I had made some tough decisions to remain with her since the day I met her in January of 1972. I had passed up a skiing scholarship that would possibly have landed me on the U.S. Ski Team under the great Willy Schefler. I had skied with him in 1968 and again in Colorado in 1971. That was the year he became coach at the University of Denver. I applied to the school through him and was accepted. Around 1976 he was elected head coach of the U.S. Ski Team and, if I was as good as I thought I was, I would have followed him. The scholarship opportunity was offered to me in the spring of 1972 and I decided then that I loved Sue more than anything. I gave up my greatest ambition for her and to this day I do not regret it; in fact, I would have sacrificed everything to live a lifetime with her. Ironically this was my reality now, I was to sacrifice who I was, what I could have been, and all my dreams and aspirations to stay alive in any capacity with her. I intuitively knew that I would never be the same if I survived, which led me to wonder: Would I be loved the same by her?

Over the long hours of the evening, we reminisced about our adventures and exploits over the years where we had spent selfishly indulging in each other. At times that night, we lay together, just holding onto each other, afraid to let go lest we lose one another. The evening sped by faster than I anticipated, but when Sue fell asleep, the night dragged on endlessly. I lay next to Sue, my arms wrapped around her in an embrace, trying to imagine what would become of Sue and my children if I were unable to support them. What pain and anguish would Sue suffer? Would she ever love someone else if I died? I wanted to believe our love would pull me through this and we would endure, no matter what the outcome.

I did not sleep at all that night. I relived my life, questioning my actions and decisions. I tried to imagine what I would do if I were single and independent. Would I make the same decisions? Would I endure the intrusion into my brain or would I run off into the sunset and live like there was no tomorrow? Would I take all my assets and cash them in for a spending spree? The love and responsibility I had was something I could not run from, but that did not stop me from wondering. I had already given up a real estate broker's career without consciously being aware of it. In the last 10 months I had done everything a dying man would do except buy a casket and cemetery plot.

On Tuesday morning I got dressed to go to Chuck's for a haircut and then to the hospital. I started to pack a bag and tried to think of what to bring—pajamas and a robe, toiletries, a CD player and some discs. When I was showered and dressed, I looked at the things I had assembled and realized two things. One, why bring any clothes when I might be severely disabled? Two, I would not require anything at all if I died. So I just grabbed the CD player and discs—I needed soothing music the night before surgery. When Sue realized what was going through my mind, she started to pack for me. I stopped her and asked, "What's the point of bringing anything?" My question stopped her cold. She turned ash-white and I could see tears in her eyes. I embraced her and whispered, "No matter what happens, I will always love you." We stood there in a stranglehold and cried together. It was the first time she allowed me to see her with tears and I could not let go of her. This was not going to be easy and we both knew it. Then Sue took hold of my hand and said it was time to get going or we would be late again for my admittance to the hospital.

Chuck was unlocking the front door when I pulled into the parking lot in front of his salon. I could tell he was apprehensive and nervous. He knew what I was facing and I could see the sadness in his eyes. I immediately set out to reassure him that I was all right and that he should relax and not be tentative. We entered the back room and he started cutting with the trimmers. As I sat in the barber's chair, I thought of what type of haircut the doctors might give me and decided to thwart any pranks they might play. When Chuck was done, I had a nice short haircut and the words "Go 4 it" across the back of my head. We both laughed and I thanked him. He wished me well, and I assured him that I would be back to see him when I got better. I will never forget the look in his eyes—he looked like someone who had just seen his pet die.

As Sue and I drove to the hospital, I could not concentrate on anything. It was as if I was not really there, this was happening to someone else. I was not really driving to the hospital, I was watching someone who looked like me drive to the hospital. This other Bill was going through the trauma. Before I knew it, I was parking the car and sitting there trying to gather the courage to get out of the car and walk to my fate. The temptation to turn the car around and drive west as far as I could go and never look back was alluring and irresistible. But with Sue by my side, I could not. I believe we are born for a specific reason—maybe this was where I would find out what life held for me. All the bureaucratic paperwork was behind me and I did not have to go through any admittance procedures. By now I knew what to do and where to go. They were all expecting me at 10 a.m. and, unfortunately, I was not going to disappoint them.

Chapter 17

I arrived at Ellison 22 and got to my room just in time to meet the nurse, who informed me that I was not going to radiology until 11 a.m., so there was no rush in changing into my short hospital gown. I had been given an hour's reprieve. Sue did not say much, just her touch or a glance from her were enough to keep me going. I had anesthetized myself with some type of defense mechanism. Perhaps it was my mind splitting myself into two Bills: one watching from an out-of-body state and the conscious Bill. The tearing apart of my life was real and the neverending conflict between facing the cure and agonizing over the outcome took all my power. I knew my spirit was strong and would shine in this life or the next, but only a fortuneteller would know the outcome for sure. The hour passed quickly as lab technicians took blood samples and Drs. Schumacher, Crowell and Gress visited. An attractive brunette by the name of Dede Buckley made her first appearance as Dr. Crowell's assistant. She captured my attention with her presence and as I lay lost in a last-minute fantasy, she informed me that the procedure room was being prepared for my angioplasty.

Just before 11 o'clock in the morning, Dr. Hacein-bey and Dede Buckley walked in with timid smiles and a little uneasiness in their demeanor. In a few words, Dr. Hacein-bey announced that the procedure had to be delayed until that afternoon because some of the equipment was malfunctioning. They were very apologetic and assured me the procedure would go on later that day without a hitch. Over the next four or five hours, I waited in my room with Sue. I was nervous and uptight about this second angioplasty. The fact that I had mentally prepared myself for this morning and now faced this delay caused me even more anxiety. Several hours passed and Dr. Hacein-bey returned with a long and distraught face. He informed me that the equipment was not functioning properly today and, in order to get the best results, they would have to delay my angioplasty until Wednesday. I was relieved at this development. By then, it was dinnertime. John and Dad had arrived and volunteered to go over to the Algonquin Club to bring back my favorite dinner from the restaurant: chicken à la King in a rich cream sauce, mashed potatoes, green beans and cranberry sauce. The preparations were complete: the condemned man was enjoying his last meal, complete with the pain, anxiety and fear of waiting another day to meet his Maker.

Next morning, Dr. Hacein-bey came to my room and said the procedure was delayed again due to technical problems. By now he and I were on a first-name basis; the bond between doctor and patient was developing. We spent several hours together, talking of our families and lives. Compassionate and a gentleman, he was from Algeria. I learned that he was trying to become a citizen of the United States. After the second evening, I still had not undergone the second angioplasty and my stress level was off the charts. Dad was full of optimism and informed me that he had seen Dr. Pyle-Spellman and Dr. Crowell that morning. They assured him the equipment was ready and that the procedure would commence in the morning.

Unknown to me, the doctors had met with Sue and Dad to discuss the success of this second angioplasty. The goal of the first angioplasty was to reduce the size of the AVM; the second procedure was to occlude an artery sufficiently to allow the doctors to operate safely. They learned that Dr. Pyle-Spellman and his team did not think they would be able to occlude any more arteries and vessels in order to operate safely. The theory was that surgery **might** kill me or the angioplasty might not sufficiently slow the rate of blood flow to let them operate safely. In laymen's terms, either the angioplasty or the surgery would kill me. The doctors felt I would hemorrhage to death on the operating table before they could stop the bleeding into my brain.

The debate was whether to do the surgery and perhaps have me die on the table or not to do the surgery and let me die with my family. During the meeting, Dr. Desanctis asked the neurosurgeons two questions that resolved the debate. The first was what would happen if they did nothing. The answer was that I would die within 18 months, the merciful outcome of a cerebral hemorrhage. Then Dr. Desanctis asked what I stood to lose if they did not at least try. The only chance for survival was surgery. The odds for surviving the surgery were between 30 and 40 percent; the odds of neurological deficits were more than 99 percent. It was an all-or-nothing gamble. They then decided, without consulting me, that they would take the risk and attempt to occlude the carotid artery.

Had it not been for Dr. Desanctis' ability to analyze all the available information from Dr. Crowell and Dr. Pyle-Spellman's team, the surgery would not have taken place and I would have died. Dr. Desanctis pushed the experts and gave the marching orders, "What does Bill Fallon have to lose? Give it your best shot and make it a good one." Dr. Crowell told Sue and my father that this was a 50-50 shot. Sue later told me that she said, "Do it, he'll be all right, just do it." If the doctors said there was a chance of survival, that was all she needed to hear.

I discovered from the nurses that the morning was going to proceed as planned. At 10 a.m. they would transport me to radiology for the second angioplasty. I forced myself to remember the three words that lifted me emotionally to endure all that I faced in this war for my life—"endeavor to persevere." Fight as if there were no tomorrow, reach into the deepest region of my spirit and consciousness, draw upon those mysterious powers that enabled humankind to rise to the top and fight. It would take every ounce of strength I had to fight this fight. I would have no reserves or surpluses to reinforce my warrior spirit—the next 60 or so hours would take all an all-out effort to fight the lure of the Grim Reaper. It is easy to die; living takes work.

I sensed Dr. Lotfi and Dede were to arrive just moments before they actually entered my room. Dr. Lotfi was first; he had a big smile and a gleam of light in his eyes. Dede was right behind him talking to Dad and Sue; she too had a look of relief on her face. Just as Dr. Lotfi opened his mouth to say it was a go, my lower back erupted in a spasm that felt as if I were passing a bowling ball through my kidneys. It was so intense I could not breathe. My back arched in a muscle seizure that was impossible to tolerate. I begged them to give me something for the spasm so that I could endure the angioplasty.

Within minutes, a tall, pretty brunette resident appeared with a syringe of serum and injected me in the lower back. She was a resident in the neurosurgery department and a lot better-looking than the army of neurosurgeons who were attending to me. "Things were looking up," I thought, as the narcotics slowly took effect. The resident's first name was Julia and she reminded me of Julia Roberts. I was catching one of the best legal buzzes of the century and liking it. I must be a certifiable lunatic; if the doctors ever knew what I was thinking, they would have to commit me no matter what the outcome of the surgery. It was only a matter of minutes before the shot took effect; to me it seemed like an eternity. Then a haze hit me that lasted through my operation. My vision was blurred; it was hard to distinguish reality from hallucinations. Instinctively I hung on to the three words, "Endeavor to persevere."

The now-familiar intravascular neuro-radiology surgical unit on the second floor of the gray building materialized to my consciousness. I had only a few moments of clarity. What a psychedelic experience this was turning out to be. I remember the release of the sodium nitrate into my brain and then JPS informed the team he was going to release the glue again, which was followed by intense heat burning in the back of my eyes and pain in the brain. It felt as if an elastic band in my brain had been stretched out to its maximum elasticity and then released. SNAP! I slipped into unconsciousness.

At 7 p.m. I was aware of being taken back to my room. When I finally regained consciousness, I saw Sue sitting next to my bed with her head slumped over, touching her shoulders. She looked so peaceful I did not want to disturb her. The strain on her must have been momentous and still she was my bastion of strength. I had mental clarity, although I was unstable and dizzy. There was a food cart by my bed and I tried to pick at it; in a moment I started to devour all of it. As I cleaned my plate, Sue woke up and I asked her how it had gone.

Just as she started to tell me, Dr. Lotfi walked in and with a big wide smile full of accomplishment. I repeated the question to him and he started to glow as he delivered the news that all had gone exceptionally well. When I began to thank him for doing a good job, he started to praise *me*! That was very odd—the doctors felt I was responsible for the good results, not their talents. They said I was starting to show signs of being a medical miracle.

The visits from all the doctors took on the proportions of a parade and exhausted me. It was difficult trying to be a living guinea pig for medical science. It was 10 p.m. before all the medical staff finished marveling at their handiwork. I was sore, but wide-awake after being drugged all day. It is really wild that they could wake me up, ask me some questions and then knock me out for a couple of hours. It must be what a light bulb feels like. I was wired emotionally, knowing that tomorrow morning at about 6 o'clock I would start the journey of no return. I kept repeating the three words that summed up what I had to do, "Endeavor to persevere." The Fallon creed is "Fidelite et Fidelitaire"—"Boldly and Faithfully." I was learning the meaning of life and fighting to live a normal lifespan.

The night was wearing on and Sue was getting tired, falling asleep sometime after midnight. Sleep was not an issue for me.

All I wanted was to be awake, alert and vigilant—to behold the stars in all their glory. I found myself in the waiting room, gazing into the heavens as though the reason for my suffering would be revealed to me. The sky was moonless and the stars so plentiful they lit up the night. If there were no lights on in the city, I would have seen a hundred times more stars. It reminded me of a night 60 miles offshore in Dad's sailboat, where there was no glare from city lights. It was a glorious night, an appropriate night.

My five senses were on full alert, reacting to every odor. The taste of the air I breathed seem sterile but sweet. I had never tasted the air before. The movement of the 30-story structure swayed below my feet. I was so sensitized; I felt, heard, smelled and tasted the environment around me. From this lofty perch, I could see the city of Boston lying at my feet. The city was slowly growing dark below as lights went out one by one. It was quiet, all too quiet, like the calm before the storm. I could hear my heart beating within, the pain in my head always present. It was as if my head wanted to explode and every ounce of my will power was needed to fend it off. I hoped and prayed I would be relieved of this pain, sometimes wishing for the surgery if it would purge me of this evil. Other times I feared the finality of it.

At some point in the early morning, I wandered back to my room and cuddled up to the one person who could reassure me. I lay next to her, embracing her, feeling that if I let go I would fall into an abyss, never landing at the bottom. Each time I dozed off for a few minutes, but I would suddenly wake up for fear I would never wake up at all. Around four in the morning, I turned on my Walkman and listened to some soothing music. I found the Bob Marley "Legend" CD and dropped it into the player, hit the play button, turned up the volume and tried to soothe my restless soul with its tranquility.

* * * * *

I found myself standing in the waiting room again. It was eerily silent as the black night sky retreated from the advance of the sun. The light started to glow orange, red and yellow on the horizon. The certainty of the rising sun signaled the beginning of an ordeal I did not want to face. Soon I would have to shower and shave for the surgery. For now I could only stare into the glow of the sun's light as it crested above the horizon. Its light and warmth penetrated all the way into the deepest recess of my soul. I looked into the light of the sun and felt no discomfort; it only ignited my passion for life and the will to survive. I knew then, staring at the glory of the sun, that I would not die—but I feared how I would live. God is truly a great power to be worshiped; if the power of God could create the universe, then He is something that cannot be overlooked. I knew I had to trust God.

During the night, Monsignor MacNamara had appeared in my room. My father, knowing that I might die from this operation, had asked him to pay me a visit. The monsignor apologized for the late hour of his visit and asked how I was doing. I was honest and told him I was scared shitless and at that we both laughed nervously. I told him that I was afraid and said that if God knew me, he might not like me. The good monsignor asked if I regretted anything in my life. I said no. I believed I was a good person and had not meant anyone any harm. Then he helped me through confession and the Lord's prayer. He told me he would administer the sacrament for the sick and say the prayer for the immaculate healing. I made no effort to resist. It must have been all the Catholic teaching I received in my youth that made me succumb to his prayers. I did not know at the time that these were the prayers for absolution and Last Rites for the dying. I was being prepared to meet God, to ask for his forgiveness and to be admitted to Heaven.

As I stood in the glow of the rising sun, I put my faith in God. The sun was above the horizon, the waiting room warming in its light. I returned to my room to shower. I crept into the bathroom, hoping not to wake up Sue. It was the longest shower I ever took. I washed my hair with Phisohex twice. To make sure I killed all the germs, I used it on my body twice. Then, not wanting to leave anything to chance, I washed my hair again.

When I emerged from the shower stall, Sue was sitting on the sink putting on some make-up.

I returned to my hospital bed and started to tie a tag Pam had given me to my right toe. I remarked to Sue that if it was my day to die, today was a beautiful day to die. Sue hushed me and said, "No one is going to die today." Then she questioned the sanity of putting the silly toe tag on my foot. I said "If I do die, I want to give the doctors one more laugh before I go." The next moment, the attendant walked in with a gurney, accompanied by Dad, Mom, John and a nurse. It was time to go!

Stress and strain were evident in my family's faces. John had a hard time looking me in the eye. Dad was tense and rigid. It was a difficult moment for all of us, especially Sue. I asked everyone for a minute with her alone. Once the room was left to the two of us, I looked at her and told her that no matter what happened, I loved her and that I would always love her and the children. I asked her not to let them forget me if the worst outcome became a reality. Embracing, we stood there holding onto each other, feeling the life flow within our souls. We were in love with each other in a way that made us one body, one soul. Our minds worked as one and each could feel the other's pain. I kissed her on the forehead whispered "I love you" and let go of my bear hug. I had to get on the gurney, cover up the toe tag and be wheeled to the operating room.

Chapter 18

"Calm, stay calm," I reminded myself. I tried a little humor with the attendant, but he paid no attention to my remarks as he hustled around corridors and into elevators. I told him not to rush on my account and got a smile out of him. He asked if the haircut was my idea, and I said yes. He laughed and said he liked my attitude. After careening down a dozen corridors, around a few dozen corners, and onto two elevators, my entourage arrived at the point of no return: the set of double doors to the operating room wing of the hospital. If I were ever to escape, I had to make a run for it now.

Thirty-eight operating rooms situated in a maze of corridors and alcoves are in that part of the hospital. I sat up on my gurney and peered through the windows lining the long hall. I could see four or five sets of doors with nurses, doctors and technicians gathered in front of each operating room. At each entranceway was a recessed alcove. We stopped in front of one of them, where I had to say goodbye to Mom and John. I gave them both hugs and kisses, assuring them I would be all right and would see them soon in intensive care. Only Dad and Sue were allowed to enter through the double doors into the pre-surgery room with me. It was a large, open room with about 20 or 30 gurneys on either side. A curtain split the room in half and it looked as if the few people on the left side of the room were just recovering from surgery. I was pushed over to the right side.

Dad was upset and nervously asking questions. Sue was squeezing my hand, afraid to let go. Soon a nurse asked them to leave, and Dad hugged and kissed me goodbye, saying "Good luck, Champ, I'll see you soon," and then reluctantly walked away. Sue and I were left alone, afraid to say goodbye for fear of losing one another forever. I don't think we had time for anything but "I love you" and then she had to go. A nurse came over with a handful of pills. As I took the pills in my hand, I watched Sue walk out of the room. I saw her take one quick look back, and I knew she was really shaken. For the first time, I saw fear in her face and a deep sadness in her eyes. It hurt so much to see her in such anguish. The thought that it was because of me hurt even more. I was starting to feel emotional and psychological pain. I knew what physical pain was like and could handle it, or so I thought. Emotional pain was new, crushing me with a weight that seemed impossible to bear. I sat there in a daze, alone. Then I was wheeled down a corridor to an operating room. It was like being at a bank robbers' convention, everyone's face was covered by a mask. They knew who was behind each mask—I did not.

Every so often, one of the team would look at my haircut and then at the medical chart. The result was one of those looks of pity. If someone commented on my message, I would reply that I was full of surprises, and they would walk away with a look of puzzlement in their eyes. You can tell a lot about people by their eyes and I only had their eyes to look at.

The nurses and anesthesiologist showed up and started asking me some questions, small talk to calm me down. The last thing I remember is a doctor introducing himself as Dr. Westmark as he placed an IV needle into my right arm. I could not resist the urge to peek through the windows into the operating room. As I sat up to take a look, the doctor told me to lay down and relax, saying, "Now I am going to give you a little of the goo juice." After that, the lights went out. I was told much later that I kept hinting to them about a surprise. Apparently my hair cut tickled them, but when they found the toe tag, they laughed so loudly that a few doctors from adjoining operating rooms came in to see what the commotion was about. The tag stated in big dark letters: "Caution! Please do not try this at home. I am a professional." It expressed the sentiments of a neurological patient who has taken everything modern medicine can dish out and still retain a sense of humor.

The anesthetic they used gives the patient pre-operative amnesia. The patient is conscious and alert but without the memory of any pre-operative anxiety. Patients can still relate things to the doctors as they are prepared for surgery. A few weeks later, I was told that I was the first patient they had tried it on. The resident neurosurgeons who attended to me after surgery explained that the anesthetics used during an operation of this type are very tricky and critical to the overall success of the surgery.

The brain needs to have blood supplied to it through the vascular system to stay alive. But if blood contacts brain cells in any other way, it kills the brain cells, causing brain damage. Oxygen is supplied to the brain through the neurovascular system; deny the brain oxygen and the brain incurs damage. In order to operate on the brain for long hours at a time, the doctors must first stop the flow of blood or reduce it as much as possible. The patient's body temperature is lowered to around 45 degrees, which impedes the dying process of the brain cells. In essence, the patient is clinically dead. Bodily functions are medically placed in a state of suspended animation and maintained by machines.

It is only then that a neurosurgeon can make an incision in the back of the scalp from one ear lobe to the other, arcing over the crown of the skull. Once the scalp is peeled back and the membrane protecting the skull is removed, the surgeon drills a hole in the skull. From this point, the skull is cut into four plates and removed, exposing the brain. The surgeon screws a halo with a surgical microscope mounted upon it into the skull. The doctors then manually manipulate the brains folds to expose the region where the AVM is located.

In my case, the second and larger malformation was in the left occipital lobe at the back of my head, at the point where the neck meets the skull. With the microscope focused on the vascular malformation, they started to cut and suture or cauterize the hundreds of vessels, veins and arteries that made up the malformation. They removed the entire back of my skull, exposing the back portion of the brain from ear to ear. In the process of removing the AVM, the doctors are bound to damage or remove portions of brain tissue around the malformation. And as the operation proceeds, the skull cavity loses some cranial fluids that the brain floats in. This fluid is the suspension system of the brain. It helps prevent the brain from sloshing around within the skull and becoming bruised. How this fluid is rejuvenated, I don't know. All I know is that a major concern of the doctors was to make sure I was not active post-surgery for fear I would bruise my brain while the cranial fluids were being reintroduced into the skull cavity. As a result of the two craniotomies, there was room for the brain to move around, increasing the potential of bruising and damaging brain tissue.

Upon the successful removal of the AVM, the doctors would begin to put old Humpty Dumpty back together again. I am not exactly sure of the process, but I can explain it in simple terms. Dr. Westmark later told me that they located some kind of clip to hold the four corners together in the middle of the removed skull plates. The pieces were then reattached to the skull by drilling tiny holes around the outer parameter of the incision, as well as on the plates. These plates were then wired into place with a monofilament thread, like fishing line—it may actually be fishing line, for all I know. The skullcap, which is like saran wrap, as stretched back into place and sewn to the skull. The scalp is then stretched and folded back into place, and the surgeon sews it down. Unlike Dr. Schumacher, Dr. Westmark and Dr. Ogilvie used thread instead of staples. After an AVM is removed, the doctors perform an angiography to verify that they have completely removed the malformation. The angiography also confirms whether there is any bleeding; if there is, the patient goes back to the operating room and the doctor goes back in to eliminate any hemorrhaging. This is why they keep you down. It is critical to the success of the surgery to monitor the patient for any bleeding or infection for several days after surgery. If the patient incurs any infection, it could be fatal. The time in ICU is spent watching for either of those two events.

Prior to the operation, Dr. Crowell had implied that I would be brought back slowly. I had wondered what he meant by that. Where was I going or, a better question, where was I coming from? The "bring you back slowly" remark comes from the fact that you are clinically dead or in a semi-frozen state of suspended animation during the surgery. If all went well with my surgery, they would move me to the neuro ICU for a few days of careful monitoring under the supervision of Dr. Gress. Twenty-four hours after I entered surgery, I was moved to the ICU. When I first regained consciousness, two days after emerging from my marathon surgery, I was disoriented and bewildered. The air seemed foggy; my vision was blurred; I could hear before I could see. There was an annoying ringing in my ears and a loud humming noise in the background. If you have ever stood near a large transformer or generator, you know what I am talking about.

The concern of walking toward the right light was not prevalent as I regained consciousness. I sensed grayness—as if fog had filled my room. The blinding light of God or of the surgical lights did not confuse me this time. I knew I had survived because I thought the pain in my head would not be there if I was dead. If I had died, I believed and hoped God would show me mercy and relieve me from any pain. With difficulty, I recognized Dr. Crowell standing over me, asking me if I could hear him and if I knew who I was. The light hurt my eyes and I had to squint in an attempt to focus.

I wanted to snap back that I knew damn well who I was, but I didn't. I had an enormous head; it felt as large and heavy as the medicine ball that boxers toss around for exercise. My vision was distorted, but it was difficult to know whether it was due to my eyes, the drugs or poor lighting in the ICU. Dr. Crowell tested the strength in my hands and the reflexes in my legs; they all appeared to be functioning normally. He asked who the president was. I mumbled out the correct answer. Then he asked the critical question, "Can you see me?" I acknowledged him affirmatively but informed him it was difficult to focus. Then he held up his hands about shoulder level and asked me to look at his nose.

"Can you see my right hand?"

I strained to say, "Yes!"

"Can you see my left hand?" he asked.

"What hand?" I replied.

"Can you see it now?" he asked again.

"No!"

"Can you see it now?"

"No," I replied again.

"What does your vision look like?" he asked.

"It is distorted and blurred," I told him.

"Tell me when you can see my hand," he pressed. Dr. Crowell moved his left hand around in the air until I could see it at the level of his waist.

He told me that I had lost about 30 to 40 percent of my visual field. He went on to say that I had no paralysis and that they had gotten all of the AVM. He added that there was a lot of old blood from previous hemorrhages in the area of the AVM. Apparently, I was very fortunate to be alive and the doctors were amazed that I was as well as I appeared to be after so much evidence of prior hemorrhaging. I asked him what day it was and realized I had lost almost three days. In his soft and compassionate voice, Dr. Crowell told me that my whole family was outside and would come in to see me, but only one at time. His last comment was to ask me to promise him one thing—that I would never lose my sense of humor. I thanked him for saving my life. He stopped me and said that it was my attitude that had saved me, and that I should thank JPS—his talent and treatment had saved my life. His surgery would not have been successful if JPS had not occluded the arteries first. He instructed me to rest, then excused himself and left. Modesty did not allow him to take full credit, but I knew Dr. Crowell was the best in the world. I had placed my confidence in him, and he had not failed me. I would not see him again until I was discharged a few weeks later, because he was too busy saving the lives of other neuro patients.

As I lay there trying to focus on my surroundings, I realized I was wired for everything conceivable. I continued to try to focus, not truly understanding the level of visual impairment I had incurred. On my head was a turban of gauze, my legs were wrapped in some kind of inflated splints from my ankles to my knees. Every 20 seconds, these leggings inflated and deflated. In my left arm was a wooden splint and an arterialgram to monitor my vital signs. The right arm had an IV inserted into an artery, dripping some antibiotics and steroids. On my chest were transducers. An oxygen tube ran up my nose, a catheter was in my penis. I began to think I was the bionic man. I had so many wires and tubes hooked up to me, I checked to see whether there was one up my ass. Luckily, there wasn't. It was all very intrusive and unpleasant.

As I took inventory of my body parts, Sue quietly entered my room and placed her head on my chest. I strained to see her face; it was not all there. I could only distinguish the right side of her face and part of her jaw. As soon as her head touched my chest, I started to cry. When she asked why, I could only tell her that I could not believe I was still alive. At that, she broke down in tears and held onto me as if she feared letting go. I asked her what the doctors said, and she told me they were all jumping for joy when they saw the angiography confirming that all the AVM was gone. They also confirmed that the arteries and veins were not bleeding. The doctors were elated at the results and said I had a strong spirit to survive the grueling 24 hours of surgery as well as I had. My throat was raw from the breathing tubes that were in my throat during surgery and I had a hard time talking. Under my left arm I felt a burning stinging sensation. When I touched the area I could not feel my finger pressing against the skin. Apparently some nerve damage had occurred while I lay motionless on my side for the entire operation.

When Sue was composed, she whispered that she loved me and that she would be back in the morning. She had been up for more than 24 hours and was exhausted. I strained to smile for her, but I was still heavily medicated and it was a useless effort. Moments after she left, Dad walked in, kissed me on the cheek and told me how courageous I was. He confirmed the doctor's report and reinforced that I would be all right in time. He said he was proud of me and marveled at my courage. I was too humble to think I was brave and thought I was too stupid to be courageous. You would have to be stupid to let someone do this to you. Then he whispered that I had earned the right to be the executive vice president of his company whenever I felt ready to take the job. I faded off to sleep. At some point Mom, Pam and John visited, but I can't remember when. I started to check on all the machinery I was hooked up and wired into. The ridiculous leggings I was wearing prevented me from moving. Every time I tried to roll over on my side or onto my back, an alarm sounded and nurses ran into my room. I hate to sleep on my back and found myself distressed and uncomfortable.

On the second day, I was more alert. I slept well, probably because I was heavily medicated with painkillers, although I remember the nurses coming in at what seemed like every 15 minutes and waking me up. They would first check all the connections that were attached to my various appendages. Then they would take my pulse and temperature, lift up my eyelids, and shine a bright light into them from half an inch away. The flashlight shining in my eyes hurt as much as the pain in my head. I noticed that everyone was whispering. When someone spoke in a normal tone, it hurt my ears. As if that weren't enough to harass me, the nurses would ask a bunch of ridiculous questions. What is your name? Do you know where you are? Who is the president? What day is it? After I answered all the questions, they would prick each foot with a needle and ask me to hold their fingers with both hands and squeeze. This routine occurred every half-hour for three days.

Sue did not come on day two. I found out later from Pam that once she saw me after surgery, she had collapsed from exhaustion with a severe headache. The doctors said she might be having a case of delayed stress syndrome. I worried about her and wished I had not been the cause of her illness. Sue suffered from this headache and fatigue over the next month until she felt comfortable that I was out of danger.

Chapter 19

The next evening, another patient was wheeled into my room. Mildred was an elderly lady about 70 who was in a coma resulting from a fall in her bathroom. When the nurses came in to check my neurological functions, they would first check Mildred's. Now I had to listen to the nurses go through the neuro check with Mildred every half-hour. There was one difference— first they would scream at her to wake her up, then they would yell, asking if she could hear them. At times it was so loud that they disturbed me from what little sleep I was able to get.

As the second day drew to a close, I tried to bribe my night nurse into taking off the booties. When that did not work, I knew she was going to be a tough one to win over. By the second night, the booties were so cumbersome that it was impossible to get to sleep. Combining that annoyance with a steady reduction of pain-killers made for a very unhappy and uncomfortable patient. My anxiety was further compounded by my poor vision. During the day I seemed to manage—bring on the night and I became a monster.

In the early morning of day three, my anxiety exploded in anger and I started to disconnect myself from all medical devices connected to my body. I did not care about bleeding or setting off alarms. I had to get rid of the goddamn wires and tubes, even if it killed me. Within minutes, I had two male nurses and two female nurses trying to untangle me from a web of wires and tubes. The concept of bribery crossed my mind again, so I attempted to negotiate my way out of some of the machines around me. I first tried to convince them to take out the catheter in exchange for good behavior.

"Not until the IVs are removed," scowled Vinny, the big male nurse. "We don't want to have to bring you a bedpan every five minutes."

"How about taking these wires off my chest?" I was persistent.

"If that settles you down, we can arrange it," answered Debbie, the night nurse. Ah ha! A victory. I had cracked her armor and she was putty for me to mold.

"While you're disconnecting wires, can you shut off the booties?" I added.

"Do not push me," Debbie warned, waving her finger at me. Suddenly I noticed that I couldn't see her hand—only her forearm was visible. I acquiesced to her demands and attempted to calm down.

The realization that my eyesight was hallucinogenic—things I thought I saw were not as I saw them—disturbed me. I could no longer trust my eyes to see all that must be seen to formulate an understanding of what I was looking at. I could not see anything in the upper right-hand corner of my field of view. My eyes could see, but the message to my brain was scrambled. I strained to understand the confusion in my brain. As the hours passed and the medication was slowly eliminated, I became more aware of how badly I was damaged. This awareness would take many months to fully identify and comprehend.

The hospital routine droned on without any relief from the constant neuro checks. One time the nurses came in with their little flashlights and tried to snap Mildred out of her coma. They screamed at her an inch away from her face without any response, their flashlights casting bizarre shadows about the room. After I had heard, "Mildred wake up!" or "Mildred, can you hear me?" a dozen times, I shouted back from behind the curtain, "God damn it! My name is Mildred." Debbie whipped the curtain back and scolded me for making light of the situation. She warned me to settle down and try to relax.

"Relax? How can I relax with all that screaming and these damn wires and tubes all over me? Can't you even turn the beeping of my heart monitor off?"

As the night rolled on, I struggled with my pain, which was sometimes so intense that I could only sleep for short periods. By about 4:30 in the morning, my anxiety was out of control. I was ready to jump up and run away screaming. Debbie had to come in about every five minutes because I could not handle the pain or the anxiety any longer. My alarms would constantly go off as I tried to free myself from all the wires. Finally Debbie came in and said, "Mr. Fallon, I think we are having what is called a severe anxiety attack." Then she popped two brownish-orange pills into my mouth and handed me a cup of water. The next thing I knew it was 2:30 in the afternoon and Mildred was nowhere to be found.

Vinny brought in a new hospital gown and asked if I wanted a bath. I was reluctant at first, but quickly realized that he would have to remove the booties to wash my legs. When he finished my sponge bath, I was given a shave and clean pajamas and started to feel human again. After the bed bath, I asked Vinny if he could leave the booties off. He informed me that the boots were to prevent any blood clots from forming in my circulatory system and promptly put them back on. The IVs and arterialgram were still in both arms, but the oxygen tubes were gone from my nose. When Dr. Gress came into my room, he announced that if I behaved I could go back to Ellison 22 in the morning.

During the quiet evenings, I found pain too great to handle and had to ask for a shot of morphine to sleep. If I did not, I would cry from the pain. In my moments of consciousness, I could hear a buzzing sound in my ears. The area of surgery was numb from nerve damage. My left side felt like pins and needles and was a constant source of irritation. My senses were on full alert; sight and sound were sensitized. My ears were so tuned in that every noise was amplified to the point where it hurt when someone talked in a normal tone. My response to questions was delayed as I struggled to interpret the questions. My body felt like it was made of lead. My arms and legs felt so heavy, I could hardly move them. I was not aware of how severely I had been affected by surgery. In the ICU everyone is so cautious and purposeful that the patient does not really comprehend the impact of the damage to the brain.

On the morning of the fourth day, I was permitted to move out of the ICU. As I lay alone waiting to be transferred, I listened to my heartbeat on the monitor—46 beats a minute. Thinking about the events of the week, I could hardly believe I had agreed to be put through this. Was it worth it? My pain and anxiety seemed worse, not better. I wanted to wake up from this nightmare and find everything all right. Once out of the ICU, the natural light hurt my eyes so much that I had to keep them shut. I hoped the disturbance in my vision was due to the lights, but deep down inside, I knew my eyes were messed up. When we reached the 22nd floor, Sue and Pam greeted us at the waiting room next to the elevator with big smiles on their faces; Sue leaned over me and gave me a kiss. I whispered into her ear, "Are you all right?"

"Yes, I'm fine now that you are out of ICU."

I knew she was lying but did not let on. Pam was excited, as she usually is for big events, and I got a kiss from her too. The attendant was rolling my gurney like a cab driver in a hurry to get to another fare. Pam and Sue were almost running to keep up with him. We entered the room headfirst so I could not see what was going on, but I had the feeling a surprise was ahead. When my gurney was turned parallel to the hospital bed, I noticed a big sign made out of a bed sheet hanging on my wall. It read "YOU KNOW YOU'VE SURVIVED WHEN YOU ARRIVE AT ELLISON 22." The sign covered the whole length of the wall opposite my bed. The sheet was decorated with drawings of skiers, sailors, hunters and pretty girls, and was signed by all my family, who were standing around the room congratulating me for a successful operation. The sign looked like a giant get-well card. As I looked around the room, bright with the midday sun, warm with the love of my family, my vision was scrambled, like the pieces of a fragmented puzzle. I could see some things in my visual field, but others were blurred and unrecognizable. It also hurt in a new way—my brain was hurting too! For the first time I felt the pain of my brain's personality and the injury it had suffered. It literally hurt to think! My brain was working very hard to understand what my eyes were telling it. All the visual messages were being sent to the brain, but the brain could only decode 60 to 70 percent of each message. The rest of the message was disjointed; my brain was confused by the uncorrelated information it was trying to decode. I was like looking at a kid's puzzle book where you have to find the hidden objects in the drawings and circle them. You know what the objects are, but they blend into the picture so well you have a difficult time recognizing them. I tried to shield my eyes but that didn't relieve any of my discomfort, neither did squinting.

I had to close my eyes in order to talk; my brain could not tolerate seeing at the same time as speaking. From what I could tell, the room was full of flowers, balloons and stuffed animals. It was all very comforting, but it hurt my eyes and my brain just to look at it all. I began to think I could not deal with any of it. I had thought I was prepared for some deficits, but this was much greater than anticipated. I hurt in so many ways I wanted to cry, but even that hurt! It hurt when I breathed, let alone move my head. If I even moved my head slightly, I felt sharp jabs of pain in many areas. It felt as if the doctors had chopped the back of my head off, which was exactly what they did. I slipped quietly into a deep sleep, hoping Sue would be the only one there when I woke up.

In the process of weaning me off morphine, the doctors had reduced my pain medication to Tylenol and codeine. As the heavier medication was eliminated, I physically got worse because the pain increased. In the old days, I could achieve relief from migraines by knocking myself out with Percocet and falling asleep. Now I faced a new challenge and a new life. My old life was gone. I was scared of the future I faced, the uncertainty of my full recovery and the discovery of my deficits. While I was in the ICU, I had not comprehended the full scope of my injuries. I believed I would just bounce back from surgery as I did from the first craniotomy. Now I felt as though my head had been used as the soccer ball in the final game of the World Cup. While Sue, Pam and the rest of my supporters were applauding my triumphant victory over death, I could only comprehend the intense and relentless pain in my head. My suffering had not been eased but compounded by pain, anger and frustration.

Later in the afternoon, Dr. Westmark, one of the two resident neurosurgeons who had assisted Dr. Crowell, came in. He seemed too young to be a neurosurgeon, so I strained to read his nametag. I could only see two or three letters at one time. The bright light of the midday sun hurt my eyes and the normal noise of the activity in the hall was unbearable. A throbbing pain pounded behind my right ear. I slurred my words in saying hello; in fact, I was talking like a phonograph record on slow speed. I began to feel retarded. Words were hard to formulate and I was having difficulty understanding simple instructions and responding to them. I first had to think about what someone was saying to me, then develop a response and finally deliver an answer in a painfully slow manner. My mind still functioned at the same speed as before the surgery, but the output was slower.

Dr. Westmark reviewed my chart and tested my major neurological functions. All of them—talking, feeling, smelling, hearing—worked! Vision was another story. I simply could not tolerate keeping my eyes open. I almost broke down as I realized I had exchanged one aura for another. When I had migraines, the aura was like bright lightbulbs; this aura was unrecognizable, like a smudge on a lens or scratches on your eyeglasses. I wanted to look in another direction, hoping not to see the deformity in my sight. Prior to surgery, I experienced the aura only when I had a headache, now the disturbance was permanent. At times I wondered whether I had made the right decision. My brain was so confused by sight that it was impossible for me to talk with my eyes open. My capacity to do more than one thing at a time was diminished and I was easily confused. Bewilderment is an appropriate term for my state of mind.

My legs could move but I had not stood up for over a week. Although I wanted to test my legs and balance, the doctors would not allow me to get up out of my bed. The arterialgram was still in my left arm, the IV in my right arm. The catheter was still in me and I decided to try to convince the nurse to remove it over the next day or two. The effect of the anesthetic was still evident—my behavior was filled with sluggish mannerisms. My pain was relentless and I felt nauseous and dizzy, almost seasick. I kept testing my eyes by looking straight at something and then measuring how much I could not see by looking at the area where I had no vision. It was weird because I could see all of an object if it was within 1 foot. When the object was moved away, I could see less and less of it. If I looked out the window at a building across the Charles River, I could not see a building to the right of the one I was looking at. Lack of confidence in myself was building up; I could not trust my eyes anymore. The realization that a lot of my functions had been reduced to almost infantile proportions threw me into a slow downward spiral toward depression.

Chapter 20

My family was filled with joy at my surviving against impossible odds, while I was crying in my bed. Were my tears full of joy or humility? Was it good that I lived or was it a curse? Just when I was sinking into a sea of pity, the doctors started to show up one at a time. First came Dr. Westmark to remove my bandages. As he lifted the bandages, I did feel not a thing in the back of my head. It was as if the entire back of my head did not exist. Because I was still wobbly, the doctors would not let me out of bed to look in the mirror. Dr. Westmark told me I would be up and about in a day or two and left me alone sitting in the dark, pondering my situation, questioning my good fortune. I decided my good fortune was bittersweet.

During the day, the room had to be dark with the shades drawn. In the darkness of night, I asked the nurse to open them so I could look out my window and confirm that the world was still there. The dim night light was soothing to my brain. My eyes were less sensitive in the night light and I surveyed my surroundings to gauge my level of visual impairment. It looked as if life were a Picasso painting: I saw half chairs and partial pictures, an eye and a chin, no nose or ear, pieces of a face—my visual world was askew and tilted. The games the visual deficit played on my mind were intense; a constant war with reality clashed in my mind. Was what I was seeing real or was my seeing unreal?

As I could not lay totally prone, I slept at a 45-degree angle, allowing me to lay my head back against the pillow without hearing the grinding of the skull plates as they floated over my brain. The back of my skull was like a trampoline flexing with every movement, every sound. I thought of Flash and his developing skull. So many years between us, yet in many ways we were alike.

Dr. Gress arrived in my room at about 10 p.m. as I was lying quietly in my bed, thinking of all the things that had happened to me in the past months. When he asked me, "How are you doing?" I did not know from which perspective to respond—from the part of me that was pissed off over this or the part that thanked God for being alive. Looking at Dr. Gress, I saw only his right eye and part of his face. I focused in on his one eye and dissolved emotionally. The reality of my previous life was lost forever; my personality and character would never see life through the eyes of the old Bill Fallon. I did not know the new Bill Fallon or what his new existence would be like. When I was finally composed enough to answer his question, I simply replied, "I don't know."

I was not sure what to say so I started to talk to him, telling him how I felt. This new emotion hurt but I felt tranquil and at peace with myself, yet at the same time I felt a sense of overwhelming loss. In a peculiar way I felt as if I had met my Maker and He had passed judgment on me, sparing me from death but not from punishment. I also felt a sense of guilt for surviving with better results than the doctors had predicted. If my chances of surviving were so slim, why did I live? Why didn't I receive more in the way of deficits, like paralysis, severe cognitive deficits or total blindness? All these confusing issues were racing wildly in my head. With a very gentle and compassionate manner, Dr. Gress listened to me and then responded by affirming that my emotions were similar to other patients' experiences. His words did not make me feel any more at ease, but they did justify the existence of my feelings. I told him the experience had changed me in many ways but had also created the desire to change other things in my life. Then my ability to stay focused and concentrate started to disintegrate. I lost track of where the conversation was going and turned to how my head felt and what I could or could not see. The entire back of my head ached, as if the entire population of China was marching on it. My neck was getting tired of holding up my head. I wanted to have my head amputated and put on a counter to rest my neck for a while.

Dr. Gress explained how vision works. When the eyes see an object, they code the subject and send the code to the occipital lobe, which decodes the message and tells the brain what it sees. The human eye learns by memory association. If it sees a red ball, it sends the code for a red ball to the brain and the brain's decoder in the occipital lobe tells the brain it sees a red ball. In my case, the eye sees the subject, codes what it sees and sends the code to my brain, which can decode only 60 percent of the message. The part of the brain necessary to finish the decoding is no longer there. That brain tissue is gone and cannot be redeveloped. The improperly decoded message confuses the brain and that confusion has a pain the brain feels. I see what appears to be a normal scene; however, part of the scene is fuzzy and indistinguishable. If I hold up five fingers, I can only see the thumb and not the rest of the fingers, but I can still see everything in the foreground and to the left and far right of what is in my field of view. The field of view appears normal but there are segments I cannot distinguish. I heard what Dr. Gress was saying but found it difficult to accept. In cases similar to mine, people see other people's faces and may know them as a brother or friend, but cannot identify them.

Dr. Gress was a good listener. The time flew by as we talked in my darkened room. When I realized it was after 11 p.m., I apologized for keeping him so late. Dr. Gress told me that I was no different from a person who has suffered two severe strokes and that, as time passed, I would uncover other side effects from the two surgeries. He comforted me in offering to discuss anything that I experienced from the operations. As he was leaving, Betty, the night nurse, arrived to check my temperature and pulse. I asked Dr. Gress whether it was all right to get rid of the booties.

"In the morning we will check with Dr. Crowell," he answered. "Good night."

* * * * *

I woke up to the whir of the floor buffers in the hall and the change of shifts for the nurses. Queenie, the food lady, came in to say hello and see if I wanted breakfast and the newspaper.

"Sure, what can I have?" It would be my first main meal since surgery. She suggested my favorite, hot cakes, and I jumped at the offer. Anne Geary arrived for the day shift and promptly informed me that I could get rid of the damn boots and, if I had assistance, I could get up. Quickly I asked if that also meant I could get rid of the catheter.

"I guess so," was her reply. Yes! I would be liberated from that unpleasant little device and a bonus was the departure of the pesky booties.

Just then, Dr. Westmark and Dr. Schumacher arrived with two other neurosurgeon residents to check on me. The routine neuro tests were implemented and my vision tested. The doctors all seemed a little curious at my condition. Their interest was not in my deficits but in how well I was after extensive surgery to the head. It was almost as if they did not believe the good results they had achieved. In the process they decided to leave the A-line in my left arm for another day, because of my low heart rate. Apparently my heart rate was around 40 beats per minute. Normally the heart beats at about 60 to 70 beats a minute. They had intentionally slowed my heart rate to a stop during the operation and now it was intentionally being kept low by Dr. Crowell and Dr. Desanctis. The wisdom of this was simple: the less blood pressure, the less stress on the vascular system in the brain. Soon the residents left and another group from Dr. Pyle-Spellman's team walked in. Dr. Lotfi led this squad of doctors to marvel at the results that were far better than any of the hospital staff had expected. I obliged their curiosity and answered all the probing questions they asked. Besides, it built me up and I needed the encouragement.

When this group left, Queenie arrived with my breakfast of hot cakes, coffee and bacon. It was my first solid meal in a week! I devoured it as fast as I could, then decided to watch the morning news to see what I had missed. Watching the news revealed the depth of my visual impairment. The screen was not all there. What I saw did not make any sense to me—the screen showed a news desk and only one person. In order to see the entire picture, I had to look at the four corners or at the right side of the screen. In this way I would see the entire picture using my left peripheral field. It was a painful effort and I decided to read the paper instead.

Reading was not as simple a task as it used to be. When I looked at the print, I could not see all of the words. I would have to look at each letter of each word and spell out each word in my mind to understand what was written. The brain learns to read in blocks of words. The brain reads by associating the words it is reading with words it has retained in its memory. If you can not see all of the word at once, you cannot read. I could not read at all! I had to spell out each word individually in order to understand what I was looking at. The whole task of reading was cumbersome and exhausting. It made me feel like a child or an illiterate! Within a minute's time, I had to stop looking at the page. In some ways it was like a computer short-circuiting. A sense of hopelessness cast a cloud over my enthusiasm at the success of my surgery. I had encountered my first intangible deficit in excess of my blindness. I had never experienced anything like this in my life. Reading was second nature, something you do without thinking about it. Now I had to think about every letter of every word and then I had to make sure I read the entire sentence. Before surgery I could see all of a sentence, now I had to scan the entire line a sentence was on to make sure I read all the words in each sentence. If I didn't, I would miss a word or two and the sentence did not make sense.

This startling discovery was very depressing. I wondered how I would be able to work if I could not read. I sank quickly from the jubilation of surviving to the depression caused by the realization that I had more problems than I was prepared to deal with. It was not so much the fact that I had difficulty reading that bummed me out, but that it made me sick with nausea and caused a pain like no other pain I had experienced before. My mind was incapable of processing data and concentration skills were nonexistent. The first signs of cognitive deficits had surfaced. When you injure an arm or leg, the limb tells the brain it is hurt, so stop using it. The difference here is that the brain is the injured party and it throws itself into shock. My frustration at this revelation caused me to discard the paper the way a child discards a toy that won't work.

At 9 a.m. Dr. Gress stopped in to see me and I raised the reading problem with him. He said that the occipital lobe is the region of the brain that processes information and other cognitive functions like concentration, rationalization and problem solving. When I asked him whether this was a permanent deficit, I received a veiled answer. His response was that some patients adjust to this problem and others regain the ability to concentrate for longer periods. It is a legitimate problem for stroke and brain-damaged patients, but the medical profession knows so little about the function of the brain that they have no clear-cut answers. The brain injury I had incurred resulted in the same neurological damage as a stroke patient. It started to sink in that I might have this feeling of distress every time I tried to read, concentrate or solve a problem.

"What other cognitive problems will I encounter?" I asked Dr. Gress.

"Some patients have memory deficits, trouble concentrating, or moments of confusion caused by too much sensory input for the brain to process. Others have problems recognizing friends or relatives. In due time we will work with you on this aspect of the surgery. In the meantime, take it easy. There is plenty of time to work on rehabilitation, what you need now is a lot of sleep. The brain needs sleep to heal. We know what areas of the brain control the major functions like sight, motor skills, vocalization and sound. We know very little about the brain function of almost 70 percent of its area. We have identified what 30 to 40 percent of the brain does; the remainder is a mystery."

During this conversation he revealed the anticipated length of recuperation. The doctor informed me that sometimes a recovery and rehabilitation period can last as long as three to five years. I was stunned; my mind had never anticipated that length of time. I had assumed that in six to nine months I would be as good as new. Perhaps I would have some problems, but I had never dreamed of three to five years of recuperation. The whole reason I rushed into the second surgery was to be healthy enough to ski that coming winter. I must have been naive to think I would bounce back from such intrusive brain surgery in six to nine months. When doctors had referred to my neurological deficits in terms of diminished capacities, I had never properly interpreted their meaning.

It was time for Dr. Gress to go on his morning rounds and, as he was leaving, Pam, John and Mom walked in. I enjoyed their visits but had an overwhelming desire to sleep and found it hard to carry on conversations for any length of time. The activity level of a few people in my room was difficult to cope with and the pain the commotion created was distracting and uncomfortable. I hoped the pain was the reason I was having difficulty coping with movement, noise and general daily activity. I prayed these problems would diminish as the pain subsided.

Sue arrived shortly after the others and brought Shannon with her. As Shannon entered the room, she was very apprehensive and tentative. Once she saw that I appeared normal, with the exception of my shaved head, she let out a smile and giggled nervously. I was happy to see her and assure her that Daddy was alive and well. But when she saw what had happened to the back of my head, she turned white as a sheet.

Over the next few days, at least a dozen different doctors checked on me every morning. They acted as if my survival and health were miraculous and they had to reconfirm I was as well as I had been the previous day. When it quieted down, and the booties and catheter were removed, I asked if I could get up and try to walk. Ann and Sue were to walk with me and each gave me a shoulder to lean on. Gingerly I swung my legs over the side of the bed. I could feel the rush of blood within my veins and there were butterflies in my stomach. My skull moved like the tectonic plates under the earth's surface. The effort of breathing was all the motion necessary to cause pain in the back of my skull. The fluctuations in my arteries and veins registered on my consciousness with every beat of my laboring heart. As I sat with my legs dangling, I felt dizzy and unsteady. Cautiously I put my feet on the ground to test my strength. Immediately, I had a rush of blood to my head, which ignited a burning pain all over the back of my brain. The stability and strength in my body was almost nonexistent and I stumbled forward only to be saved by the beautiful maidens at my side. The knowledge of this revelation was astounding: Only seven or eight months ago I had the ability of a world-class extreme skier; now I was reduced to the feebleness of an old man, fragile and helpless.

That first step enlightened me to the severity of my deficits and the realization that I was starting from the same place a new-born infant starts from. I thought of Flash and said to myself, "My boy, we are going to grow together." Right now I was slow and uncoordinated, my legs weak and unsteady. I literally had to think to put my right foot in front of my left foot or I did not make any progress. I made it about 15 feet from my bed into the corridor. It was the beginning of a difficult and painful road. I returned to my bed fatigued and in pain, wondering what would become of me.

When I woke up hours later, everyone had left. I wanted to see for myself what the incision looked like, so I buzzed for Ann to see if she had a mirror that I could use to look at my scars. Gingerly she helped me to the bathroom and handed me a small mirror. As I held it up to look into the mirror on the wall, I focused on the huge horseshoe-shaped incision that literally went from ear to ear over the crest of my cowlick to the nape of my neck. It was much larger than the scars from the first operation and, with my bald head, I looked as if I had a large softball for a head. The incision was sutured with black nylon thread, unlike the staples of the first operation. It was a clean bloodless incision, which appeared to be healing already. On my forehead was a _-inch-diameter scab. Anne said that was where the doctors screwed the halo into my head to hold the surgical microscope. There were two more holes on each temple at the hairline and I wondered why they had to place a screw in the middle of my forehead.

I spent much of the first week sleeping, talking to the various doctors who frequented my room, or being entertained by Pam. At times I found myself testing my eyes, trying to define the limits of my vision. The visual deficit was annoying because it was like having a dime-sized spot of Vaseline on both lenses of your sunglasses. If you have ever scratched the lenses of your glasses, you know it is a nuisance to wear them. That is what I was dealing with in my visual field, only I could not take off the glasses to eliminate the irritation.

I would often sit with my eyes closed because it was fatiguing to keep them open. Occasionally I listened to my CDs, trying to find some comfort in the melodies and guitar licks. Unfortunately I did not get the same reassurance from the music that I had received before the surgeries. One or more times a day I would hold my pointing finger out horizontally, pick an object in the room to focus on, and move my finger right and left. Amazingly, the tip of my finger would disappear and then reappear, unattached to the rest of my hand. When two or more people came to visit and stood three abreast, I could only see the person to the left of the group. I would have to scan the room to see all three visitors. I imagined this to be like taking LSD and hallucinating or having your eyes out of focus and trying to focus.

The flowers and fruit baskets poured into the room, the phone constantly rang with well-wishes and good intentions. Apparently the phone at home started to ring whenever the receiver was put down; it got so bad that Sue turned the phone off so the kids could sleep. She was also struggling with a delayed stress syndrome of her own and unable to visit every day. The doctors had asked all the family to run interference for me to limit visitors and activity so I could get the amount of sleep required to heal.

Nights were the worst. I was rested from sleeping all day and could not read because of my eyes. Watching TV was out of the question—it was awkward and cumbersome trying to scan the set to see all that was on the screen. It was easiest to sit with my eyes closed and listen to the programs rather than watching them. Every evening after dinner, Pam would come and stay all night to help me deal with the pain. She would relate all the activities at home and keep me informed of Sue's progress dealing with fatigue. My father, having seen me through the two surgeries, refocused on work and assumed I would fully recover and get back to work brokering deals. Mom was depressed about my condition, but thankful I was alive. She prayed for me every day at church. Even when I was a child, she had believed in me, although she never could find the words to say it.

Everyone acted as if my survival was the end of my ordeal and that, with time, I would recover and return to my life as it was before. Only the doctors and I knew the real story—it would take many months and even years to recover from my injuries. In the days that followed, I settled into a routine that involved waking up, eating pancakes, bacon and coffee for breakfast—accompanied by a handful of pills—and quickly scanning the headlines on the front page of the newspaper. That was all I was able to cope with before the demand on my brain became too taxing. I had not shaved or bathed since the sponge bath in the ICU, so when Barbara Dunderdale paid her daily visit, I asked her when I could shave and shower.

"Today," she said, "but someone has to be with you."

Quickly I invited her to join me in the shower, but she was too smart for me and said she would hold my hand from outside the stall and behind the curtain. Once I was in the shower stall, she cautioned me not to get the incision wet and to hold onto the rail inside for support. She vigilantly stood outside the stall in case I lost my balance. I tried as best I could to wash myself with one hand while I held on to the rail with the other. My balance and coordination were definitely not working and it took almost every ounce of energy I had to perform the simple tasks of waking up, washing, shaving and feeding myself.

In fact, shaving was not as simple a task as it used to be—when I looked in the mirror I only saw one eye looking back. As I found myself struggled to focus, I started to cry. The sudden breakdown caused Barbara to sit me down on the bed and assure me that it was all right to cry. She said my ordeal was difficult, but I was doing much better than predicted, and that in itself was cause for celebration, not tears. I knew what she was saying, but from my standpoint, I could not accept the infantile state I found myself in.

My elation at beating the odds was nullified by the reality of my diminished capacities. There was no joy in Mudville. Every morning I woke up and hoped to be normal and every night I hoped I would not wake up in the wee hours in severe pain.

I napped all day and struggled all night; Pam's companionship helped me deal with all the questions we discussed in the dark hours of the evenings. My dreams and aspirations were smashed into fragments of a life that were uncertain and insecure. Pam steered me through this mine field and reminded me of what wealth and power did to our father's health and life. I mourned the loss of my old life and found the anticipation of an unknown future bewildering. Much of the time I was left alone. This gave me the opportunity to explore my deficits in private. As the shock of surgery wore off, I hoped these problems would evaporate. But they didn't. Eventually I would have to raise these issues with the doctors, but at first I did not want people to know that I was suffering other problems. I had never faced such fear and had feared for my life only once before.

Chapter 21

In the mid-1980s, Dad, H.L. McSorley, Peter Starck, Francis O'Neill, Doug Wilson and I were sailing Dad's 40-foot boat home from Key Biscayne, Florida. We had been at sea for four days and had reached the Gulf of Savannah, about 120 miles off Charleston, South Carolina. That night on the 2 to 6 a.m. watch, the sky was clear with a heaven full of stars. The wind was accelerating slowly to about 15 knots; by sunrise we were in 25 to 30 knots of wind and the sky was a cloudless blue. At first, we shortened sail by one of the three reef points but, as the wind accelerated to 40 knots, we were forced to remove the Genoa and put up a storm staysail. The main was on its third reef point by 10 a.m. and the wind was still gaining strength. I had never seen a gale with clear skies before. Pots, pans and personal belongings inside the boat were tossed around as if they were in a clothes drier.

Remarkably, Dad and Francis lay calmly in their bunks. Why should I be concerned if they were not? I had on my life harness and was shackled to the safety line attached from the bow to the stern. The line was 1 1/2-inches thick and securely fastened to the hull. I had tied the knots myself. We decided take the mainsail down and try to sail into the enormous sea, taking the waves on our starboard bow, trying to sail over the huge seas at a 45-degree angle with just the staysail on. That way we would not pitch and turn turtle, a maneuver with disastrous consequences. When we released the tension on the main halyard, the portion of the sail still unfurled shredded like toilet paper. The only thing that kept the halyard from going to the top of the mast was the line stitched into the luff of the sail where the track slides are fastened.

Waves were towering 30 to 40 feet high in front of us. Our bow tossed left and right with the swell of the waves as we lumbered up one side and down the other. When we finished lashing the pieces of mainsail to the boom, we huddled to make a life or death decision. The deck was under white water and we were not making any headway into the enormous sea with our tiny sail and our motor. Eventually we had to shut off the motor because it was overheating from straining against the powerful sea. For the first time in a long sailing career, I was afraid of the sea.

We decided to alter course and reach off toward Charleston since it was impossible to make any headway on our present course. This clear-air gale had caught us off guard; none of the weather services we listened to had predicted these horrifying conditions. We had battled these winds and seas for eight hours and planned a course of action should we have to abandon ship.

Our position put us 90 miles east of Charleston. At our present speed, it was going to take another 20 hours before we could reach the safety of the harbor and Fort Sumter. The waves were so violent that the cockpit was waist-deep in water and the hatches and portholes leaked like a sieve. It was literally raining inside the boat. We bailed out the bilge every half-hour. Sometime in the late afternoon, I made my way up to the mast to try to get above the constant wash across the decks, repeating to myself the man overboard drill and abandon ship procedures.

It took us 18 hours to reach the safety of the Charleston harbor. If it were not for our sailing experience, we would have surely perished that day. The sea is a cruel place for those who are unaware of its power. I had learned to respect the sea and allow myself the humility to recognize its strength. We had struggled, but our struggle was short and easy compared to the battle I now was waging for my life.

* * * * *

During the first week in the Ellison building, my environment was controlled. The doctors had taken me off the medication for my blood pressure along with the heavy painkillers. In the daytime, I was given Co-Tylenol. With visitors or doctors constantly walking in and out of my room, there was enough distraction to help manage the pain. When darkness fell over the city and things quieted down, I could feel the pain all over my head. Sometimes I would feel the artery that ran from the back of my head to the right temple bulging. The sandpaper-like grinding of the skull plates was annoying. In a way, the back of my head was nonexistent—it was as if the doctors had welded a steel plate over the back of my skull.

Between the constant flow of visitors and the unending parade of doctors, I was exhausted. The technicians from the lab had a thirst for my blood like ticks feeding on a dog. Rarely did I wake up rested. I felt trapped inside a body that was not mine. I wanted to get out and act, think and sound like everyone around me. I had to think about everything I did before I could do it— walk, talk, drink or eat. I was so infantile that I had to tell myself to chew my food before I could actually eat something. All the same, I experienced an inner calmness and tranquility that helped me appreciate life more and made me spiritually stronger.

Every morning when the parade of doctors came to my room, the discussion centered on the problems I was experiencing. I did not want to share those problems with my family because I thought I was imagining them. I had to confirm with the doctors that what I was experiencing was a result of damage to the brain. Accepting the fact that I had brain damage was not going to be easy—my mind wanted to think of those deficits as imagined and not real. Psychologists call it denial. Coping with denial was exhausting and my brain frequently had to shut down and rest. Throughout the day and night, I took many short naps. Whenever I could not take it any more, I would roll over and sleep. Every doctor who visited me encouraged sleep; they all told me that sleep was the only way for the brain to heal.

After lunch, I would ask whoever was my guest to help me walk in the hall. Each day I would try to walk a few steps farther than I had the previous day. By the end of the first week, I was able to walk to the nurses' station, rest a few minutes and then walk back to my bed for a three-hour nap. At the end of the first week, I sneaked out of my room to a supply and storage room and found a walker. This device allowed me to take little walks on my own until the nurses discovered me. After that, one of them would walk with me until I returned safely to my bed.

One night I awoke to the annoying sound of a buzzer out in the hall. At first, I thought I was hearing the constant buzz in my head and expected to roll over and fall asleep by ignoring it. Eventually I realized it was not in my head and sat up to see what time it was—3:30 a.m. I decided to investigate where the noise was coming from. I grabbed for the walker and eased myself to my feet, moving slowly but deliberately. Once I was standing, I told my right foot to move, then my left foot. Five steps later, I was at my doorway, only to run into the night nurse, who was coming to give me my four o'clock neuro exam and pills.

"Mr. Fallon, where do you think you're going at this hour of the night?"

I told her that for obvious reasons I was going out of my room to see why that goddamn buzzer was going off outside my door. She turned me around and headed me back to bed, explaining that an IV alarm was going off because a patient kept trying to pull the needle out of her arm. She said that maintenance had been called to fix the alarm. I asked why the alarm was still on. She claimed that fluid from the IV had shorted the circuits in the wiring so they could not shut the alarm off. I was disturbed by this development and voiced my distress vehemently, whereupon the nurse forcefully returned me to my bed. Then she almost shoved the pills at me, handed me a glass of water and told me to go to sleep!

As soon as she left my room, I planned an assault on the lady and her IV. I would take a pair of scissors from the drawer next to my bed and find the buzzer, unscrew the faceplate, and cut the wires with the scissors. A simple solution for a simple problem! Stealthily I sneaked up the hall with my walker, scissors in hand, determined to silence the buzzer forever. Like a cat in the night, I progressed to the alarm on the wall, eagerly awaiting the silence that would be achieved when I cut the wires. Before I could get 10 feet from my door, two things happened: one, the buzzer went silent and, two, the nurse found me again. In the morning, Barbara told me that the night nurse had made an entry into the log depicting my attitude as disturbed.

I have a hazy memory of the last two weeks in the hospital, other than spending a lot of time testing my vision by holding my hands out in front of me and moving them left to right and right to left. The urge to squint in an attempt to focus was constant and the effort drained me physically. The only relief came when I sat in the dark or with my eyes closed, although even then I could see an aura. At times I thought someone was sneaking up behind me or that small gray squirrels were scurrying about the floor. The temptation to ask the doctors about these visions was compelling, but I feared they would blame the hallucinations on the pain medication and stop prescribing them. My pain level was hardly tolerable and the fear of having to endure it without medication kept me silent. When I was alone, I would sometimes challenge the hallucination and ask the empty room if anyone was there. At times like that, I began to question my sanity.

While I slowly slipped into a state of depression, my stay at the hospital came to an end, three-and-a-half weeks after my admittance. I eagerly anticipated my discharge day but was not sure how my senses would respond to the stimulus of the environment outside my hospital. I called it my hospital because I knew every nurse on Ellison 22, as well as all the lab technicians from the blood bank and the whole neurology department. In a strange way I was a celebrity to those people—many of them had not expected me to survive. On the last night of my stay, Dr.

Gress and my other doctors appeared in my room one by one to tell me that I would get out the next morning. My head was full of questions—I felt lost and confused. What do you say to those special doctors who saved your life!

I had formed a unique bond with Dr. Gress. I was able to tell him what I was thinking and how differently I saw life compared to before my surgeries. In return for my second chance on life, I would try to be a more understanding individual and contribute to society. This second chance gave me an opportunity to improve myself physically and emotionally. I was committed to a healthy diet and exercise regime to take better care of my body and mind.

I believed that I saw the beautiful things in life and that my inner vision was clearer. The analogy I used to describe my new perspective went something like this: Before, when I looked out the window to the west, I saw the Charles River and the trees lining Storrow and Memorial Drives. Interspersed were buildings, cars and streetlights, along with a sea of humanity. Now, when I look out the window, I see the ripples in the waves and the shimmer of the wind over the water. I see the texture of the bark on the trees and the veins of the leaves. Buildings have definition and contours; colors are bright and alive. In short, I had seen the emptiness of death, and I reveled in the richness of life. I appreciated what I could see and touch, my senses tingled with awareness; I was alive and it was far better than the deep darkness that awaits us on the other side of life. Instinctively, I responded with a will to survive that was stronger than the mysterious forces of death and darkness.

A period of discovery began during this introspective discussion with Dr. Gress. Damage assessment and control is what I would have to deal with. For almost two hours we sat talking about my vision and memory difficulties. I felt overwhelmed and confused and had difficulty formulating sentences. At times I felt a tension inside my brain and up the back of my neck. When I asked Dr. Gress about these difficulties, his answers were general and of little comfort. We discussed the activities I could and could not do. Heavy lifting or straining in any way was out of the question. Driving was not allowed—if my eyes improved, we could consider driving later. I had to avoid tension, pressure and stress of any kind. I was told to take it easy, enjoy my life and, after four or five years, see how I had progressed. Sleep was the prescription for a long recovery and I was encouraged to sleep whenever I felt the urge.

When I asked about work and when I could return, he said, "Bill, when it comes to brain damage or stroke victims, we know so little about the brain that every patient is different and unique. In some cases a patient may recover fully with few or no neuro deficits. Another patient with the same damaged area of the brain can experience many or all of the deficits you have and more. You are a very special patient and fortunate to be alive. Take all the time you need to get back on your feet. After all, you have the rest of your life to figure that out."

When I forced this issue, Dr. Gress said that I might never go back to work! Some patients have such intense fatigue that they physically are unable to return to the pace of life that they were accustomed to. This was the first instance when I heard that my permanent disabilities might prohibit me from picking up my life where I left it back in November of 1990.

My last night in Ellison 22 passed like all the rest, a nervous sleep because I was unable to place pressure on the back of my head in the effort to get comfortable. The doctors wanted me to be vigilant about my head. The simple task of raising my voice, sneezing or coughing created an immense pressure pain in my vascular system. Clearing my throat caused the arteries in my head to bulge with the pressure caused by the increased blood flow. Anything I did to increase my heart rate or blood pressure caused me great discomfort and pain. It felt as if something was going to rupture and I was always wondering if I was going to blow an artery.

The sun was not yet over the horizon as I swung my legs over the edge of the bed and reached for my walker. With a great deal of effort I made my way to the lounge area that faced east. As I arrived, the sun slowly climbed over the horizon, its rays stretching west between the highrise office buildings. Its warmth revitalized me as it struck my face. As the sun's intensity grew, so did my desire to live. As I relaxed in the glory of the sun, I could feel my weakness and instability growing and sat down. When a nurse found me gazing into the sun, she scolded me for wandering off like an Alzheimer's patient and walked me back to my room.

Looking around the room made me realize I was loved by many people. The gifts, cards and posters strewn about touched me and I started to weep. An event like this always weeds out the superficial friends an individual picks up over the course of a lifetime. Fortunately, I had only a few of those encounters. My dad had taught me how to read and pass judgement on an individual's intentions. I had been a good student and learned well. When I struggled to read the wishes on my wall-size get well card, I realized how many true friends I had.

My usual breakfast of pancakes arrived at the same time as Dr. Westmark. Behind Dr. Westmark was Dr. Gress. The two of them were happy to announce that if I passed the morning's EEG test, I would be discharged that afternoon. I knew that this EEG was an important test to pass: If the results showed low risk of convulsions and a normal brainwave pattern, I would be allowed to go home. A great distress grew within me because I knew I had been in a controlled environment. Dr. Gress stayed only long enough to arrange for the EEG test and then left.

Dr. Westmark, who had assisted Dr. Crowell, was the resident assigned to me for the duration of his tenure at the hospital. We had spent many hours talking about our families and ourselves. He was a genuine genius with only nine more months to finish his seven-year residency for neurosurgery. And he was only 28! His caring and compassion during the most difficult and unpleasant time in my life made it easier to bear. I can honestly say that about all my doctors; if they had not done their best for me, I would have never survived. The compassion and kindness they demonstrated was superb and I am eternally grateful to them for making a bad time tolerable. I made a commitment to myself to never forget them; if there was anything I could do for them in the future, I would do it without a second thought.

Sue and John arrived around 10 a.m. to load up my personal effects and flowers. It looked as if I had won the Kentucky Derby, with all the flowers and baskets littering my room. Within minutes, a gurney and an attendant arrived to take me to the radiology department. The fact that I was wheeled there in a gurney is indicative of my condition after three weeks in the hospital. Frail would be a good word to describe it. This was my second EEG, the first was after the first operation, and I remembered the very pretty blonde lady from Germany who was in her 50s and looked 30. The test takes about an hour. Several sensors were glued to my head, and I lay down on a bed. Above me was a strobe light that I was supposed to look at. I looked at the light with one eye at a time, wondering whether it would affect the results. After about an hour, the test ended and I was wheeled back to my room.

Sue and John had packed all my belongings, except for the sheet inscribed by all my friends. I decided to have all my doctors sign it as they came to visit me one last time. Around noon, Dr. Crowell came in and sat on the end of my bed. He reminded me to take it easy and rest, not to do any straining or lifting. I was told not to get hit in the head, drive a car or fall down. He again told me that I had a great attitude and never to lose my sense of humor. I asked him what I could do and he said anything I wanted except fly a plane or be an air traffic controller. For the near future, I should rest and take it very easy, no stress!

"In six or seven months, we will have you back in for a follow-up. At that time we will talk about returning to a normal schedule of activities. You have the rest of your life to figure out what you want to do and can do. In a couple of months, we will have Dr. LaSalle test your eyes and then again six months after that. I am going to let you go home this afternoon. Sue, I want you to keep it quiet around the house and restrict visits. What Bill needs now more than anything else is a long rest. He has my orders to become a first-class couch potato. See you later on, Bill!"

Despite repeated warnings from doctors that it could take three to five years, I anticipated a recovery of perhaps one year— maybe nine months. If I was lucky, I might get to take a few ski runs in April. Was I in for a shock!

The adrenaline in my veins was flowing with the anticipation of the familiar surroundings of home, fresh air and a new reality. I was going home to a new life and a new me, a chance to start life over. It was a rebirth of the body, the spirit and the soul. The thought of viewing my plight from the perspective of what I had lost versus the new persona and a chance to correct what I perceived as deficits was compelling. The term one doctor used was that I had a new lease on life. My reality would be what I would make of it. I had to start thinking in terms of what I could do to make myself better: healthier, smarter, stronger mentally and emotionally. If I was going to start with walking and build up to the point where I could care for my own personal hygiene and be able to function throughout the whole day, I might as well fix what was wrong with all of me.

Dr. Westmark asked if the Percocet helped my pain. I said yes, and he recommended two pills every four to six hours as needed. He figured that a prescription for 100 tablets with three refills was enough. I questioned him about the risk of becoming a junkie. He assured me that people in serious pain rarely develop a drug habit. As I took the handful of prescriptions for everything from anti-convulsants to stomach tranquilizers, I thanked him, not only for his medical expertise but also for his friendship and advice through a difficult time.

When the attendant came around with my wheelchair, I exchanged phone numbers with Dr. Westmark and warned him that

I would stay in touch. One of the wrongs I wanted to right was my poor organization and inability to stay in contact with the many people who crossed my path. I decided to get a new address book to keep in touch with anyone I cared for. It was time to go home and I began to make the transition into the real world. The attendant wheeled me down the polished and shiny halls. On the way down to the entrance, I passed some of the nurses, lab technicians and attendants I knew, and we exchanged greetings. Trying to absorb all the activity and process it so my brain could comprehend the data caused me great distress and pain. I was beginning to believe that it hurt to think.

Outdoors, the day was sensational. The sky was cobalt blue, the temperature in the 70s with a gentle southeast breeze. I had not been outside for more than three weeks, and I cannot tell you the sense of relief I experienced. The rush of sensation as the elements assaulted my body was a powerful antidote to my soul and spirit. I was alive. Sue had decided I should return home in style and had hired a limo. The air was warm and sweet, the sky cloudless. On the ride home, I quickly realized I could not look out the window at the passing sights because it caused me to get motion sickness. The visual distortion combined with the speed of objects rushing by was too much for my brain to handle and I just sat quietly with my eyes tightly closed. The day was so warm and beautiful I wanted to absorb every ounce of its energy, hoping it would recharge my lost strength.

We decided to stop at the drugstore on the way home again to fill my prescriptions. The list of medications was frightening. There was Phenobarbital, 230 mg a day, for anti-seizure; Tagamet to keep the Phenobarbital from eating a hole in my stomach; Percocet, two every four hours or as needed for pain; and Valium for anxiety. There was some other pill, a steroid for brain swelling, and another one for something I couldn't remember. While I was sitting in the limo in front of the pharmacy, feeling the warm breeze on my face as it drifted through the window, a hand gently grabbed my arm. It belonged to an old friend I had grown up with in Weston: Steve McShane, now a policeman in town. He asked how I was and wished me a speedy recovery. I thanked him for the encouragement, asked about his family and wished him good health.

Anticipation was growing as we got closer to the house; I wanted to see my daughter and my 6-month-old son. I longed for the familiar smells of my house and the warm softness of my own bed. Sue loved a lot of pillows and our king-size bed has a regular mattress and a down mattress on top of it. When you lay down, you sink into it about 6 inches—it feels like sleeping in the clouds. As I rode in the car with my eyes closed, I listened to my surroundings to make up with my ears what I had lost with my eyes. Or should I say what I had lost of my brain. Each bump in the road registered in my head. I felt like my brain was sloshing around in my head—it was like having a fish bowl for a head.

I tried to look out at the beauty of the New England countryside, with its majestic oak and maple trees lining the roads like giant sentinels. I grew up in the heart of the birthplace of America. Towns like Lincoln, Concord and Lexington surround Weston and Wayland. These towns are the essence of colonial Massachusetts, with its corn and hay fields lined with stone walls. White farmhouses and colonial-style homes line the streets and ancient trees provide shade with their huge canopies. It was all relevant and beautiful to me. The strain on my mind to see portions of life as it zoomed by was overwhelming my sensory receptors. Looking at life race by at 40 miles an hour caused too much pain.

When we came to a stop and I heard Riley, my German shepherd, bark, I opened my eyes to see the whole gang standing in the driveway. Katherine held Flash in her arms and Shannon came running from the swing set in the back yard. I was home—oh God, I was home! Only now could I allow myself to think of the worst that could have befallen me and I fell apart. A rush of emotion exploded within me and marked the beginning of a long healing process that I would undertake to heal my body and repair my soul. The spirit had been taken out of me and I had to start to renew my spirit then and there. If I did not, I would be crippled for the rest of my life.

I would be treated differently from now on and it was going to be a tough transition. I was always a free spirit, independent and strong. Now that I was home and in my house, the reality of the world outside my hospital had shaken me. I realized the magnitude of the changes I would have to make to adapt. The doctors had not lied to me and I prayed to God that they were not lying about my learning to adapt and adjust. The longest walk I had taken in the hospital was about 30 feet on a flat plane; walking 30 yards into my home with steps to deal with was exhausting. I felt the pressure of each step in my veins and when I reached my den, I sank into my leather armchair and rested.

Chapter 22

The first day at home was exhilarating and exhausting. Reading all my get-well cards took up most of the afternoon. I ended up napping on the couch for a few hours. A few of the skiing gang dropped in for a visit, the first of many for Robert Mann, Ross and Bernice Hamlin, and Grover and Starr Daniels. Late in the afternoon, I summoned up enough courage to walk out onto the deck that adjoins my den. I began the practice of sitting in the sun for hours on end with my eyes closed. After the kids were put to bed, I sat in my den in the darkness listening to CDs and tapes. Music satisfied my one sensory mode that wasn't damaged too badly. If I controlled the volume, music became a form of entertainment I could process. I could escape my reality into a fantasy inspired by soul-filled rhythms and the riffs of blues guitars—a place where I had no pain and everything I looked at was whole and complete.

It must have been nearly 10 p.m. before Sue finally had enough time to sit alone with me in the den; her first instinct was to switch on the lights. The harsh change in my environment violated my senses and aggravated my pain. Instantly, Sue turned the lights down low with the rheostat. Alone together for the first time in months, we listened to the music. My selection of tunes ignited memories of cross-country trips and summers fishing in the Canadian Rockies—the early '70s, fast cars, rock and roll, and the social revolution. Somewhere in the night we made our way to our bedroom where, we indulged ourselves in a long, slow and passionate night, a rekindling and reaffirmation of our love for each other. This catastrophe had tested us to the core of our existence and our love was growing stronger. For the first time in a long while, I slipped into a sleep secure in the knowledge that when I woke up, I would be alive and entangled in the arms of the most precious thing in my life.

When I awoke with searing pain in my head, I found Sue sitting up in bed watching over me. She had a sad face, teary eyes, and she was fumbling with a Kleenex. Awake while I slept, her long vigil not yet over. The sorrow and pain she endured on my account hurt my heart.

I slowly sat up and asked if I was talking in my sleep.

"No" she replied, "but I know you are in a lot of pain."

"Is it that obvious?" I asked.

"Yes," she said.

The pain was like striking your head with a hard object, never subsiding, a relentless ache. Sue handed me a glass and a couple of pills to deaden the pain. I tried to explain what it was like to have your brain violated and a hole in your visual field. We talked about where my emotions were and how we were going to do to deal with my disabilities. The Percocet did not take long to diminish the pain, although drugs never totally relieved it. They did, however, take the edge off so that I could get a little more sleep. I must have passed out in mid-sentence because the next thing I knew, I was being served breakfast. Katherine was treating Sue and I to a welcome-home breakfast in bed. Coffee, eggs and bacon for me; toast, strawberries and tea for Sue. I carefully ate my food to avoid spilling anything. It was a constant struggle to see everything and even, when I was most vigilant, I usually spilled my coffee or knocked over a glass or the salt shaker.

Katharine had brought the newspaper, but I did not dare try to read it. Instead I chose to watch an early-morning television news show. When I looked at the picture on the TV, however, I still could only see part of it. If it was a face, I could see a cheek, part of a nose, and an eye. I could not see the host sitting next to the anchor unless I directed my focus to the right side of the screen; otherwise the person seemed to be talking to herself. I had to strain to focus in an attempt to understand what I looked at. At times it seemed as if I saw in two dimensions only; my perspective had no depth.

There was no reason to rush and get out of bed—what was there for a blind man to do? Nevertheless, I would get up, shower and shave. As the effects of the drugs slowly faded, I became more aware. When I looked at myself in the mirror the first time I shaved myself, I could only see the right half of my face. At all times I tried to see where I could not, which created a state of high anxiety within my consciousness.

My routine started to take shape: I would get up, get dressed, and have coffee and breakfast. Then I would move into the den to select a half-dozen CDs to stack in the player, a painstakingly slow task. I could not read the labels and tried to decipher what the album was by the cover. Of course that wasn't so easy because my memory wasn't good either. Then I would open the windows and door to the deck and move out to the hammock. It was a slow, tedious process but I needed to follow a routine. To make any progress at all, I kept my movements slow and purposeful. Every word or action had to be preplanned, otherwise my mind would wander and I could not finish what I started to do.

The days passed slowly. I rarely wore a watch, time no longer had meaning. If I paid attention to the time, the days seemed endless. When I reached the hammock, it did not take long before I slipped into a sound sleep. I was told not to resist the temptation to doze off, so I didn't. Usually I slept for a couple hours, then would wake up and amble into the kitchen for lunch. The televised Persian Gulf War got me into the habit of watching the 12 o'clock news.

After lunch I went for a walk. At first it was around the deck, then to the steps. At the pace I was going, I figured it would be a month before I would have the strength to walk the 50 feet to the mailbox. If a task caused me distress, I had to stop or my anxiety and pain would grow, rendering me incapable of judgment. Any mundane task that we all perform many times a day without thinking turned into a monumental task. The pain was like no other feeling I had ever experienced. It was motion sickness, acrophobia, anxiety attack, headache, migraine and hangover, all at once. How different my life was going to be! How could I function throughout the day? No longer could I contemplate how I was going to provide for my family—first I would have to learn how to feed and care for myself, dress myself, and get to the other end of the house before I had to take a four-hour nap to recover.

Talking was not going to be my strong suit—I found it mentally fatiguing and cumbersome. Words were hard to formulate in my head, let alone speak coherently. I had to keep to the basics like "What's for lunch?" or "Do I have to do anything today?" If I didn't, I would forget I was on my way to do something and go off in another direction.

Occasionally I could count on someone like Robert to come by and visit or have lunch on the deck. Robert and I had spent a lot of time skiing together over the years and our friendship strengthened when we started to sail together in the summers. My friends supported me during those dark days. Most of them accepted my limitations, others could not. In a sad sense, I have grown away from some people. Some could not come to terms with the loss of the old Bill. Perhaps my inability to drive to visit them or share in some activity due to my visual limitations was too difficult for them to accept. I realized that I was experiencing some of the discrimination disabled Americans face.

My strength was nonexistent. I could not lift or strain without feeling pressure on the arteries in my head. My right temple felt as though it was bulging and an artery over my right ear twitched all the time. I would wonder whether I had sprung a leak in the neurovascular system or whether the sharp pain in my head would subside or intensify until I died.

My reality was slipping away. Before, when I looked at a table, I could see everything on it. Now when I looked at a table, then looked away, I thought I knew what was on it. If I looked back at the table again, I would notice a book where I had not seen it before. I began to question my vision and my judgement; it was a constant form of irritation that eroded my confidence. Add that to the phenomenon of hallucinating—I saw people sneaking up behind me or objects moving around in my peripheral vision. I would notice dark objects floating around my legs and attempt to step around them. Knowing what was real and what was hallucination frustrated me even more. The only refuge to deal with this anxiety and pain was sleep.

At lunchtime, I took some more Percocet, a Phenobarbital and a Tagamet. Memory was a problem because I could not remember whether I had taken the pills or not. While Sue was at work, Shannon was at school, and Flash slept, Katherine and I would eat lunch, then I would walk to the mailbox. The round trip exhausted me. Afterward I would lay down in my den with a bunch of blues CDs to drown out noise and doze off until three or four. By that time Sue was back from the office, and Shannon would bounce in full of excitement and energy from her day at school. My days ended as they began—two or more cups of coffee, which enabled me to stay awake long enough for dinner, and the evening news on television.

After about four weeks of visual special effects and constant hallucinations of someone sneaking up from behind my right shoulder or the furry squirrels at my feet, it was time to visit Dr. LaSalle, a patho-neurologist, to test my visual field and compare it to pre-surgery. It was four weeks since leaving the hospital and I had not been in a car since. Sue was taking me into Mass Eye and Ear for the test. The bumps in the road registered in my egg-like head and the passing scenery strained my eyes and brain. I felt nauseous and queasy, my brain ached and the arteries in my head burned. My consciousness screamed out for the relief and safety of darkness. I closed my eyes to the real world. Imagery—closing my eyes and imagining where I was by the sounds around me—was the only way I could see while in a car.

When we finally reached Mass Eye and Ear, we parked the car and headed for the main entrance. I was all right once the car stopped, but my movements were rigid. When I encountered someone on the sidewalk, I sometimes did not see another person walking with him or her, or I would notice a pair of legs. It dawned on me that I could not navigate in a crowd without bumping into someone or something. As I walked to the main entrance, I almost knocked down an old lady on the sidewalk. When I turned to apologize, I said, "Excuse me, I did not see you there."

"Why don't you look where you're going?" she snapped.

We entered Dr. LaSalle's office just in time to meet him in his reception area and exchange polite greetings. I did not want to be there; I did not want to go through a test that would tell me what I already knew. I was partially blind and disabled—what else was there to know? The first part of the exam was the basic eye test, which I passed with a little myopic problem. Either I was getting old and nearsighted, or I was suffering from more than I knew. It turns out that the swelling on my brain was putting pressure on my optic nerve, causing the difficulty with my distance vision. The doctor was not going to prescribe glasses until we knew how much swelling would dissipate, which by itself would result in improved vision. Next we moved over to a device for testing field of view; it was shaped like a beach ball cut in half with a chin support. The inside of the sphere is white with a spot in the middle straight in front of your face. In my right hand was a button. As I rested my chin on the support, I was instructed to look at the spot in the middle of the sphere. The doctor moved a little white light around in the sphere and whenever I saw the light, I pressed the button. It was difficult and cumbersome to stare at the spot and resist the temptation to move my eyes to the light. The test continued on the right eye, then the left. Dr. LaSalle graphed the blind spots in each eye and then reviewed the results with Sue and I. The test clearly indicated a visual deficit in both eyes of about 35 percent. The weird part is that it was not my extreme peripheral vision that was deficient, but the center right. Imagine two circles representing the field of view for each eye. Each circle represents the face of a clock. If you look at the center of the circles, the field cut would eliminate the upper right-hand quadrant in each circle. Yet I could see the outer line delineating the circles. In other words, there was a big hole in my field of view.

I asked if I could try to drive. Dr. LaSalle advised that I not drive for a while. When I did, he emphasized that I would have to be very careful. The news that driving might not be a casualty of my surgery still did not give me much hope—deep down I knew my vision was going to give me trouble. Just when I thought the appointment was over, Dr. LaSalle asked me to describe what I saw and whether I had hallucinations.

"Am I supposed to?" I asked.

"Sometimes when a person suffers damage to the brain, specifically to the occipital lobe, they experience hallucinations."

When I heard these words, I wondered whether I should admit I had hallucinations or not. Finally I decided to tell him. To my relief, he informed me that seeing people and little furry creatures running around my feet was normal. I was relieved to hear this because I had thought I was losing my mind. For weeks I had been sitting on the deck in my rocking chair seeing little furry creatures and some guy who kept sneaking up on me. I feared telling or asking anyone about it because I thought they would think I was nuts. The doctor told me that as long as I did not talk to these hallucinations, things would be all right. If I talked to them and they talked back, then I should get some help. I questioned my ability to see cars on the side of the road or a pedestrian crossing the street. With a laugh, Dr. LaSalle said I had enough vision to see a pair of legs walking across the street. On a serious note, Dr. LaSalle praised the work of Dr. Crowell and Dr. Pyle-Spellman; if it had not been for the skill of each surgeon, I would have been in much worse condition. He had special praise for JPS and credited him for saving as much vision as he did.

"That JPS is terrific! His procedure saved your eyes and Dr. Crowell saved your life. God must love you, Bill! You had the best there is taking care of you. I want to see you in six months for another field test. I have to be honest with you and say that I do not think your vision will improve, but I want to check your eyes again. You were very lucky to keep the vision you have left. I thought the damage was more likely to be in the 70-percent range. You have sustained a field cut of about 35 percent. If it had been your peripheral vision, you would have adjusted easily. The odd fact is that yours is in the middle."

I thanked Dr. LaSalle for the encouragement but, nonetheless, I was glad to leave his office. The confirmation of what I had figured out on my own was no consolation. The hope of improvement had been extinguished by the confirmation of my visual reality. Up until the visit with Dr. LaSalle, I had thought I would drive again. My handicap had made me dependent.

It was a beautiful day as we emerged from the shadows of Mass Eye and Ear. The rays of the sun warmed my flesh and rekindled a spark in my soul. In the car on the way home, Sue assured me that the news, although final, was good. Instead of looking at the dark side of things, I should start to look at the good side of my ordeal. I was alive!

Five weeks had passed since I was discharged from the hospital; the foliage was starting to take on the brilliance of autumn. Everyone was talking about the beauty of the season, yet somehow I could not share that sentiment. My thoughts were of days gone by, when I was hunting with Rick Burtt. The bow season was in full swing. Would I ever hunt again? How could I see the elusive whitetail deer or the flushed cock pheasant taking flight? Would I be able to shoot a gun or bow? What joy was there in stumbling blindly through the trees? My stealth and skills were severely damaged. With the ability to be the hunter gone, I felt like the prey I used to stalk. All fall I sat on my deck or at the point on the Cape, trying to follow the movements of the birds and critters with my ears and not my eyes. When I thought I had located the sound a bird or squirrel was making, I tried to find it with my eyes. Usually I could only catch a fleeting glimpse of the prey I was looking for. It would be a long time before I hunted again, maybe never.

Sleep was all I did—besides eating. What else could I do? Just about nothing, according to the doctors. I indulged in sweets and drank lots of coffee in order not feel tired all the time. As the doctors had recommended, I became a first-class couch potato. Instead of watching TV, which I could not tolerate because of my eyes, I listened to music. There were times when I craved something like a cookie or brownie. On the way to the kitchen I often forgot what I was there for. At times I would stop and try to remember what it was I was going to do! Sue would find me sitting or standing in one place, glazed and dazed, as we called it. When she asked if I was all right, I would lash out at her in anger. I was not angry with her, I was angry with myself and humiliated because I felt so stupid.

It had been well over a month and a half since the second craniotomy and I was like a sedated turtle in every capacity. All my manly duties and responsibilities were stripped away. Learn to exist, eat, dress and care for myself was all I could do to get through the day. It took all my mental effort to do those things, let alone take responsibility for anything. I was no longer a provider, a successful entrepreneur or athlete. Would I ever play catch with Flash? How could I see the ball to catch it? I was drowning in a sea of uncertainty. Every day brought some event that raised more questions. Emotionally I felt about 3 years old.

Chapter 23

Every Columbus Day weekend there is a three-day golf party organized by my longtime friend Joe Clair. Joe and I went from kindergarten to college together and share mutual friends from the different arenas of our lives, a rare event in this world of technology. After college Joe dreamed up an annual weekend of revelry with some of his closest friends at a mansion his father owns in Sebago, Maine. Sue and I attended most of them. I had missed the previous two years and was determined to make an appearance so as to not lose my status as a regular. Another reason was that my self-imposed isolation needed to come to an end; I had to find out if my distress was real or perceived. Besides that, I wanted to show off my scars. Sue was reluctant to take me, but I promised I would behave and sleep as much as I did at home. Yes, there would be drinking all night, cigar smoke and card games, but I knew I could not cope with any of that.

When we arrived at the lake, everyone greeted me with affection and joy. The primary function at the tourney is to socialize with old friends, party and golf. I wanted to see if I could swing a club and hit a few golf balls. Swinging the club was easy; hitting the ball was challenging; making contact with the ball was excruciatingly painful. It was bizarre to hold the club and see only half of the club shaft. No club head at all! On every swing of the club, I hit about two inches behind the ball, which meant I had to concentrate on the ball in order to hit it. But I could see only part of the golf ball. I could not see my backstroke at all. Relentlessly I swung at the ball until one mighty swing connected. Whack! Ouch! Where did it go? What a dilemma golf had become! Pain reverberated from the contact point on the club head all the way up the shaft to my head. In one glaring instance it dawned on me that this "minor visual deficit" had changed my life. Trying to play a few holes exhausted me and I decided to ride the rest of the way around the course in a golf cart. Even that became uncomfortable and I soon asked Sue to take me back to Sebago Lake for a nap. On the way we saw Joe, who asked if I had had enough for the day. I nodded in agreement.

"You are doing great, Bill, and you deserve a rest. We will see you at dinner tonight."

I did manage to play a full nine holes over the next two days. On one of the days I rode around with Joe, who was so glad to see me doing well that he gave me a bear hug. As we discussed my surgery and how amazing it was to be alive and healthy, all I could do was lament my losses. In mid-sentence Joe interrupted me, "Bill, if I was on a handful of Phenobarbital and Percodan with a few beers in me, I would be in a coma! Look at what you are doing after only a month following the most invasive and dangerous surgery there is. I think it is a miracle."

On the third and final night, Joe always awarded prizes and joke gifts at the dinner. That year he stood up and praised my courage for enduring more than any human should have to, and expressed his genuine love and happiness for my well-being. I was unable to hold back the flood of tears as I thanked him and everyone else for their encouragement. Friends like Joe make surviving worth all the pain. The time I spent at the golf tourney lifted my spirits and I went home with a sense of accomplishment.

Adjusting to a new perception of time was part of the recovery process; no longer did I have every day of the week planned in advance. To make this adjustment took a momentous effort, I had always been on the go. In the winter I spent my free time skiing; in the summer I was sailing or golfing; in the fall I went hunting; and in the spring we went to my parents' place in Golden

Beach. Between work and play I was a perpetual motion machine. The adjustment to having nothing but time and nothing I could do was harder than I ever could have imagined. When Shannon was born, I hardly remember her years as a baby. I was home with Flash, however, almost every hour of the day. The bond between father and son would be strong, carefully crafted to avoid the mistakes of earlier generations. The father-daughter relationship is as strong, but special in a different way. As I contemplated my children's future and lamented over my losses, I learned to treasure sharing experiences with my children. I was learning that life and reality are not just three-dimensional. I was learning what was relevant and what was not.

Winter was coming and Sue and I needed a little time together, somewhere warm and romantic where we could rest and sleep unencumbered without the responsibility of children. We set out to find someone responsible to take care of a 6-month-old baby and a 5-year-old girl. Sue's sister Sherrill came to the rescue. Before we knew it, Sue and I were on our way to the Royal Pavilion Resort on tropical Barbados for 10 days. After our vacation, we would go home, pack up the kids and move to Florida for a couple of months. The ghost of my past life haunted me so much, I needed to get away.

Both Sue and I had suppressed our emotions so much that we had to get reacquainted with each other, to expose our fears and anxieties so that we could draw on the tremendous strength and power of our relationship. We needed to be vulnerable enough to confide in each other and try to sort out all our confusion and uncertainty. Our love for each other was the strongest thing we had left in our lives—only it had been put on the back burner. In Barbados we hoped to relight that flame.

* * * * *

As we moved through the crowd in Boston's Logan International Airport, the sea of people in my twisted vision made me feel as if I was going to bump into someone. My movements resembled a drunk walking on an uneven floor. I probably would have been better off if I was totally blind. A few pills and a Bloody Mary or two calmed me, but by no means helped steady my instability.

The brochures did not misrepresent the beauty of Barbados. When we stepped out the door of the plane to walk down the ancient gangplank, the warm Caribbean air rushed in on us. It was a breeze getting into the country. Customs hardly checked anyone's bags, but they scrutinized everyone carefully. Occasionally they do check, which was unfortunate for some guy who was busted for smuggling cocaine as we were processed through. I wondered if I was going to be searched and, if so, what would they say about the entire Phenobarbital cargo I carried? A doctor had told me they were worth $6.50 a tablet on the street. But the officials just looked at our passports, stamped them and handed us a visitor's visa. The Royal Pavilion van was waiting for us and we boarded the van and headed east along the coast.

The country was lush with vegetation and had a gentle hilly topography. The interior was full of tall green mountains reflecting the island's volcanic birthright. All along the roads, the usual sidewalk vendors and shops dotted the coast for the first few miles. The buildings and homes were modest and well maintained. Soon after leaving the commercial area around the airport, we drove by the seaside resorts that mark the northeast coast of this beautiful island nation. Barbados is one of the southernmost islands that run from the Bahamas to Belize. Actually we were off the coast of Venezuela. After a half-hour, we passed the Sandy Lane resort. Along with the Royal Pavilion, these two are the best resorts on the island. They both are five-star resorts offering exquisite food and beautiful private suites along a half-moon-shaped cove.

Our suite was on the second floor with a balcony only 10 yards from the surf lapping gently ashore. Lawns and gardens were manicured to perfection and tropical canaries and parrots filled the air with their music. While we checked in, we were informed that high tea was served between 1:30 and 3 p.m. It was already about 3 p.m., so we decided to go to the patio bar for a hit of caffeine to refresh our weary bones and enjoy the wonderful weather. That night we ate in our room and sat on the balcony, drinking champagne and listening to the tree frogs gently announcing their presence with their soft two-toned whistle. The low lights on the beach did nothing to detract from the brilliance of the tropical stars above our heads. There was no radio or TV in our accommodations, only a sitting room, bathroom and bedroom; the balcony looked out on the whitest beach I have ever seen.

By 10 p.m. Sue had slipped into a deep sleep and I found myself sitting on the balcony staring into the beautiful heaven full of stars, wondering why all this trauma and pain had befallen me. Questions filled my mind and I was bewildered by the magnitude of what I had suffered. I slipped into bed and soon fell asleep entwined in Sue's arms—the only place I felt safe and secure, comforted by her softness and sweet smell. The tranquility of the resort and the warm Caribbean climate helped drop my defense systems enough so that I realized I had truly danced with the Grim Reaper and lived to say I saw his face and felt his touch. The gray pallor that had come over my complexion began to fade. As I lay in bed listening to the gentle chirp of hundreds of tree frogs that sounded like crickets in a corn field, I wondered how long I would feel this bad. I could hear the soft rhythmic slap of the waves as they rolled onto the beach through the open balcony door. It was a moonless starlit night and I was unable to sleep. Sue was sleeping soundly. Her striking beauty made me want to curl up against her smooth body; instead I let her sleep. As I scanned the heavens I found myself asking the powers that be when I would be free of pain.

In the morning, I awoke to find breakfast at the foot of the bed. Sue was sipping tea and reading a local newspaper. On the table were two eggs sunny-side-up, English muffins and bacon— the only thing missing was pancakes! As I was remarking on that omission, Sue reached under the table and held up a warming plate to reveal pancakes. "She is truly an angel," I thought to myself. Our only objective was to lie in the sun, play in the surf and fool around whenever the urge arose. For the first three days we never left the beach in front of our room or the room itself. The food was excellent at the hotel, but by the fifth night we had exhausted all the options at the resort and needed a romantic night out. On the advice of the staff, we made a reservation at a place up the road called the Maison. When we arrived, the restaurant was almost empty. We were seated on the patio at the water's edge facing the setting sun. We ordered a bottle of white wine and proceeded to have a very romantic dinner. After dinner we went back to the Royal Pavilion and skinny-dipped in the warm Caribbean. Later that night we immersed ourselves in each other and slept entangled through the night. A few weeks in paradise was exactly the right prescription for both of us.

Near the end of the vacation, we decided to try some deep-sea fishing and ended up going out in a boat like the one in the movie "Jaws." I was worried about the lack of safety equipment like life jackets and a pump; when I checked out the boat there were none. Unfortunately we were already about 3 miles off-shore when I made this discovery. Within a few minutes of letting out the lines, we hooked a 5-foot kingfish and then some mahi mahi, which we gave to the captain. It did not take long to experience some real excitement, but I was fading fast and needed to head home. The captain and his mate were friendly and we enjoyed the few hours at sea with them. I was starting to feel a little sick from the swells coming in from the open Atlantic— between that and my visual handicap, I needed to get off the boat fast. After telling the captain of my situation, he obliged and set a course for home. In fact, he dropped us off right in front of our hotel room on the way back to his harbor. All we had to do was wade through the surf. When we reached shore, we plopped our tired bodies on the first lounge chairs we came to. Within a few minutes I fell sound asleep. When I woke up, it was almost dark. Sue was still sleeping.

Our time in Barbados was very special; Sue and I engulfed ourselves in each other. Our future was so tenuous that we had both unconsciously built emotional barriers against each other. It was an instinct in order to protect ourselves. We both had prepared ourselves for the possibility of my death. In the process, our emotions had taken a back seat. We had to learn to touch each other, hold each other and express our affection again. We snorkeled in the ocean, even though I am terrified of sharks. The thought of being eaten alive by an animal without warning or defenses is my greatest fear. Another brain operation would be preferable to a shark attack! In Barbados we got lost emotionally and avoided thinking about the future—you could call it neurological Novocaine.

The tropical paradise and the beauty of the beaches made you to want to take off all your clothes and frolic in the surf, which is mostly what we did for two weeks. There was no radio or TV; movies and tapes did not exist; telephones, for all intents and purposes, did not exist either—they were unreliable and expensive. Eating, sleeping, swimming, and sex were the main activities and we enjoyed them all. This vacation affected our sexual intimacy, emotionally and physically; medication or mental depression has its adverse affects. We were trying to rebuild bridges and drop our defenses enough to ignite the passion that had been sacrificed by the catastrophe that had befallen both of us. Sue was as much a victim as I was; we had to help heal each other. A lush tropical oasis was just the right prescription. In Barbados we decided to do things differently: We would choose the directions we wanted to go in and not continue in the directions that had controlled our lives so far. I tried to put my old life behind me and develop the courage to move on.

Chapter 24

Back home in Wayland, we checked the mail, packed the kids' bags and moved to Golden Beach for two months. I wanted to spend more time recuperating at the beach when seaweed does not get blown ashore and the weather is not so hot and steamy. We had promised Shannon a trip to Disney World and stopped in Orlando on the way down. It was great fun for Shannon, but I could not keep up with the energy or excitement of a 6-year-old girl. It really hurt me not to be able to share the fun of the rides with her. I did go on Thunder Mountain, but regretted my decision after the first turn.

I settled into a simple routine. I would wake up around 7 a.m. and get myself a pot of coffee and a muffin. Then I would amble down to the cabana and take a seat on a lounge chair and enjoy my breakfast while I watched the morning beach traffic. The beach walkers were usually the same people every day. By 9 o'clock in the morning, a steady flow of tourists was walking along the waterfront from the hotels at either end of the golden mile. Occasionally a young beauty in a bikini or thong would stride by, warranting scrutiny with the binoculars.

While I lounged on the beach watching Shannon or Flash, I was unaware of the gathering storm building in my psyche. I was content napping off and on throughout the day or taking short walks at the edge of the wavelets. During those walks I moved slowly, masking my fatigue by searching for seashells. Sometimes I sat day and night in the tropical climate, staring off over the eastern horizon. The Gulf Stream is just a mile or so off the beach and hundreds of northbound and southbound ships passed by. I often wished I could get on one and disappear over the horizon, leaving my pain and discord behind. November, my birthday and Thanksgiving came and went without fanfare. I did, however, take note of the one-year anniversary of the date I was told I might die because of a rare neurovascular disorder called arteriovenous malformation. In one year I had been reduced to an infantile state—how humbling life can be.

I was becoming honey-bronzed and, I hoped, desirable. The only one who got more attention than me was Flash. With his blonde hair and honey tan, he looked like a California surfer. Flash has his mother's looks and my personality, which could be a dangerous combination. The four of us spent our days playing at the beach, collecting seashells and eating. Chowing down was one of the few things I could do without myself causing pain. One night we feasted on crabs, shrimp, steak and corn on the cob. Since eating was one of the few pleasures I could enjoy, I indulged in all kinds of culinary treats, so much so that I started to gain a certain amount of girth. I figured that I would soon be able to exercise and lose the weight I was gaining.

For two months I was content to sit on the beach and contemplate.

There is a great power at work in the universe; if God is what we call it, I believe in God. The Indians called this power the Great Spirit. I call it My Friend. This unknown great power over life and death had chosen to spare me and this time of metamorphosis was my way of thanking him. There was nothing else I could do, including sex, that did not agitate me or cause me discomfort. By the time we left Florida in late December, there was no perceptible improvement in my health or vision. Sometimes I wondered whether I would ever ski again. Secretly I was hoping that by spring I could try a run or two. It was time to set another series of goals. I had lounged around long enough. Christmas was closing in fast and we wanted to be at home so Santa Claus could find us—it was Flash's first Christmas.

The trek home with two children in tow was a nightmare. Sue is an organizer and a doer. I am a lazy thinker, and Sue always takes care of our travel arrangements. While I roamed around trying to think of what I needed to pack, she had already taken care of everything. Before I could organize my thoughts enough to know what to do to help, we were at the airport curbside checking in. Navigating the mob scene at the airport was traumatic. The movement of people in my visual field created a commotion that was uncomfortable for my brain. The plane was a refuge from the noisy terminal and calmed my frayed nerves. When we finally reached the house, we were burned out but glad to be home in familiar surroundings. I felt safe and secure in the one place where I knew where everything was.

*   *   *   *   *

When Christmas finally came, all I felt was ambivalence and frustration. This celebration is for children and parents always want to provide their child with something memorable. Inevitably that gift is delivered in pieces with easy-to-understand instructions. It's the father's responsibility to assemble the gifts or install the batteries, with a few laughs along the way. But for me, this was not going to be the case, as I encountered unimaginable difficulties. I could not read or understand assembly instructions. My inability to problem solve along with my reading difficulties made me feel stupid and out of control. As I fumbled with parts, batteries and directions, I had to swallow my Irish ego and succumb to Sue's offers of assistance. I was humiliated. If we were ever going to get the toys and games assembled in time, I would have to forget my stubborn pride and let Sue take charge. On Christmas day, I watched Shannon joyfully open her presents. Since Flash was just short of 1 year old, he showed little interest in the holidays.

Two days after Christmas, we packed up the car, placed the kids in restraints in the back seat, and went north to ski country.

It was vacation week and Shannon was enrolled in the Ski Wee program with Lindsey Mann, the daughter of my friend Robert. I agonized over the fact that I would never have the joy and satisfaction of passing on to Shannon all my knowledge of skiing. She had already inherited the physical skills needed to become a great skier. Secretly I aspired to have one of my children surpass my accomplishments in skiing and become a champion. I think every father shares the same dream, whether in sports, academics, or artistic expression.

We soon fell into a familiar routine. Sue and Shannon headed up to the hills early for the 8 a.m. lift opening. I took my time getting up and caught a bus later in the morning, depositing Flash at the nursery. Then I grabbed some coffee and tried to catch the gang at their 10 o'clock break for coffee and muffins. They always filled me in on the conditions. If there was fresh snow, it was a story of how they had carved up some unbroken snow somewhere above us. When they left, I would grab my second cup of coffee and amble over to the ski shop. By the time I made my way into the ski shop it was almost 11 a.m. and the morning rush was over. I still suffered from the phobia of too much visual activity, allowing pain and anxiety to creep into my day. John Lapointe, an old and dear friend, managed the shop where at one time or another, I had worked in the repair shop. Just being around skiing made me feel better. I would leave the ski shop after about an hour and meet Sue for lunch. We had arranged with the ski area that I could ride the chairlift up to the lodge for lunch and then back down. By that time, it was 1:30 p.m. and I headed to the bus for the short ride home. Around 2 in the afternoon, I would gingerly place my battered head on a pillow to seek the refuge of deep sleep. Only in the sanctuary of sleep did I escape the discomfort and distress that enveloped every moment.

There were days when I would do nothing more than shower, shave and dress. By the time I accomplished that, it was lunchtime. On other days I could function well enough to go to the mountain for half a day. That is how I spent most of the 1991-92 ski season, which turned out to be a great ski year. It was also the beginning of my year of discovery, a time that marked my awakening to all those other little functions too numerous to an activity, making me ever cognizant of the damage to my brain. There was nothing in my life that made me feel good, not even sex. New Year's Eve came and went with no celebration.

Amongst our family of friends, winter meant vacation time at the best resorts in North America. I was out of the picture, but many of my friends went their separate ways in search of fresh tracks—and Sue was no exception. She and a couple of girlfriends took a chicks on sticks heli-ski weekend at Snowbird in Utah. She drove me insanely jealous when she called me from a hot tub sipping white wine with Shauna and Starr. What a trio they are, three beautiful women who can outski almost anyone! I had visions of losing her to some handsome heli-guide with a rugged mountain-man look. Needless to say, she came back to me and the kids, rested and rejuvenated.

For Sue, taking care of me was a lot like taking care of Flash. My mind was not organized, my memory of recent events questionable. Often I would think of something I wanted and start to get it. By the time I entered the kitchen, my mind was blank. Sue would find me standing in a daze, unable to recall why I had gone there. My mind was like a sieve—thoughts poured through but nothing was retained. When I answered the phone, I would be able to conduct a comprehensible, well-thought-out conversation. When the call was finished, Sue would ask me a short time later who was on the phone and what we discussed. Most of the time I could not remember what we talked about or relay specifics.

All winter I tried to act happy that I was alive, but not being able to ski made it a difficult task. Every time I started to talk to Sue or anyone about the struggle building within me, I would elicit the same old answer, "But Bill, you are alive!" Amazingly, that was no comfort to me. I tried to fool myself by saying it over and over again, but the more I thought it, the less value it had.

Chapter 25

I had developed terrible eating habits and ballooned to about 198 pounds, which meant I was carrying almost 15 pounds of fat. One of the first self-improvement goals I set was to lose 20 pounds. Making myself into a conditioned, trim, healthy body was a difficult problem. Any increase in activity or heart rate affected me physically and physiologically. I felt spasms and muscle twitches in my head and my mind wondered whether I had hemorrhaged. Fear paralyzed me every time I experienced a strange sensation in my head. How was I to condition myself with this constraint? When would I ever be able to exercise?

In the waning months of winter, I started to think of ways to exercise without lifting or straining or even elevating my heart rate. Late one restless night, I lay in bed watching a martial arts movie when the idea struck. I should try the martial arts! There might be some form of martial arts or yoga I could study. My balance was all screwed up, I could not concentrate and mental focus simply did not exist. For the most part, I slept through winter like a hibernating bear. The only activity I endured were the weekend trips to Waterville to keep some connection to skiing. Ski season was ending, however, and it was difficult to resist the urge to mount those splendid splinters called skis. It had been more than six months since my second operation and I had succeeded in convincing Sue and my friends to allow me to put on a helmet and skis for one run—one run, to prove to the world that my skiing days were not over. Besides, I needed to lift my spirits out of the quagmire I was falling into.

On a warm and sunny day at the end of March, I put on my ski clothes, grabbed a helmet and skis, and Sue drove me to the mountain. It seemed like forever since I had last put skis on my feet. The thought of doing something that was supposed to be impossible was exciting. The mere strength required to lug my equipment to the base of the lift was exhausting. Every movement was slow and laborious. Robert, Ross and Sue escorted me up the mountain to the top. Emotion filled me as I rode up the new high-speed quad chairlift the mountain had installed during the summer. I stood on top of the mountain scanning a panorama that I thought I would never see again. My eyes were a problem, for I could not see well. Deep inside, I wanted to yell "fuck you" as defiantly as I could to the Grim Reaper and the whole world. But I knew that physically it would not be wise.

The day was perfect and the crowds nonexistent, a perfect scenario for a dangerous test of my abilities. For the past six months, my physical activity had consisted of short walks. Luckily few skiers were on the mountain. As I stood at the top, my knees were weak, my heart beat quickly and my courage was shaky. Gingerly I pushed off with my poles and started to glide to my first turn. Incredibly I could still turn—my speed was that of a snail. My eyes constantly strained to see the terrain in front of me. I glided precariously, awkwardly trying to maintain my balance. As the world rushed by me, my eyes made me feel queasy. I saw images and people come and then disappear. After a few hundred feet I stopped to rest and my energy drained away rapidly. Slowly I picked my way down the trail with a phalanx of friends around me ready to ward off any stranger who skied close to the parameter they had created. Cautiously they cheered me on and encouraged me to fight my frustration. I felt a little like the president with an entourage of Secret Service agents. Sue was dead set against my attempt to ski but realized I had to make this test or lose my sanity. She led the way down. It took every ounce of concentration and energy I had to stay on my feet. I stopped a dozen times to rest my weak legs; my eyes pained with the strain of seeing. When I reached the bottom, I had mixed emotions, but certainly felt elation that I had accomplished something the doctors said I would never do again.

Ultimately, all I could focus on were negatives. Remorse and grief became new additions to my ever-expanding pool of emotions. The final result of my attempt to ski did more to drive me into depression than lift my spirits. I had proved the doctors wrong, but did I have the drive to continue the fight? My attempt ended my perception of a quick recovery. That one run in one hour brought the reality of my horror to the front page of my life. Life for me was a delicate balancing act, with enormous pitfalls and very few victories. From my point of view, the casualties kept mounting and I foolishly kept hoping for a small victory to lift my spirits.

*   *   *   *   *

The first post-surgery consultation with Dr. Crowell was scheduled for April. Sue and I arrived at the A.C.C. building at Mass General, next to the emergency entrance. It was the first time I had been to the hospital since the second surgery. My legs were weak, my stomach full of butterflies. I feared Dr. Crowell would order an angiogram to make sure they had gotten all the AVMs. Sue took my arm and gently squeezed it, reassuring me as she pulled me toward the front door. When I caught someone looking at me with the look of "that poor bastard, look what some doctor did to his head," I became self-conscious. The elevator to the third floor was always slow and crowded, but very few people got out on three, where most of the neurological offices are. We stumbled to the third door on the left and then took a right toward Dr. Crowell's office. The waiting room was empty, another reminder of the loneliness of this ordeal. Down the hall sat Julie, compassionately aiding some other patient's request for help. Always smiling, always comforting, she went out of her way to help. With the phone held to one ear and a pencil and appointment book in front of her, she gestured at us to take a seat. Dr. Crowell was still in surgery.

Each meeting with Dr. Crowell prior to surgery had been laced with the news that I was in greater danger than previously explained. In my mind, I reviewed the issues I wanted to discuss. When Julie invited us to enter the doctor's office, it was like being summoned to the principal's office as a result of some schoolyard prank. Apprehensively I walked in to greet him; his tall slender frame and warm smile comforted my nerves. Then the words that I hated to hear, "Well, you look marvelous. How do you feel?" I started to tell him of my discomfort and distress, all the issues I had rehearsed. Then I broke down in tears and a flood of emotions poured out of me. It took a few minutes to compose myself and as I did, Dr. Crowell started to talk. First he assured me that I was cured and that the risk of a massive hemorrhage was 99-percent eliminated. When I heard that, all I could imagine was what Dr. Spierings had said after ordering the MRI: "There is a 99-percent chance we will find nothing." The words flowed from deep within him; I could feel his empathy and compassion. He said that often when a person like me, competitive and successful with a Type A personality, cannot do the things he used to, life becomes a struggle. The symptoms I complained about and the pain I experienced were real and not imagined. Some patients recover fully, some did not. Unfortunately for me, it looked as if my deficits would not go away. He recommended that I see Dr. Christopher Gates, a psychiatrist.

As the session ended, I asked Dr. Crowell whether I would need to see him again. "No," he stated, "my job is done. The two AVMs are gone and that there is nothing else I can do for you." I felt an immediate sense of loss. I had to restrain myself from hugging him. To me, Dr. Crowell was God and I owed him my life. As we left, I felt empty. We thanked Julie for all her help, and she informed me that she would set up an appointment with Dr. Gates. The finality of this meeting really shook me—it clearly stated that there was nothing physical left to do. I had to come to grips with my new reality and try to move forward in my life. On the drive home from the hospital, Sue and I were silent. There was such a sense of finality about our meeting with the doctor that there was nothing to talk about. The idea of needing a psychiatrist was so alien to me, I could hardly comprehend the words. The words "cannot do what I used to do" revolved in my head.

* * * * *

In May we went to Golden Beach during Shannon's spring vacation. By the time I returned from my exile in Florida, it would be time to meet my new keeper, Dr. Gates. The necessity for psychotherapy made me feel ashamed. I was insecure and my insecurity made me consult Dad at his house in Florida and ask for help in developing a new job description for me. If the doctor was right, I would need to change my life, adjust for my deficits and move on to new things. I needed Dad's help if I was to continue at the company and the sooner I solicited his help and understanding, the sooner I could set a goal. Sue and I decided to talk to him two days before we moved north, hoping we could spend some time discussing my dilemma with him. It would be reassuring to know that there was something to look forward to and I was eager to figure out what it was.

Early on a Friday morning, Dad and Mom were sitting out on the patio looking at the beautiful Florida surf. Mom gave me a hug, said she loved me, then broke down and cried. Sue and I sat down with them to talk over our situation. Months earlier I had written both of them to try to get them to understand that behind my normal-looking shell was a twisted and shattered person. Unfortunately I got no acknowledgment of it from Dad. How could I start this conversation with a man who had never known what it meant to lose something? He always won, and if something did not come naturally, he worked very hard at it. As far as I knew, he had never felt the pain of defeat or the sadness of not accomplishing a goal.

I was able to summon up enough courage to tell Dad about the meeting with Dr. Crowell. He seemed to hear the words, but after two days of honest discussion, I left Florida with no direction or goal. Dad's denial of my tragedy was immense. I looked so healthy that no one could believe I would not make a full recovery. My parents could not understand that I was a zombie. My activities could be counted on one hand: eating, sleeping, walking, rarely talking, and listening. It was awkward and uncomfortable to form sentences; the simplest tasks were difficult. Sometimes Sue ridiculed me, forgetting that everything was not functioning upstairs. Humiliation hurt me to the point where all I could do was explode in an irrational rage.

Back home in Wayland, the rebuilding process started. I went through all my clothes and gave away anything old and tired or too small. It was like a great purge—letting go of the clothes of a healthy young man with a 30-inch waist for those of a middle-aged man with a 34-inch waist.

When John called a week later and remarked how great it was to get a dividend check, his statement caught me offguard. I called the company's chief financial officer to inquire about my dividend. He stated matter-of-factly that my dividend went to pay the company back for the money it had spent to provide for my family. Since I owned 8 percent of the company—my brother, sister and father owned the rest—I was deeply hurt. I never had the chance to say that somehow, some way, I would pay my father and the company back.

The knowledge that my father was more concerned with being reimbursed rather than the fact that I could not return to work broke my heart. I felt totally worthless. He believed that I only had a slight visual deficit and that there was nothing else to prevent me from returning to the life of a broker. Disability insurance would have paid my bills. Sue and I would have to trim our budget. I felt stripped of my dreams and ambitions.

For the first time in my life, suicide was a consideration. The knowledge that not even my father was willing to create some type of job for me, the insecurity of having no viable means of earning a living, and the clinical depression that can be a byproduct of surgery weighed heavily on me. I wished I had never submitted to the brain operations—all I wanted to do was run away and never look back. When I seriously contemplated taking off, I realized my problems would only follow me. Ending my distress could only be accomplished by ending my life.

I hoped the strain on my marriage would not escalate. If it did, I believed I would lose the only thing I had left, my wife and two children. Sue and I fought frequently because my irrational behavior and mood swings were explosive. I began to inflict pain on those that I loved. The days preceding my first appointment with my shrink were tumultuous, my rage completely out of control and focused at Sue. Sue was noticeably upset and our relationship was shaky. May was spent in exile and isolation. I did not want to see anybody and let it be known.

The whole time this was going on, Sue was planning our 15th wedding anniversary party. Five years earlier, we had held a two-day blowout at a resort in New Hampshire with 130 friends. We golfed and partied all day on Saturday and then threw a dinner party and danced all night long. The band was outrageously good, playing all the classic hits of our generation. It was so much fun and such a success that we all agreed to do it again on our 15th anniversary. The date was June 4, 1992, and it was coming up fast. So was my first appointment with Dr. Gates. At this same time, Dr. Gress was weaning me off Phenobarbital and I was hoping to get some physical therapy for my neck.

In order to operate on the back of my brain, all the neck muscles and ligaments had been cut and reattached. As a result, my head slumped forward and down, making my posture look horrible. After checking around for a physical therapist, I found Ann Inngard in Framingham and contacted her for a consultation. Before we met, I told her of my plight and gave her all the doctors' phone numbers so that she could talk to them prior to my appointment. Ann was instrumental in helping me rebuild my life. Our first session was short but gave her a chance to see the trauma to my head and neck and size me up. When Sue and I first saw her, I kept thinking I had seen her somewhere before. She examined my neck and we practiced some exercises that she wanted me to start doing every day. When we finished and started to leave, she said, "You don't remember me, do you?" Ann was a former girlfriend of a good friend of mine, Peter McGraw. Sadly I had to tell her that Peter was battling cancer. During my visit we talked about exercising and I asked her if she knew anyone who taught some form of martial arts. Ann agreed that something like yoga or tai chi would be helpful and thought her friend Walter Mattson in Framingham might be the right teacher. He taught an easy, flowing style of martial arts from Okinawa. With Dr. Gress' approval, Ann said she would call Walter and set up a time for an interview. This was the beginning of my physical and emotional rehabilitation.

As we left Ann's, I had a new goal to look forward to. That night Ann called to inform us that Walter would take me on. She went on to tell me that under doctors' orders I was not to overdo it and sparring was out of the question. It was clearly understood by Walter, Ann and the doctors what I could and could not do. Nine months after surgery, I had deteriorated in muscle tone; atrophy had replaced the rock-hard muscle that had powered me through knee-deep powder two winters earlier. My fat content skyrocketed when I stopped skiing—my inactivity and lowered metabolism could not burn off the food I indulged in. Emotionally I was so twisted that I inflicted pain and anxiety on the one person who meant the most to me. I wanted to make love to my wife, but never had the urge. I had no idea what to expect from my sessions with Dr. Gates, but Sue and I knew that if I was to come to grips with all the stresses in our lives, we had to start there. Our strategy was to rehabilitate the mind, the body and the soul.

Chapter 26

Entering Dr. Gates' office is like entering a maze. You enter from the back of the building into the basement. Once you get through the storm door and the heavy basement door, you enter a small foyer about 3-feet square. In front of you and to the left are closed doors. I chose a door and entered a small waiting room with two more doors. If you choose the right one, you win an expensive 40-minute consultation. Suddenly a door lurched from its sprung frame and a gray-haired giant poked his head through the doorway. "The Fallons, I presume. I'm Christopher Gates. Welcome, won't you please come in?" His manner had a calming affect on us. Dr. Gates looked well over 6 feet tall, towering over my height, which is a fraction under 6 feet. We entered a small office in his basement, outfitted with a couple of chairs, a desk and a couch. All over one wall were volumes of books and files; there was only a small window and a blackboard. When Dr. Gates spoke, his voice was soft. We exchanged pleasantries and small talk, then he invited Sue to come and go from the sessions as she pleased. Then he asked me to tell him what happened and how.

At that, he leaned his chair back against the wall and closed his eyes. I immediately got pissed off because he looked as if he had fallen asleep. I spent the next two hours telling him my story and just when I was convinced he was asleep, he asked a question relevant to the issue I was talking about. "Wow!" I thought, "The guy listens in his sleep!" When I finished telling him a brief history of events, I felt like whacking him on the leg and shouting, "Wake up!"

When he asked, "How did that make you feel?" I exploded in emotions. Up until now it had been too painful to think about how I felt. It was less painful to focus my mind on anything else but how I felt. But Dr. Gates had opened a floodgate and I crumbled. When I stopped crying, I was embarrassed, ashamed and felt no better. The tears did not remove my pain or ease my suffering. Dr. Gates encouraged my tears because he believed crying would help me bare the pain. It was impossible to tell him in just two hours how I felt—it took two hours just to tell my story.

What I did discover from the very first session was that I had suffered far more damage from this event than I had known. Incredibly, I felt worse when I left the doctor's office than when I arrived. But I had gained a slight insight into the pain and confusion. Two hours was just the beginning of the intense psychotherapy that was needed to repair my battered soul.

Over the weekend I had time to sit on the porch and ponder the Friday session. The excitement of starting physical rehabilitation in the form of the martial arts made the weekend speed by and by Monday evening I was ready for my ride to the dojo in Framingham. As Ann suggested, I called Walter Mattson to ask him what time I should arrive for class. He suggested I arrive 15 minutes before the normal class time of 6:30 p.m. I found the four-story brick structure right in the middle of Main Street. A small sign on the building confirmed that I was in the right place so I entered the building and immediately confronted with a two-story flight of stairs.

By the time I reached the door leading to the dojo I was ready to take a nap. My legs trembled from fatigue, my lungs gasped for breath, and I could not imagine how I was going to study the martial arts effectively. To my right was a bookshelf loaded with shoes and I got the message that I should leave my shoes there. Confronted by another flight of stairs, I lumbered up. Part of the dojo on the third floor consists of two dressing rooms and a small workout room with mirrors on two walls.

Lumbering up the last flight of stairs to the fourth floor brought me to a much larger exercise room with high ceilings and hard-wood floors. On the walls were pictures of Asian men in ghis; in one corner were punching bags and a stack of bos, resembling thick broom handles. Diplomas, certificates and trophies documented Walter's accomplishments.

In a corner of the fourth-floor training room was a small office. Sitting behind a desk was a white-haired man with a gentle smile. When he stood up, I saw that he was a 6-foot tall, broad-shouldered, trim-framed man. There was no menacing glare, no intimidating expression, just a twinkle in his eye and a friendly tone in his voice. We exchanged greetings and he handed me a white cotton ghi and white belt and asked me to tell him my story. As I did, he escorted me to the men's locker and showed me the proper way to wear the ghi and tie the belt.

I started to feel like Bruce Lee, with visions of flying side kicks and karate chops. I imagined fighting 10 men single-handedly! Then I saw myself in the mirror next to Walter; I looked as if I had been used as a punching bag. I was heavy, frail and pale. I also felt humbled by Walter's quiet forceful presence. When he moved, it looked as if he had not taken a step; instead he floated. Slowly he showed me the warm-up routine and then started to explain the kata sanchin, the most essential yet basic exercise of the style okakukia, or uechi-ryu, karate. It is a style introduced to the Okinawans by the Chinese monks and priests who developed kung fu and almost every other martial art. They all originated in some ancient Chinese form. As Walter instructed me in the 12 movements that make up the kata sanchin, I realized my motor skills were seriously impaired by my surgery.

The kata sanchin has three stages, each one repeats the same 12 steps but at three different speeds. The first sanchin is done in slow motion, the second a little faster but with pauses after each movement, and finally the third sanchin. This kata is done at full speed and its emphasis is on continuous flowing grace and speed. The first sanchin was easy for me physically; remembering the

12 movements and coordinating my limbs was where I struggled. All my life I had been an excellent athlete and my diminished capacity made me feel ashamed and deficient. However, Walter did not know the old Bill. He had no preconceived notion of my ability and he treated me as if I were as uncoordinated as every other beginner karate student. Walter made it okay to make mistakes; it was the only way to learn. As I watched him demonstrate sanchin two and three, I was awed at his speed, grace and power. His movements seemed effortless and without sound, except for the snap of the cotton-sleeved ghi he wore. It made the same sound as when you snap a wet towel. If this was the basic kata of this style, I could not wait to see what it would do for me. I am not impressed easily by anyone, although I have met many famous and great people, but I was very impressed with Walter Mattson. I plunged into the art form with both feet. The benefits so outweighed the negatives that I did not object to the pain and discomfort.

Shortly after Walter's introduction to karate, the regular students began to arrive and stretch out. At exactly 6:35 p.m., about 12 students around my age—half of them black belts, a few of them women—arrived and lined up according to rank. Walter introduced me without explanation and began the warm-up exercises. I felt like a dork. My motion and balance made me look like a drunk! My head ached and twinged with flashing spasms in my brain. I could feel every movement within my neurovascular system.

The exercises required concentration and relaxation at the same time, teaching me to visualize what I was to do. In a way, that is how I tried to overcome my visual impairments. About 40 minutes into the class, we paired up for what are called toughening exercises. One is called katicete, where one person punches, the other blocks, then the defender attacks while the opponent blocks, and you go back and forth like this 20 times. It is designed to develop blocks and to toughen up the arms by deflecting the blows with them. Then you assume the sanchin stance and rub forearms together like a tug of war, only you are pushing with all your weight, pressing forearm to forearm. After that, you practice leg kicks. You and your partner practice kicking each other on the upper and lower leg to strength the muscles.

I pushed way too hard in the beginning and, when I did, my color and complexion turned purple. At that point, I also would feel lightheaded and dizzy. Fortunately, Walter noticed and excused me two or three times to rest during the 90-minute class. My brain and body were on two different frequencies, the body wanted to work out and the brain would not cooperate. I kept apologizing for my mistakes, sometimes I just froze, empty-headed.

As time passed and Memorial Day came and went, I engulfed myself in daily walks, karate class two or three times a week, and psychotherapy. I soon developed a routine: Monday, I rested from the weekend; Tuesday, I went to karate from 10 a.m. to noon, in the afternoon I spent an hour or more with Doctor Gates; Wednesday, I recovered from Tuesday; Thursday, I went to karate in the morning and therapy in the afternoon; and Friday was a lot like Wednesday—the most I did was a walk in the morning after coffee and a scan of the daily newspaper. Some afternoons we took off to the Cape or Waterville Valley, although most of the time we stayed home because riding in a car still made me queasy.

My need for some sense of self-worth and independence led me to do a little driving around Wayland and Framingham. If I stayed under 35 mph, I could see things in the lower right-hand quadrant of my visual field. If a target entered that visual field, I had the reflexes to identify the object and stop in time. This could be a car at an intersection or a truck on the side of the road. People riding bikes or jogging along the side of the road were not so fortunate, because I usually did not see them in time or did not recognize them as people. Stop signs and stoplights were invisible to me because of their placement in the upper right-hand quadrant of everyone's visual field. To compound my difficulties, I would see a stop sign, recognize it as a stop sign, but my mind would not always realize that it meant I was supposed to stop!

Chapter 27

In June, Sue and I celebrated our 15th wedding anniversary. The whole crowd from our 10th anniversary made it to our 15th and, in true form, partied hard. For my friends, it was a celebration of my triumph over death; for me, I saw little to celebrate. Dancing for even a few minutes exhausted me. Someone placed a chair in the middle of the dance floor and I sat there swinging and swaying. Before long, others were chair dancing next to me. What a scene!

My psychotherapy was geared to getting me to accept each day—one at a time—and to not think about tomorrow. That was especially difficult considering the pressure my father placed on me to return to the life of a broker. Relentlessly, he put the question to me about my future interest in the business, forcing me to look into the future while I was learning to live within my diminished capacities one day at a time. Planning for tomorrow, or the next day or next week or even next month, was out of the question.

The only progress I detected was in karate. I could remember the 12 movements in the first kata sanchin because I had done so many repetitions. My improvement was imperceptible to me, but to those around me, the improvement was dramatic. In the toughening exercises, however, I noticed that I often momentarily lost track. In defending a blow, I knew what was coming but could not defend or think of a counter-attack. But after all was said and done, karate gave me goals and a sense of accomplishment. Not only was I learning a martial art, I was also learning a form of meditation and relaxation. Karate taught me how to concentrate and focus my mind on performing the immediate task before me. Martial arts combined with psychotherapy were rebuilding my self-esteem and confidence in myself.

Summer was in full swing and the sailing season upon us. John and I usually took turns racing the Marna. This summer was my turn and I decided to race in the championship series, six races. There was no way I could have anticipated the troubles I encountered out on the racecourse. The level of concentration that sailing required in light air was beyond my diminished capacity. When I was in close combat with another boat, I could not sail the boat efficiently nor could I formulate strategy. Being the helmsman, tactician and navigator was easy for the old Bill. After my surgeries, I could not perform those tasks all at once, not even one at a time. My frustration grew as each race was held and I was unable to compete up to the level of my reputation. My judgment was so impaired that I made stupid errors, which embarrassed me. I felt humiliated by my poor performance and abandoned the last race in the series out of frustration. I think it was the first time in 40 years that a member of my family was not in the top 10 places.

Weekends at the Cape brought solitude. I spent hours on the point, where it was quiet and peaceful, my sanctuary from the hustle and bustle of daily routines. My damaged and battered spirit welcomed the sweet sounds of nature—the wind gently blowing through the trees and the warbling of the songbirds. As the fall season approached, I tried to imagine going back to work. However, I detected no improvement in the tingling in the back of my head or in the level of pain. The more time passed, the more active I became and the more errors in judgment occurred. I was not getting healthier—I was getting sicker! How was I going to earn a living and provide for my family? I had disability insurance and there was not a doctor in the world who would not vouch for my disability, but I despised the thought of living on a fixed income. I had dreams and aspirations of greater things than what I had so far achieved! I clung to the hope that I would recover to my pre-surgical existence with no more than a visual deficit.

In early September I received a letter from Unum, the disability insurer, offering me a $1.5 million annuity or a $475,000 lump sum payment. I was stunned that the offer was so low compared to my policy payout. How could I support my family on the monthly payment the annuity would provide? The lump sum payment would cover my bill for only four to five years. All of the luxuries I had worked so hard for had to be sacrificed in order to provide the necessities. Sporting activities like sailing, golf and skiing would be out of reach financially. Medical insurance would not cover the cost of therapy with Dr. Gates, who had been making steady progress with my various problems—forgetfulness, inability to perform multiple tasks, mental fatigue. My perception of reality was so badly shaken that I needed constant psychotherapy to keep my grip on what reality I had left. Through therapy with Dr. Gates and at karate class with Walter, I was learning to lose my former perceptions and adjust to a new lifestyle.

The fall of 1992 marked the end of my physical ordeal, as well as my real estate career of 14 years and nine months. On the outside, I had made a miraculous recovery, appearing healthy and strong. I had a great tan and, for now, financial security. On the inside, I understood why it hurt to think and accepted that there were certain things my mind could do and some things it could not do. Some of these problem-solving tasks would improve over time, but in most instances it is a permanent disability that you must learn to adjust for and live with. I had to learn to do almost everything in a different way. The time I first felt the pain from thinking occurred when Sue and I tried to sort and count the change from a huge piggy bank that swallowed our change every night. As I began to sort the pennies from the silver, I started to feel a tingling sensation in the back of my head, growing in intensity. I tried to shake it off and ignore the growing pain and confusion. Finally I became so distressed by the activity that I felt like throwing up. I could not even look at the coins in front of me.

As winter drew near and ski season was only weeks away, I intensified my efforts in karate. After three or four months I had performed enough repetitions to remember the warm-up drills and sanchin. The martial arts had captured my imagination and I immersed myself in the search for more knowledge. This was the only activity that actually made me feel as if I was getting better. I started to learn kenshewa, the second kata. At times Walter would pull me out of the class to rest. I still had no idea of my limits and did not know when to take a break.

My 39th birthday came and went without notice. I hardly wanted to acknowledge the past year. Dr. Gates and Sue were working overtime to help me heal emotionally, but it became apparent that I had some pre-existing conditions that complicated my personality. I wrote a letter to my parents outlining my health and where I was in my life. The uncertainty of my future and how I would support my family was an issue. In a way I was reaching out to my father for guidance. All he had to offer was my old broker's job. In my letter I wrote that I could not work in that capacity any more. He was in as much emotional pain as I was over my fate and facing his own physical and emotional battles.

Christmas was closing in and my emotional gas tank was on empty. I did not even have the ability to buy Sue a fitting Christmas present. Living on disability made us scrutinize every penny. My fear that I was so changed that I would lose Sue ripped me apart. I started to think I had lost her; we were fighting constantly. In her frustration over my mistakes, she would sometimes lash out in anger. We were building emotional defenses again. The fights intensified, mostly my fault, because I could not handle the rage within me. If wishing I were dead were the thoughts of some suicidal maniac, then that was me. Sue was so concerned that she wanted me to get rid of my guns or at least lock them up and give her the key. Eventually I did lock them up, but I did not give her the key.

The pain that my tragedy had inflicted on Sue was the thing that hurt me most. Sue was the most precious thing in my life. At times I started to think Sue was losing interest in me. We rarely were intimate with each other and sex was not a regular occurrence. Often I made advances to her, but rarely did she reciprocate. My insecurity made me believe that Sue had a lover or that she had lost her love for me. The more Sue rejected me, the more my rage intensified. I finally exploded, accusing her of having an affair and of not having any desire for me. My assault was not gentle and Sue, being strong willed herself, attacked back. After all the yelling and crying ended, we stood looking at each other through our tears. She said she did not know me anymore! I had changed so much she did not know who or what I had become. She said she loved the Bill she married, but she was afraid of me. My anger was so intense I scared her!

What had I become? My wife feared the anger that was exploding within me, as well as fearing the man she used to love. She did not know what to do or how to confront me because she was afraid I would kill myself in an act of irrational rage. The knockout punch came when she totally crushed my manhood with the revelation that I was unable to satisfy her any longer. I was totally humiliated, ashamed and embarrassed. I slumped over my knees, trembling in tears on the floor, wanting to be dead but too much of a coward to do anything about it. How do you win your wife's love back when you are no longer what she used to love? If I could drive or had any money, I would have packed up and headed west on the Mass Pike and disappeared. Why stay? My wife feared the stranger I had become. I could not satisfy her as a lover.

I knew that the old Bill Fallon was dead and the new Bill had to figure out what to do next. Giving up the past meant selling the luxuries I could no longer afford. The first to go was my red Porsche. It didn't seem to make sense to own a car that expensive and that fast when your finances and driving ability are limited. The decision was difficult because the car represented my former success. Dr. Gates asked me what the car meant to me: It was a symbol of my career and one of the last possessions I had that gave me independence. I went for one last drive, slowly, the last mile to the house, going about 10 mph with the radio blasting rock and roll. Pulling into the driveway, I realized that the old Bill was all about material things—what was the new Bill all about? I did not know.

I had to get deeper into psychotherapy to save my marriage and get a handle on the rage that erupted from deep within my inner person. I also had to try to make myself attractive to Sue again. We decided that Sue would join me at one of the two weekly sessions with Dr. Gates to assimilate her into the rehab process; it would help her understand why I was the way I was. Instinctively I knew I had to be proactive in my rehabilitation and implement some of those promises I had made to myself and Dr. Gress the night before I was discharged. The real miracle of humankind is our ever-expanding ability to overcome all adversity, to compensate for inadequacies. The enemy of the human spirit is failure to attempt to overcome obstacles and to lose the drive and energy that has enabled us to endure for thousands of years.

During that winter I went to see Dr. Gress to discuss the feeling of distress that constantly weighed me down. Desperately I wanted to hear him say that in time it would go away, although deep inside I knew it would not. During our consultation, Dr. Gress confirmed that the pains and distress I complained of were common complaints from other patients who had incurred massive brain damage. It did not matter how they got the brain damage—whether by stroke or accident—the complaints were the same as mine. His words were comforting to know I was not alone with this pain. The knowledge that others shared the same pain and distress and that, in time, I would adjust gave me hope.

Chapter 28

I really understood what karate had done for me when I started to ski again that winter. Karate was the right prescription to help me adapt to my neurological and physical deficits. The art form did not make me feel dumb or humiliated—since it was a new activity, how could I feel dumb about something I knew nothing about? The art form is like meditation—it requires you to think about every movement and only that movement. The repetitive nature of karate trains the mind to think and concentrate. The other students were around my age or older, which made me feel comfortable, although I felt compelled to explain to each student why I made so many mistakes. Dr. Gates was schooling me to tell people why I do some things in an attempt to get me to accept my deficits and not feel ashamed of them. I had been studying karate for six months and my endurance had improved slightly. I was learning how to develop mental discipline and how to concentrate on one task at a time in order to avoid the intense pain that concentrating caused me. The ancient art of self-defense was building the mental, emotional and physical skills that would allow me to compensate for my neurological deficits. Every weekend I skied, I felt the control and discipline in my skiing skills. It may sound corny, but I felt as if the ski and I were one. I still lacked strength and endurance; no longer was I able to ski the bumps at 20 miles an hour. Adjusting to this new reality on skis was out of the question—I had to go heli-skiing in Canada to prove everyone wrong.

By early February, I was making plans with the gang to return to Whistler/Blackcomb. Although still weak and disabled, I was determined to return to the high alpine, the glaciers of British Columbia. This was a challenging goal—in order to get the most out of an experience like that you need to be in great shape. Skiing the glaciers would mean a return to something I was not supposed to be able to return to. A small victory, but significant. As my weekly routine continued through the month of February, it was apparent that British Columbia was not getting its usual 20 feet of snow, and our little band of adventurers started to look for alternative ski areas.

In my mind the only alternative to Whistler/Blackcomb was Sun Valley, Idaho. In the '70s and '80s, Sue and I had spent a lot of time in Sun Valley and we had a good friend there—Chris DuPont, who had gone to Whistler/Blackcomb with me before the first surgery. I called him to see if the weather reports were right and talked to his wife Holley. She was a former racer/ freestyle skier with a passion for skiing. Holley informed me the snow was so high they had to dig out the windows on the first floor of the house to let in the sunlight. She urged us to come out and stay with them, but with Robert and Ross in our party, Sue and I declined the offer. Holley would not take no for an answer, so we compromised and added a week to the trip in order to visit with them. In less than 24 hours we had rescheduled our flights, re-routed to Ketchum, Idaho, and rented a condo for the first week at the base of Exhibition chairlift.

All week long I had butterflies in my stomach and a constant ache and anxiety in my head. Subconsciously I knew I was not ready to take on a big mountain like Sun Valley, but I was determined not to give in. When I skied in the '70s, I would have at least one race or freestyle contest a year on Baldy Mountain, then on to Colorado for the Rocky Mountain championships. In those days we traveled on a chartered plane and the whole tour was one big party. Once a trio of hang gliders streaked naked over the mountain and a man in a gorilla suit crashed onto the mogul course wearing no pants. It was a crazy time but I developed an affection for the place. When we made the decision to go to Sun Valley, I hoped the heli-skiing would be easier than in British Columbia since the runs in Idaho are shorter. I thought I would have the strength and stamina to get three or four runs in before collapsing from exhaustion. The true test of how far I had come back would be revealed within the next 48 hours; we were packed and primed for another extreme adventure in the alpine.

Dr. Westmark had insisted that I wear a helmet while I was skiing, although under his breath he said it would not help me if I fell hard or hit something. "Why?" I asked. "What will happen?" His concern was not about the integrity of the skull but about bruising and cell damage that would occur from the jarring. He politely said that the repercussions would devastate me.

We arrived in Sun Valley and, to our joy, there was so much snow the street signs were buried. Holley picked us up at the airport and took us to her house, where she promptly tossed me the keys to a hotrod Jeep with a souped-up V8 350 HP engine. This rig was great, with headers, straight pipes and a roll cage. I could not wait to try to drive it. If I was not safe in this thing, I would never be safe in any car. Now that we had a set of wheels, we headed to the real estate office for the keys to the condo, then everyone rushed to grab the best room.

The first day or two at Sun Valley we couldn't fly, so we skied the regular trails. Then the weather in the high country cleared and we went heli-skiing. Heli-skiing in Idaho is very different from heli-skiing in western Canada. The runs are a lot shorter than at Whistler, but the ravines are very narrow, steep and dangerous because they are like funnels. Avalanches follow them down to the valleys. The skiing is fast and takes a lot of strength. We flew in small groups in a little Bell Ranger, which takes three people besides the guide and the pilot. Our guide, Sean, his wife, and Sue and I were one group, Robert and Ross were in another. It had snowed for a couple of days and cleared to a fresh, beautiful blue-sky day. I had explained to Sean and the pilot what I had been through and what I thought my limitations were. The first couple of runs we tried were fairly easy. They weren't very steep and the snow was light, just below the kneecap. I went down 500 feet, then stopped. Then down another 500 feet, and we were at the bottom. After the second run, I wanted to try something a little steeper and more difficult. Nobody seemed to object, so we flew over to a place that was considerably more challenging.

When I started out, I looked down and saw a hundred vertical feet of a clear snowfield falling away from me. From the air we had seen that this open field funneled into a narrow steep ravine with a lot of trees. Most ravines increase in incline and degree of difficulty. When I started off at the top, it was easy skiing. Entering the ravine, I noticed I was a little fatigued from the first two runs, so I started off very tentatively. Before I had even entered the hard part, I was feeling weak. Fatigue was building rapidly and I was doing short jump turns, going 6 or 7 feet right or left. As I descended the slope, it got harder and harder. Usually I didn't even notice my body weight, but this time I felt as if I weighed a ton. I started telling myself that it was the snow conditions or the skis; my edges were too sharp and were hooking like crazy. "Give me a file," I thought, "and I'll file them off." I started crossing my skis inadvertently and falling down.

But I could not admit defeat. I could not say, "This run is too much for me." That would mean that the hill had won, and no hill had ever beaten me. I didn't realize that as I went down the slope and my fatigue increased, my emotional state descended with me, first into panic and then into despair. As I skied into the ravine, it got narrower and narrower, and then all of a sudden there were trees in the way. I thought I had adjusted to my impaired vision. If I stared fixedly at one thing, part of the picture would be missing. I knew there was a complete picture, and I could see it all if I moved my eyes around. If I moved my eyes rapidly, I could make enough of a whole picture so that I could usually cope with what I saw. However, the pitch of the ravine was getting steeper, I was speeding up, and what little strength I had left was draining away.

The scenery was going by too fast. I got confused and started doubting what I saw. I'd see a tree, then look left and realize that I didn't see it anymore. It was as if there were four or five images projected onto one screen and the images kept changing. I began to think, "Did I see that? Am I hallucinating?" I'd find myself heading for a tree and say, "Come on, legs, turn," but they wouldn't take me into the turn. Everything started happening at a pace that I couldn't process, so I stopped frequently. When I stopped, my legs could not take the stress of my inertia, and I fell. Each time I stopped, I thought I could recover my wind and ski another 20 or 30 yards. But every time I tried to go another short distance, I was weaker than the last 30 yards—I wasn't regaining strength on the stops. I was soaked from the inside with sweat and from the outside from falling down so often; my goggles were beginning to fog up; I was physically exhausted; and my head was killing me. I was totally confused and could not think rationally.

My talent for skiing was leaking away as I descended further into the ravine. About halfway down, it was all trees, with only about 1 to 3 feet between the branches for maneuvering. As I plunged into the incomprehensible tangle of trunks and branches, I lost my hold on reality. All I could think was, "I can't do this. I've got to grab a tree and hope I have the strength to hold on before I hit the next one." Finally I hit a tree, and I sat down in the snow and cried. For the first time since the second operation I knew without doubt that I was not what I used to be. I was just an empty, useless shell lying in the snow, crying. The hill had won. Stupidly, I thought, "Thank God Robert and Ross can't see me." I cried for at least an hour.

Sean advised Sue to leave me alone. He knew that I had been through the surgical wringer and was impressed from the first that I was even out there. When I finally stopped crying, Sean walked over to me and said, "Don't be embarrassed. It's unbelievable that you're even out here. It's a miracle that you're standing on skis, let alone doing what you've done."

I pulled myself together and sidestepped down the rest of the way, like a kid who had never been on skis before. I would traverse, fall, turn around and go back, traverse, fall, turn around, and so on. Finally we got to the helicopter. "I just want to go home," I said. "If you can't take me home, just leave me some place where you can pick me up at the end of the day. I'll occupy myself with squirrels or something."

Sean just said, "Let's get in the helicopter." We got up to the top of the next stop, and he wouldn't let the helicopter leave until I got out. I said, "Sean, I'm defeated. I can't do this. Forget it. I can't go through that again." Sean was polite but insistent, though the pilot was looking at me as if to say, "Get the hell out of here."

Sean said, "I guarantee you I'll have a smile on your face by the end of the day." Sean, his wife and Sue all made it clear that they were prepared to spend the night if I didn't get out of the helicopter and ski the run. So I got out of the helicopter, put on my skis and made the run. The trail was much wider without all the trees. It was virgin-white snow, as if someone had exploded a down pillow over the mountain. I don't remember the run, but Sue said I looked like a million dollars. Somehow Sean knew that I hadn't lost all my ability, that I had just had a bad run. That night, I felt embarrassed that I had gone to pieces. Though there was hardly a smile on my face, I at least could consider some possible future. I began to realize, however dimly, that I hadn't lost my soul. I was still recovering, and further recovery would take a long time.

The next day, skiing conditions were even better. We also had a freelance writer for some skiing magazines with us. Waves of adoration seemed to flow from this reporter, as if she were saying, "My God, this guy is just unbelievable. Look at him skiing, and he's part blind. Eighteen months ago his head was lying open on some operating table." Naturally, I was flattered. At the same time, Sean and the other guides, instead of treating me like just another customer, were praising me and encouraging me to keep focused on the fact that I should be dead or, at best, in a coma.

We stayed in Sun Valley for a full two weeks. They took us to mountains where there were no trees so I didn't have the encumbrance of having to follow a certain path. I could go wherever my skis went as long as I could hang on to them. I didn't have the mental overload of trying to sort out trees that came and went with alarming rapidity in my field of vision. I was still in denial, looking for something to blame for my difficulties. I had focussed in on the fact that I was on some new skis that were supposedly all-terrain extreme skis, very forgiving, very easy to turn. For several days, I was still falling all the time. Every day I went out skiing, I had to do something to compensate. Ski fewer runs but make them better quality skiing—better three good runs than 10 mediocre ones. By not exhausting myself, I regained some of the tremendous joy, elation and exhilaration that I used to get from skiing. Slowly, slowly, the conviction grew on me that there was not just emptiness in front of me but a whole lot more recovery. There was always the next season to look forward to.

Sun Valley was a turning point and, though I didn't know it at the time, the beginning of a different kind of recovery, the discovery of who I really was. I tired easily, but I learned to go home when my stamina failed. I had been in denial for 18 months and had wanted to prove to myself that I could go heli-skiing. I desperately wanted to confirm that I wasn't diminished. I was going to get it back by taking it back. But now I had to face it: I did have limitations and I had lost capacities. I was foolish to think that I could just jump in a helicopter and go out and heli-ski. When Robert and Ross left, Sue and I moved into Chris and Holley's house, where we skied Mt. Baldy. On the last day of our stay at Sun Valley, Holley talked us into a three-hour snowboard lesson. We headed down to the board store to rent all the necessary equipment. Once there, I got into an argument with the guy renting the snowboard boots and snowboard. I hated those awful contraptions that turn people into something like a cross between a burlap bag and a troll. The salesman wanted me to stand on this thing with my toes pointing front and back respectively. I wanted to place my stance like a surfer on a surfboard, but he insisted that was not the way snowboarders do it. After that struggle ended, the salesman asked if I wanted pads.

"Do I need them?" I asked.

"As many as you can wear," he replied.

Like a dutiful soldier, I rented knee pads, hip and butt pads, elbow pads, wrist pads and a helmet. I was suiting up like a gladiator to try a sport I despise. The only thing left to do was go to the class and hope to survive the three-hour lesson.

At Little Dollar Mountain, a pure-white pile of snow, we dragged our boards over to the meeting area and were taught how to fall, stand and walk on a snowboard. Most importantly, we learned how to get up after falling, which was what I seemed to do most. Sue and Holley took to snowboarding like fish take to water. The only lesson I learned was don't try to teach an old dog new tricks. For the last 38 or so years I had studied and perfected a technique of skiing on traditional alpine skis. Why would I give that up and turn my skis in for a snowboard and baggy clothes? Even though the baggy clothes did hide the spare tire I had acquired. It turned out to be a fun day, but painful. When you fall on a snowboard, you either fall on your face or your fanny—my fanny took extra abuse on that beautiful blue-sky day on Dollar Mountain. We all had a big laugh over dinner recounting the day's events.

The next morning we were off to the airport bright and early for our flight home. I realized it was going to take many years to regain the stamina and strength I had lost. After nearly two years since the surgeries, I was not much stronger physically. Mentally I seemed to make even more maddening errors. My self-esteem was not getting any better because I did not feel as if I had any purpose. I needed to find something I could do that would give me some self-esteem.

One of my friends I confided in was somewhere between a close friend and an older brother—Kevin Deverich. We did not see each other a lot because he was busy running Hilton Hotels and networking. Kevin often suggested that I not rush the recovery process and insisted that I deserved to do nothing but enjoy myself. That is what all my doctors kept prescribing, but my competitive nature and the need to have some independence made me dismiss these recommendations. Twice after surgery I had asked my father what I could do for the company besides being a broker. Indirectly I was waiting for him to fulfill the promise he had whispered while I was hooked up to a bunch of monitors— when I was ready, he had said, the position of executive vice president was mine. As time went by, I realized that I was not going to be promoted to that position. Through a lot of therapy and soul searching, it became apparent that the only thing I liked about my old job was the fat paycheck. In any case, that winter my father decided to sell his real estate company. In the end, it was Kevin who came to my rescue.

Chapter 29

Kevin had left his job with Hilton Hotels and was working for Merv Griffin in Los Angeles. One day he called me with an interesting question, "What would you do if you could choose anything in the world?" Instantly I replied, "I have always wanted to run a ski resort." To my surprise, Kevin said that if I found a ski area that looked like a worthy investment, he would speak to Merv about buying it and hiring me to run it.

"Bill, I'm serious," Kevin said, "this fits with Merv's plan on acquiring underpriced resorts and hotels. You are the perfect guy to find these properties."

All I could say was, "Hold on, let me get Sue. Tell her what you told me so she won't think I'm wacko." Sue confirmed Kevin's comments and looked at me in a way I had not seen for two years. She smiled, hugged me and said, "Bill, hope is here, your faith is paying off."

"I know just where to start," I told her. "Waterville Valley— my home ski area."

After 25 years of the same ownership, Waterville Valley ski resort was in deep financial debt. If someone did not infuse the company with new capital or pay down some of the existing debt, the company would end up bankrupt.

The fall raced by as I pursued my three objectives—karate, psychotherapy and researching Waterville Valley. All the while, I gained physical strength, although my confused mind still failed me. My dreams of getting my black belt in karate, the intense therapy sessions with Dr. Gates, and Sue's encouragement kept me going. My situation seemed to be looking brighter, yet even as I increased my activity level—making telephone calls to get information about Waterville Valley and writing it down in a coherent form for The Griffin Group—I paid a physical price.

I had to rest and sleep more often to counteract the pain and anxiety. My anger at my deficits and forgetfulness was taking its toll. Sue and I were fighting constantly. My father could not understand that I really did have serious neurological problems and constantly pressured me to get involved in the disposition of his company. At times I was irrational; mental faux pas were unsettling and enraged me. In my need to act normal, I was still driving and had several close calls. I almost hit a jogger, and once, I did not see a cement truck parked on the side of the road and nearly killed myself.

It soon became apparent that the pursuit of Waterville Valley was going to be a hostile attempt, which raised difficult issues both with Mr. Griffin and my father—Mr. Griffin had made a strategic decision not to pursue any hostile takeovers, and the owner of the ski area was a close friend of my father. The dream of running Waterville Valley was slipping away. The owners of the ski area were in denial that they were on a sinking ship, or else they did not want to lose control. After a year of talks, The Griffin Group offered to hire a financial workout specialist to structure the company for a Chapter 11 reorganization.

There were two stipulations: First, The Griffin Group had to control the board of directors and, second, The Griffin Group had a specific option to buy control of the company. To our astonishment, the ownership of Waterville Company rejected our offer. All bets were that the company would probably be liquidated to pay off the creditors in six months. In fact, only five months later Waterville Company filed for Chapter 11 bankruptcy and was rejected by the courts. Two months after that, the company went into Chapter 7 insolvency and was liquidated.

By that time I was well-liked by The Griffin Group leadership. We decided to further our business relationship and I anticipated working in a new career. I had dreamed up a business plan to acquire several small ski areas with 200,000 to 300,000 skier visits a season. I planned to seek out small regional ski resorts one to two hours away from a major airport, spread across the northeastern and northwestern United States. My scheme would complement Mr. Griffin's growing chain of high-end hotels. I hoped that ultimately the package could be consolidated into a Real Estate Investment Trust and go public with a huge stock offering.

When the discussions with Waterville Valley came to an end, Kevin encouraged me to put together another deal. I set my sights on a ski area in Wyoming: Grand Targhee. In my freestyle years, I used to slip over to Grand Targhee to ski unbelievable powder at what was then a little-known ski area that usually got 500 inches of snow every year. I had heard the owners were interested in selling, and I also knew that they had spent a bundle of money trying to get government approval to expand the resort. There were, however, two small problems to overcome: First, the owner and his wife were in a polite divorce and their estate included the ski area; second, Congress had to sign a bill allowing the government to trade parcels of land with the owners of Grand Targhee so that they could mortgage the real estate to build hotels to sleep the new customers. I believed I was still capable of ferreting out deals. Around this time, however, there was an air of change in The Griffin Group. A refocusing on the base investments took priority and Grand Targhee was shelved.

I thought I was going to get back to a productive lifestyle, but deep down inside I was a shambles. My brain was in constant pain and fatigue. My moods fluctuated. I was living on the emotional edge of insanity, losing my grip on reality and the will to live. One minute I was flying to the West Coast for meetings with The Griffin Group, and then I was at home struggling to assemble my children's Christmas toys. I spent more and more time practicing karate, where every move was carefully choreographed. Each student knew what the opponent was going to do and vice versa. It was like programming a computer.

Sue and I had discovered that Social Security has a trial period for people with disabilities who want to try to go back to work. If unsuccessful, the disabled person can reactivate the benefits. We decided it was worth the gamble. I applied for the trial work period, negotiated a settlement with the disability insurance company and started my own consulting company called A.D.Ventures, Inc. The Griffin Group retainer equaled what I collected from Social Security. With the settlement from the sale of the real estate company, I could pay off my house mortgage and invest the rest in case my attempt to return to a productive life failed.

Once in a while, I would hear about an entity called Resorts International and finally picked up a financial paper to check the value of its stock. What I found was a company that was in Chapter 11, trying to reorganize its financial condition in order to stay in business. Then I realized it was a Merv Griffin asset and looked at the stock price of 85 cents per share. The people working in The Griffin Group were extremely intelligent, with a conservative philosophy. I took a gamble and bought 25,000 shares of Resorts International stock while it was still in Chapter 11. Then I placed the stock in my IRA pension account.

Months later, I was sitting with Kevin after a meeting on the West Coast when he casually mentioned that he and all the Griffin people had enjoyed their association with me. "Oh," I thought, "here comes the axe!" Then he said that Merv would like to meet me and wanted to place me on the board of directors of Resorts International. He said they owned a huge amount of land spread all over Atlantic City, New Jersey, and needed a creative mind with experience in real estate to complement the other directors. The directors were very big hitters in the business leagues and I could not believe they wanted me to join their ranks. I jumped on it as if it were the last horse out of town! Kevin also mentioned that there would be fees, a modest quarterly retainer and, of course, stock options. I felt I was in over my head; I had served on a few charity boards but not in a league this big.

When I returned to my room, I wanted to call home and tell Sue the news but it was the middle of the night on the East Coast— the news would have to wait. Brain surgery had catapulted me into the booming world of high-tech entertainment. The Griffin Group association was intellectually stimulating and far more creative than the starched-white-shirt, blue-striped-suit world of Boston. The potential to eclipse all my father's success was in front of me. I think the adrenaline was what empowered me to endure the interaction, travel and sensory overload. When I returned from a business trip, I was fried for a week before my system calmed down.

Mr. Griffin was successful in Hollywood and owned casinos, riverboats, hotels, greeting cards and "Wheel of Fortune." I was not going to sit on the sidelines and miss playing in the big game. Yes, I was injured, but I had always skied or played football with aches and injuries, so why not try to work for The Griffin Group in a capacity my father had groomed me for? My father was the ultimate corporate chess grand master, and if I had learned my lessons well and could follow my instincts, I would be fine. Never in my wildest dreams did I think I would be flying around the country looking for hotels, resorts, dude ranches, ski resorts, electronic amusement centers, and dealing with Fortune 100 companies. The best part was collecting a steady check; that little fact made it easier to deal with my pain. I thought about the things that hurt my brain and the ones that did not. If Sue wanted me to screw in some brackets for a curtain rod, the pain in my head and the intense distress, anxiety and sickening feelings grew to unbearable levels with every twist of the screwdriver. In the capacity of a consultant, all I had to do was state what I thought of a deal or project.

My new assignment—casinos—put me on the trail with Donald Trump and the Native American Indians who were opening up Indian-controlled casinos on reservations all over the country. This was a new market for hungry state governments with deficit spending. The next morning I packed my bag, then called Sue to let her know about my seat on the board of directors, subject to a gaming audit by the state of New Jersey and the formal vote of the board to confirm my election. Sue shrieked and wished me a safe flight home. I grabbed my briefcase and headed for the limousine waiting to rush me to the airport. Dr. Gress had advised me to take limos because I never could have navigated a car in a city.

Back home, Sue noticed my irritability and wild mood swings. I snapped at her and the kids; they paid the price whenever I worked for two or three days. I could not wait to get to the dojo to get grounded. I was making steady progress in strength and stamina. At the dojo, I was not self-conscious about my mental mistakes since everyone, including the higher-ranked students, made mistakes. Karate was making a difference in my skiing too. During my early ski years, my feet felt like blocks of cement; after practicing karate, they were like hi-tech sensors. I felt more in control of my mind and body as a result of more than two years of regular training. The martial arts were also teaching me to be humble, patient and modest, while training my mind to learn by starting with small steps and building a foundation. I had become quite attached to Walter. Quiet and gentle, at the same time he is a dynamic and imposing figure with great humility and compassion.

When it came to working for The Griffin Group, I could endeavor to persevere long enough to get the job done. Then it was home to reality and Sue, Walter and Dr. Gates for an assessment of the battle damage I sustained after each business trip. I gladly paid the price as people at The Griffin Group listened to what I had to contribute and showed they respected my opinion. When I returned home, I broke down and exploded. Sue loved me, listened to me and encouraged me, but still I raged on like a lunatic.

A few weeks later, I was headed to Atlantic City for my first meeting with the entertainment giant Merv Griffin. When I broke the news to my father, he had some cynical remarks and a caution that they were using me to get to him. The possibility that I could have some value to The Griffin Group never occurred to him. I put on my best new suit and packed a couple of shirts and ties for my two-day trip. During the flight, I worried about being asked intelligent questions over financial matters and having no idea what to reply. When people first hear my voice, they think I am drunk or sleepwalking. How embarrassing to fumble my words the first time I met Mr. Griffin! As I stepped off the plane and headed toward the baggage claim, I saw someone holding a sign with "Mr. Fallon" in big red letters. I checked with the driver to make sure he was from the Resorts Hotel.

"Yes sir, Mr. Fallon, let me take your bags, sir."

In front of the terminal building, a super-stretch white limo as long as a football field was waiting. I received first-class treatment right to the hotel. The manager greeted me at the front desk and asked me to report to the executive offices as soon as I had finished moving into my room. I was as nervous as the first time I had asked Sue out on a date. Out of the elevator and to the left, past a security guard and through a door, and before I knew it, I was standing in Mr. Griffin's office. There he was, sitting regally behind a desk talking on the phone. As I sat down, he hung up the phone and started talking to me. Like a schoolboy, I jumped to my feet. He laughed, shook my hand and gestured me to sit down. We talked about Boston College, skiing, the real estate company and, of course, my recent triumph over tragedy. He insisted that I call him Merv. Then he informed me that he was happy I was joining his dream team and said he looked forward to seeing me at the first meeting in January.

This first trip gave me the opportunity to familiarize myself with the facility, see what The Griffin Group was doing in the way of capital improvements, and meet some of the executive officers. The key man was Mat Kearney, who gave all the board members a tour of the hotel. The company owned 70 or more individual parcels of land—large and small tracts and small single lots—scattered in and around Atlantic City. I noticed a large parking lot next to the main entrance with frontage on the boardwalk and asked whether The Griffin Group owned it. Mat informed me that they had a lease on the property. "Too bad," I thought. The next part of our tour included a walk through the resort and around the outside of the property. As we walked out the door, a thunderous downpour broke out and everyone scrambled back to the shelter of the lobby. I wondered why they didn't have a portico so patrons could enter the hotel with some protection from the elements. As I gazed out at the big open-air parking lot, it was not even full. There was something about this parking lot that drew my attention, but I couldn't put my finger on it.

As the tour looked as if it was drawing to an end, I asked about the evening schedule. The plan was to have dinner in one of the casino's best restaurant at 8 p.m. I excused myself and slipped over to the Showboat casino next door. In any competition you must learn everything you can about your opponents. I quickly cruised through the place, noting all the glitz and glimmer; if you looked closely, it was all cosmetics. The Taj Mahal was the same, but with different packaging. As I walked back to Resorts International, the problem was obvious: it was antiquated and leaky, like an old boat that you just keep putting money into and it barely stays afloat. Right then I started to formulate what needed to be done.

The time passed so quickly that I suddenly realized it was getting late and I wanted to report to Sue about my first introduction to Mr. Griffin—I mean, Merv. When I reached my room, my head pounded and a sharp jab of pain coursed across my right temple and into the back of my head. My defenses had weakened as the day wore on and I was feeling the effects. I grabbed some Co-Tylenol and a bottle of juice from the stocked bar. The room resembled a small palace with mirrors everywhere, a huge hot tub in the bedroom, and baskets of fruit and candy. On the writing desk there were several Resorts International gifts, like a Mont Blanc pen and a key chain, plus two mountains of documents: financial statements, IRS filings, demographics studies, market analyses, income projections, and the little sheets that showed how all the casinos had performed over the last quarter. How was I going to focus my battered brain on all this information? I could not read the stock quotes, let alone a couple of thousand pages of legal and financial mumbo jumbo.

When I called home, everyone was getting ready for bed, even Sue. Quickly I recounted the day's events and what I thought of Merv and his gang. When I expressed my apprehension about doing the job, Sue exclaimed, "Listen, the sharks in the business community you grew up in make this job a piece of cake. If you could make it in Boston, Atlantic City is a walk in Boston Public Garden on a beautiful June day."

After all we have been through, she still was there for me. I said, "I love you." Sue blew a kiss over the phone and we hung up. Alone, I sat thinking that I actually wanted to be out in the snow, skiing a dozen runs! But I had only had a few minutes to change my shirt and put on a new tie before dinner. A quick look in the mirror and there it was, that half face with one eye staring back at me. If the high rollers in the Board Room had any idea what life was like through my eyes, they would throw me out. I laughed out loud and went down to the lobby.

The other board members were waiting for me in the dining room. We had a few drinks and talked a little about what the future might hold. I had one vodka and ginger ale to take the rough edge off my attitude and was relieved that drinking was not going to be a big activity on this tour of duty. As soon as our food was served, I stopped talking because I could not eat and talk at the same time. Besides, an experienced broker had once taught me that it was better to listen. He also taught me that silence is a good technique when negotiating. After dinner we parted company and headed to our respective suites. I was hurting pretty badly, so I swallowed a handful of antidepressants and a Co-Tylenol and slipped into the dark abyss that medication brings on.

Next morning, as I walked out the front door to the long chariot waiting to drive me to the airport, I glanced up over my head, wondering how long it would take to convince the board to build a portico before the Atlantic Ocean weather blew all the customers away. On the flight home, I started cruising through the documents in my brief case and quickly surmised that I could never read it all. I decided to review the numbers—they do not lie. The company had just come out of reorganization and every penny was watched by at least three government agencies from the state as well as the federal authorities. I thought about the company stock I had bought many months ago when Resorts International was in Chapter 11. "Boy," I thought, "wait until they see my 25,000 shares in the quarterly statements at the next board meeting."

Before I knew it, I was back to the refuge of my quiet home with a couple of weeks to recover before the first official board meeting in Atlantic City. I had the dojo and Walter to help me deal with reality and, of course, Dr. Gates. In between sessions and karate, I tried to read the enormous pile of legal and financial material. With Sue's help, we sorted out the pertinent data and discarded the information that I knew nothing about. The strategy was simple; talk about issues I knew well and avoid areas out of my field of expertise.

Chapter 30

My twice-a-week sessions with Dr. Gates were helping clear the fog in my head.

I was becoming aware of the things that I used to think were important—ambition, wealth, power and status. Surgery had stripped me of all these things and I came to realize that I had not been living my own dreams. For the first time, I acknowledged that this strange twist of fate had blessed me. I could turn to a new path to pursue what I truly wanted out of life.

The day to be whisked off to Atlantic City finally arrived. During the flight, I reflected on what I had learned about the gaming industry. The business was spreading like wildfire as state governments, trying to balance their debt-laden administrations, were eager to get a piece of the action. The Indian Gaming Regulatory Act passed by the federal government had everybody jockeying for a place in line. Massachusetts was no different and my own network, plus my father's contacts, would get me into almost any door I wanted to enter. Working with The Griffin Group gave me a chance at a fresh start. Unbelievable, I thought to myself; two years ago I was dying. Now, permanently disabled, I was in the casino business. With my growing self-esteem and a new course to chart, I was leaving the past behind.

When I arrived in Atlantic City, I discovered that the casino had assigned a driver and limo to meet me at the airport. The closer the meeting approached, the more at ease I felt. This was quite different from the adversarial nature of negotiating millions of dollars of real estate. I hoped I could maintain this calm.

At my first board meeting, a course of events would be put into motion that would determine the fate of Resorts International. The other board members knew me without much of an intro- duction—unfortunately I could not remember them. The infor- mation packet I received prior to the meeting included the agenda and enough pertinent information for an intelligent person to make responsible decisions. The agenda included a capital budget and, as I glanced through the line items, I laughed. It was my custom to send The Griffin Group a few pages of my observations and recommendations about the projects I tackled. After my tour of the Resorts International hotel and casino, I had fired off a letter recommending the construction of a carport or portico over the front entrance to receive clients in a friendlier environment; it would also provide the whole complex with an identity. The capi- tal budget contained a request for funding to design and build a portico. "Hell," I thought, "I have not even been sworn in yet and my suggestion is in the budget for approval."

There was a commotion outside the door of the conference room and I knew it had to be Merv. Sure enough, Merv strolled in, walked directly over to me to shake my hand and thanked me for joining his team. I felt right at ease—no wonder he had one of the most successful talk shows ever. After the introductions, I was politely asked to excuse myself while they took a formal vote to approve my addition to the board. Within a few minutes, I was invited back in and the meeting began in earnest.

The first item for discussion was the huge inventory of real estate—it looked as if the architect of the acquisitions depart- ment had used a dartboard approach to choose locations. Mixed in were some valuable sites with some residual value that could be used as bargaining chips with other casinos or developers. The Griffin Group owned 86 properties all over the city. The value they carried on the books was outrageous compared to market conditions. With my real estate background, I felt confi- dent and presented my positions quickly. In a very diligent and professional manner, I made several recommendations that were adopted by the board.

The meeting went on for most of the day. Merv absorbed information like a sponge and did not miss a trick. He had impeccable timing about when to jump into the discussion or lead off to the next topic. As the other items on the agenda were addressed, I turned into a careful listener, cautiously commenting when I felt I had to say what was on my mind. The problem was that I did not understand the jargon of the gaming business. The reports included definitions, but I could not look them up fast enough to follow the conversation. I could not jot down notes without forgetting the issue or else the discussion would proceed to the next issue. It was like getting lost in the forest—panic would set in. Then Merv would speak up and, bang, I was back on track. I was starting to feel pretty good until we reached the discussion of the legal and financial minutiae. At that point, I had no idea what they were saying.

Just as I thought a motion to adjourn the meeting was coming, an item that was not on the agenda surfaced—the parking lot we leased across the street, the one that had caught my eye weeks ago. Apparently the owner wanted to terminate the lease. The point was made that the parking lot was not useful because there were buses and the city offered free parking; vehicular traffic brought nearly all the patrons to Atlantic City. The owner was offering $3 million to terminate our lease. I had spent years negotiating the purchase of long-term office leases in highrise towers in Boston, so I knew quite a bit about this subject.

There was a time when tenants were able to negotiate 20- or 30-year leases with predetermined rates. When the market value exceeds those rates, there is a residual value—the difference between actual rental rates and the market rental rates. The '80s were record-breaking years for wild increases in the cost of renting space. The financial term for the value of the cash flow of such a long-term lease is present value. Quickly I grabbed my calculator and did a present value analysis on the value of the lease on the parking lot. I was staggered when I saw the number come up on the display. I did the calculations again using more conservative assumptions—the number was still huge. When I heard someone make a motion to accept the $3 million, I intervened.

I asked some specifics about the lease terms and conditions and renewal options. The answers only made the value of the lease go up. Jay Green, CFO of Culbro Corporation, had perked up at this conversation and I suspected he knew where I was heading. I told the other board members that depending on the discount rate, the payment Resorts International was entitled to was somewhere between $70 and $80 million dollars. Quickly Jay confirmed what I was saying and within minutes the two of us had turned the deal around. Jay and I surmised that the owner might not be aware of the value of the lease and would sell the lot to us for the cheapest amount resorts had to pay for land on a per-square-foot basis. This one act would lead to one of the greatest business turnarounds in years and proved my worth to the board of directors and the shareholders.

"Wow," I thought, "my first day on the board and I made the company a small fortune."

Luckily, Jay was right with me. In the back of my self-doubting mind, I was not sure that I alone could have convinced the board to buy the parking lot. Shortly afterward, the meeting adjourned. I took my leave and returned to my room to calm my senses, ground my ego, and do a reality check by calling Sue.

* * * * *

My outward appearance did not reflect the conflict that raged inside. Hallucinations, loss of emotional control, confusion and lack of focus surfaced in every effort I made, from getting dressed in the morning until nighttime when everyone was asleep and the house was quiet. Then I would lay my head down on the pillow, hoping for respite from the pain.

I was unaware that as I became more active, I put greater demands on myself. The consequences on Sue and our relationship were becoming obvious. If I wanted something to drink, I would get a glass and then leave it on the kitchen counter. I would become distracted, forget what I was doing and move on to something else. Sue would see the glass and put it in the dishwasher if it was dirty or in the cabinet if it was clean. A few minutes later, I would remember I was thirsty and go back to the kitchen to get the glass and it would be gone. My mind would then question the reality of the glass and whether I had actually taken one down from the cabinet earlier.

One day I went golfing at the local public course. It was a busy day with a full course and a tournament underway. When the starter turned to let me approach the first tee, he remarked that no alcohol was allowed on the course, accusing me of intoxication. My rage at the insult I perceived pushed me to the point where I demanded an apology. The only time I felt normal was the time I spent in the dojo. There I felt a camaraderie, a sense of being part of something. And each time I earned a promotion, I felt a renewed sense of accomplishment.

Skiing also built up my pride. The trick was to stay on the right edge of the trail at all times, making sure I had a good visual fix on the other skiers and where they were on the trail. Just when I thought I was normal, an incident on the trail caused me think otherwise. One March day I came at my usual high speed over a headwall. I was hanging on the edge, carving monster turns at 40 to 50 mph. I scanned the trail ahead and counted five people. With a quick analysis of their directions, I decided to accelerate toward the lift tower on the right and split the space between the target farthest to the right and the tower. I hit the jets to get through the opening before a second person closed the gap. My eyes scanned ahead and I suddenly saw there was a sixth person on the trail—a little girl heading toward the tower, directly in my path. At my speed, I figured I would hit her in a second. With no time to spare, I realized that I could go to the left of the tower or hit the little girl. Without hesitation, I edged hard and turned right to avoid the little girl. The problem with that decision was twofold: first, there was a wall of ice and snow where the groomers had veered to the left of the tower, effectively closing the trail between the tower and the trees; second, there was an orange rope strung 4 feet off the ground. There was no time to think—the only thing to do was accelerate, jump the pile of ice and snow and the rope, and hope I carried enough distance down the hill to land back on the groomed part of the trail downhill from the tower. If it were not for my skiing ability and karate training, I could never have pulled off that stunt. I heard people on the chairlift above me scream and whistle in appreciation of the move. At the bottom I started to shake. My nerves and brain knew I had made a mental mistake that almost caused someone serious injury. I was so shaken that it ended my day on the mountain.

That winter I had invited Dr. Westmark, the resident on my second surgery, to go skiing. We had a great time but he scared the hell out of me because he was skiing a lot faster than his ability level and he was watching me, not looking where he was going. It was marvelous to watch his joy in his eyes when he saw how well I skied. All the way down every run he kept yelling, "Look, he can ski. He can still ski—look, everybody, he can ski!" To tell the truth, I am not sure how I can ski. In flat light conditions when even healthy eyes have no depth perception, how was I able to see the terrain changes and react to them at such high rates of speed?

* * * * *

I fretted constantly about financial problems. My trial work period for Social Security disability had been temporarily deferred and the sale of my fathers' company had stalled due to the shenanigans of the principles involved. The insurance company had settled on a lump sum payment that enabled us to pay off the mortgage on our house. Still the expenses in our life were far greater than the revenues we were generating. It was clear we had to cut some costs. I was working, but only for a few days a month. Most board of directors meet every three months, but the Resorts International board was different—as we all wanted to turn around this business, we were more of a hands-on operation. We talked almost every week by phone and met in person once a month. I needed the time between meetings to recover. Fortunately, the meetings were well organized with all the pertinent information necessary to function sent out well in advance, giving me time to review the material at my own pace.

At Resorts International, the financial viability of the company was good. The financial drain was the old tired facility we owned. It was clear to me that either we enter into a huge redevelopment of the facilities or sell the whole damn thing. The only asset was the real estate in Atlantic City—one antiquated facility and a multitude of small real estate holdings. Mat Kearney presented the board with an offer to buy the big parking lot along the boardwalk for a reasonable sum of money; the vote to accept was unanimous. We gained a real asset. Mat was authorized to close the deal and continue negotiations on another parcel behind the existing hotel that was key to the size of the development. In gaming, revenues are a direct correlation to the amount of square feet of casino floor. It was critical to maximize the footprint of the entire property in order to achieve the hotel rooms and casino space necessary to make the whole plan financially feasible. It was becoming apparent that the parking lot was to be a key ingredient. At that time we started to formalize a long-term strategy for the company. The months and meetings whirled past. After almost a year in the capacity of director, I came to several conclusions. First, the old facility was too old and costly to run. Second, we needed to diversify into other markets. The plan was to make the company an attractive merger or acquisition target in the hopes of maximizing the value of the company stock and getting a decent return on investment for the shareholders.

We developed a plan to build a $500 million, 700-room complex on the old parking lot and integrate it with the existing facility without disrupting the existing business. Management had skillfully followed our strategy and acquired the right combination of abutting properties so that we had enough real estate to get to the planning stage of a major redevelopment on the boardwalk. After years of downsizing and consolidating to cut costs, it was the first sign of corporate life in 10 years. We made sweeping changes that included reverse stock splits, name changes, and relisting on the New York Stock Exchange from the American Stock Exchange. In a few short years under the guidance of Tom Gallagher and Merv Griffin, Resorts International had been restructured and reborn as GGE (GGE). The stock had gone from $1 a share into the teens. The only thing holding back growth was our limited gaming venue; if revenues were to grow, casino space had to expand. We were a one-casino company trying to compete with the Trumps, ITT Sheratons and Hiltons of the world. The likelihood of eventually being bought out was so great, in my mind, that I felt it necessary to make the new GGE as attractive an acquisition target as possible.

Around the same time, the sale of Dad's real estate company heated up. Dad called the shots and decided to sell the company's assets piece by piece. In his eyes he had built it, he could tear it apart. That sale and the potential sale or merger of GGE looked like the end of my financial road. If I were to have any financial security for my family, I would have to maximize any benefits I could out of these two transactions. The directors of GGE owned a few thousand dollars worth of stock options, but we had not been directors long enough to accumulate any substantial value out of them. In the end, I would only have the stock in Resorts International, the new GGE, in my IRA. I would not be able to retire on that alone, however. First, it was not enough and, second, I couldn't touch it until I was 59, if I lived that long.

If I was going to have a future in business, something would have to come from the Griffin side of my efforts. The company had a giant real estate puzzle, cash and an idea. The challenge was to figure out what to do with the puzzle pieces that would derive the best outcome for the shareholders. Possibilities were limitless; it just depended on the level of risk we wished to take. I am a conservative when it comes to real estate and money, and that was the position I argued for. The due diligence and fact finding we had requested from management continued and we had not yet assembled all the abutting parcels. Soon after we bought the parking lot, neighbors smelled gold and were holding firm to some of their demands.

GGE was actively developing a long-term business strategy that would bring the company to new heights. The board had determined a course of action on two fronts: consolidate its real estate holdings into a single large development property on the boardwalk and improve financial performance, which would reflect in the value of the company stock. With the two strategies implemented, we could then think about mergers and acquisitions. That spring we had reached an agreement with an old fleabag hotel that abutted our parking garage. Then we initiated feasibility studies on the financial impact of expanding our parking structure. At every meeting, we had another piece of the puzzle and a scenario that would shape the future of GGE. I was in the middle of a potentially huge real estate development where I could use my best attributes on something I knew well. I was certain the company's future rested on how we approached and implemented the redevelopment plan.

* * * * *

Although there were many reasons for me to be grateful for my blessings, I was not conscious of them. To me, my health above the neck sucked. If I acted and looked anything like the way I felt, I would be locked up in a dark cell and forgotten. I could not control the part of me that was in pain or teeming with anger. The four years of pain and confusion since surgery seemed like an eternity. The sense of powerlessness started to inch its way into my head. In my sessions with Dr. Gates we had reached the mourning and grieving stage.

I feared this part of the rehab most because I knew I would not like the conclusions that psychoanalysis reached. My confused emotions were causing me to develop relationship problems with friends, co-workers and my family. And, worst of all, Sue and I argued constantly.

On several occasions Dr. Gress had talked about subjecting me to a complete neuro-psych testing, but it was still too early in the recovery process. He anticipated a five-year recovery period first. The three of us—Dr. Gates, Sue and I—were beginning to wonder if we were almost at that stage now. Everyone looked at me with eyes that begged me to explain why I could not function like a normal human being. They all said I looked wonderful and saw no sign of my neurological errors—no wonder my disability is called an invisible handicap. I started to know what hell was and I feared I was going to have to live that way forever.

Chapter 31

During my sessions with Dr. Gates, I had no way of hiding my emotions—that took too much brain power. Think of the brain like the starship Enterprise. Whenever the ship came under attack and lost power, Captain Kirk would shut down systems in order to divert energy use to the weapons system. My brain was doing the same thing. The more energy I expended, the more systems would shut down. Finally, Sue called Dr. Schumacher to talk about my struggle and he advised that I see a neuro-psychologist at the Lahey Clinic for a full evaluation. He cautioned, however, that the tests could have a negative affect emotionally and psychologically. Then he referred Sue to Dr. Penny, saying he would talk to her first.

At dinner that night, Sue informed me that she had talked to Dr. Penny, the doctor had my medical history, and the appointment was in two weeks. I had no meetings scheduled with GGE and ski season was over for the year. We had one weekend to put my boat into the water before seeing Dr. Penny, so we packed up the car and headed for the Cape to prep my speedboat and paint its bottom. I hoped these activities would be a distraction. I was afraid the tests would show I was not as messed up as I thought and my problems were simple psychological issues that could be fixed. Another fear was that they would find out my brain was like a couple pounds of hamburger and I was really messed up. Sue constantly assured me that the tests were the only way of knowing what was wrong with my brain.

All too soon, Sue and I were standing in front of Dr. Penny. She was sitting at her desk writing in one file while talking on the phone at the same time. I thought back to the time when I was able to do that. Dr. Penny was a petite woman with long silken hair who resembled Jane Seymour. She said I was not what she expected after reading my medical history. As I told my story, we made a connection and I knew that this doctor could help me.

She asked about my relationship with Sue and wanted us to be totally honest. I knew we were in conflict and that I had lost some of my sex drive. Hearing Sue say she did not understand me and that she did not know me any longer hurt incredibly. Sue even admitted that I sometimes scared her. Dr. Penny's questions seemed to intuitively know what I was dealing with. Finally I had found someone who understood what I was trying to say. On several occasions I tried to articulate what was wrong with me, and several times she anticipated what I was trying to say and answered my statements for me. In this first meeting she described the tests, the functions they were testing, and where those functions originated in the brain. Twice she warned that the tests themselves might be painful and unpleasant. I should stop her at any time if I was not able to continue. In addition she told me that testing would take a toll on me and that I had to prepare to accept the consequences of the testing. Having elevated my anxiety enough, she finished reviewing my medications and instructed me to head home and rest up.

"Rest up," I thought, "what for? How strenuous could a bunch of word problems and puzzles be?"

Two days later we arrived at the hospital ready for a full day of testing. The wait was not long and soon Dr. Penny stepped out of her office and beckoned me to follow her. Sue excused herself and said she would return in the afternoon. Dr. Penny asked about the therapy I had been doing. I told her I was trying to learn an Okinawan style of karate called uechi-ryu. That seemed to shock her but she only asked how long I had been studying and what degree belt I had achieved. She said that she was very impressed by how well I was functioning. In fact, she was amazed to hear that I had returned to work, especially in the capacity that I was working. But as quickly as she blew smoke up my nose, she floored me with a haymaker.

"I suspect I know how you are doing it and I am impressed by your efforts, but I am not sure how long you will keep it up."

I broke down completely, as if a dam had burst. She had hit a nerve with her first statement. She suspected what I suffered from, she just did not know all the pieces to the puzzle. They had to be discovered via testing before the full picture could be seen. There is no way I can recount the events of the day and the vast array of tests, but they started with an abbreviated intelligence test. The intelligence test, including the infamous inkblot test, was followed by a variety of language skill tests. Occasionally I had trouble with the sensory overload, but I fought through the anxiety and pain. From time to time I had to close my eyes, take a couple of deep breaths and try to calm the assault on my senses. Compassionately, Dr. Penny would stop and try to soothe me, allowing me to regain my composure and continue. My heightened level of interest in learning how the brain and the mind work helped. The scary part was that I enjoyed the intellectual stimulation and thought I was performing normally in most tasks.

On day two, a series of test required me to point to a certain letter that appeared mixed up with a few other letters on a white card. No problem, I thought. When I completed that task, however, Dr. Penny held up a card with twice as many letters. That was more difficult. Finally, she held up a third card completely covered with a bunch of mixed-up letters and I broke down in tears. I cried several more times as I struggled through math and memory tests. Even the cognitive test disturbed me, but I pushed to finish all the tests on each scheduled day.

Sue was inquisitive about the testing and my answers but I was evasive, almost hostile. The more she tried to drag answers out of me, the uglier I got. I tried to intimidate her into not probing into everything I did. Of course that annoyed her even more and the argument escalated. The reality was that I was humiliated at not being able to recount the day's activities. My defense was to blow the issue out of perspective and hide the true nature of the moment's pain.

The final day of testing involved memory and visual processing. One test I recall vividly was a test where you are shown a picture and given three minutes to study it. The picture was a detailed design with different shapes and colors. After I analyzed the picture, Dr. Penny handed me a blank piece of paper and some crayons and gave me a set amount of time to duplicate the drawing. Then she gave me a series of tests where I was asked to repeat sequences of words after she read a list of words. After about an hour, Dr. Penny pulled out the same abstract picture and showed it to me for 30 seconds. I tried to add some details to my first drawing. This happened several more times and each time I was given less time to work on the picture. Finally she gave me a blank piece of paper and asked me to draw the picture again, except she did not show me the picture. Then Dr. Penny said she had a few dexterity tests to determine whether my fine motor skills were affected. By the end of the three days, I was exhausted and relieved. When I reached home, I went straight to my den and listened to the sweet soft sounds of a guitar and drifted off into a nap. I did not even wake up for dinner. When I finally awoke, I staggered to my bed and slept for almost a week. I could not even get up to go to karate.

When Sue and I last met with Dr. Penny, she told us to enjoy the next six weeks. She cautioned me to be prepared to accept the test results; they tended to be less favorable than the patient hoped. I wanted to know the test results as soon as possible and asked why the delay. She said it took that long to analyze the tests and she wanted to take all the time she needed to do a good job for me. With those words in my mind, we headed off to the Cape until late August.

During the summer, my father's company was sold. Not too long after the testing, the planetary alignment of my future started to unfold. At the last meeting of the board of directors of GGE, we had made the decision to move forward on the development of a new complex on the infamous parking lot. Feasibility studies were conducted during the summer, with an eye on an August or September date for a commitment to proceed on the expansion of Resorts International in Atlantic City.

There was nothing left to do but enjoy the summer and that is what Sue and I did. With the two kids growing up and a little more cash in the bank, the summer went blissfully by. One day we returned home to Wayland to find that Dr. Penny had called and left a message to meet her the following week and asking us to call to confirm the date. We called and discovered she had a cancellation the next day. Next morning we got up early and headed to the Lahey clinic for our appointment, only to find ourselves in a huge rush-hour traffic jam. I was very edgy and tried to push Susie into seeking an alternate route, but she prevailed over me to wait the traffic out.

When we arrived at the hospital, we did not bother checking in at the main lobby reception desk but instead went directly to Dr. Penny's office. Thankfully she was waiting for us. She stood behind her desk with a serious look on her face, held her hand out, and said she wanted to shake my hand. I did not know what to expect next. She said I was the most remarkable man she had ever met and wanted to let me know that before reviewing my test results. As she continued, she said she was initially impressed with my appearance and ability to shave and dress myself in the morning. I looked around the room to see whether she was still talking to me and, sure enough, I was the only one there who had had brain surgery.

She went on to say how remarkable it was that I had achieved the rank in karate that I had and that I had returned to work at the level I had achieved. Considering my history, those were tremendous accomplishments. "Hell," I thought, "I must have aced the intelligence test." Dr. Penny added that she was not going to tell me I could or could not do anything because it was miraculous that I had recovered as well as I had. Then she looked deep into my eyes and as I looked straight into her right eye, she said, "but I know how hard your brain is working and you will never be able to keep up what you have been doing or it will kill you before you reach fifty."

I felt like the dagger that had been thrust into my heart in 1990 was twisting to finish me off. Dr. Penny said that I had a Ferrari for a brain, but that my Ferrari engine was running on only four of its 12 cylinders. The testing showed that my short-term memory was toast; cognitively I had the brain of an eighth grader; and my learning abilities were severely compromised. The best she could determine was that my brain had developed a sophisticated visualization technique to compensate for my memory and cognitive deficits. How ironic that my only physical deficit—my vision—had taken over for my lost cognitive abilities. To overcome and adapt, I had to create a picture in my mind to do just about everything. Then it hit me how I remembered phone numbers—I saw the pattern my fingers made when I touched the keypad.

Together we deduced that the visualization methods I used to memorize a racecourse during my years of ski racing was how my brain had adapted to lost cognitive functions and memory. My obsessive-compulsive behavior was not psychological, but rather a neurological deficit resulting from the surgery. Dr. Penny said my ability to get back to work was a result of my reliance on old memories to function. That was true for skiing, and perhaps the reason my golf game never improved. And she pointed out that constant repetition was the key to learning karate. She credited the way I was functioning to my ambition and courage. If I had incurred this brain damage as a 10-year-old boy, I would have remained intellectually a 10-year-old.

My brain was working five times harder than a normal healthy brain. If I were to compete with a healthy person, the typical 40-hour work week would take me more than 200 hours to perform the same tasks. My ambition to compete with a healthy person would ruin my marriage and my life, and eventually it would kill me. This was a sobering moment. In her summation, Dr. Penny read the four-page report and went over each test result and her conclusions. The statement that really drove the nail home: In all her years of testing she had never put in writing that anyone ever qualified for a total neurological disability, I was the first; and she was going to make this clear in the report. Up until then I only had a visual deficit; Dr. Penny's report made it sound as if I were brain dead. I did not know whether to cry or to laugh for joy that I would requalify for Social Security disability. In a very serious manner, Dr. Penny advised me to stop all work and stress-related activities. She warned me that if I did not adopt a quiet and peaceful lifestyle, I would die.

Dr. Penny impressed upon us what we had to do: First, develop an immediate financial plan; second, contact a variety of organizations and get financial aid to pay my bills. Work as I knew it was over and that included GGE—never had anyone been more explicit. She said she would assist me in any way with disability insurance, Medicare or anything else. In closing, she let me know that my mental mistakes were not imaginary and that I had serious cognitive deficits. It would be important to seek out a behavior specialist to modify my behavior to avoid the things that stressed my brain. That included a therapist for my sexual dysfunction and our relationship problems.

The message she was sending was loud and clear, but I could not help but pose the question: "What, if anything, can I do?"

"Bill, you are an ambitious and competitive man. I can only give you the following advice. Move away from the stress and conflict that is in your life. Find a quiet place to live, nest, and get comfortable. Take a year or two and enjoy being with your wife and watch your children grow. At some point, you will have to do something, that is in your nature. Whatever it is that you attempt, make sure it is something you are interested in, something you are passionate about. It must be something you know and enjoy more than anything else. When you have figured out what that one thing is, just do that one thing."

I asked her how much effort I could put into that one thing.

"Whatever effort you think you should give, cut that in half and then divide the sum by seven."

"That is hardly breathing," I thought. We thanked Dr. Penny for all her help and she again tried to assure me that it was a live or die situation. Now that I had the answers to my condition, the reality of living life pain free was not an option. Deep down I think I already knew that, but at least we knew we could limit the impact by limiting the stress in my life.

Sue and I were in shock during the car ride home. Before we had reached home, we decided that over the fall we would look for land to buy near Waterville Valley. The real estate company and Sue's travel business had been sold. With those proceeds and the disability insurance settlement, we had paid off our mortgage and all our debt. If we sold our house and moved north to eliminate the Massachusetts taxes, we could put the equity we had in our Wayland home into a more modest house in the mountains. We were going back to the place where we met and fell in love.

Then it dawned on me: What about GGE? A board meeting was scheduled for September. For the time being, Sue and I decided to proceed slowly, say nothing, and ride out my term until it expired in a year and a half. For the moment I needed to digest all that Dr. Penny had said. In one way I was devastated to hear that my cognitive deficits were severe and the root of most of my troubles. On the other hand, I was relieved that I had answers and was not imagining things—my problems were real and severe.

It was hard to attend board meetings, listen to all the different development scenarios and concentrate on the company's future. Mat Kearney, absent at the beginning of the September meeting, arrived late looking like the cat who ate the canary. He had been approached by the owners of Sun International, the people who purchased our Paradise Island facility in the Bahamas, which had enabled GGE to come out of Chapter 11 reorganization. Now they wanted to buy my parking lot, the one Jay and I had stopped the company from selling the lease for pennies at the very first meeting—the one we were planning the company's future on. In his typically Irish way, Mat had told Sun International that if they wanted the parking lot they should just buy the whole damn company and they had said OK! The conversation in the room exploded with excitement, and I sat back thinking I must be pretty smart after all. I had envisioned the future in the company when I first saw the parking lot. When we convinced the company to buy the damn thing, it was thought of as a burden; now it was the company's salvation.

I was exhilarated and getting the high of my life. I had finally done something that I knew I had done! Not my father or one of his henchman, but me. What a way to exit a business career and retire, not with a whimper but a nuclear bang. Selling GGE was a deal worth hundreds of millions of dollars. It would provide me with a graceful exit and the satisfaction that I had made a difference and done something with my life. But the hardest job was ahead—closing the deal. The next few months were spent flying back and forth from New York for dozens of meetings with bankers, lawyers and stock market experts, doing the due diligence required of us and to fulfill our fiduciary responsibilities. Negotiations by management went on most of the fall and into early winter.

Sue and I had started to look for land in the Waterville Valley area. If GGE were sold, we would make the move permanent and buy some land by the end of December. The Wayland house went on the market the beginning of November. Months had passed and we were getting close to what is called the short strokes in the negotiations with Sun International. As a board, we had only the golden parachutes to negotiate for the management team and we would be ready for a decision and the formal vote by the board of directors. I flew down to New York and caught a limo to the lawyers' offices. Upon my arrival, I was led into a monster conference room where the other board members, including Merv and an army of consultants, had convened the meeting. Merv motioned to me to have the seat next to him and for the next five hours I listened to all the points that had been negotiated.

We had finalized the compensation package for management and had just heard from a dozen lawyers that we had exhausted all the opportunities, considered all the issues, and it was time for us to make a decision whether to close the deal or not. There must have been 20 experts assembled in the room, each individual an intricate piece to the whole puzzle: Jay Green, CFO of Culbro Corporation; Tom Gallagher, CEO of The Griffin Group and past partner of Gibson and Dunn; Vince Namoli, managing partner of the Tampa Bay Devilrays and part CEO of Harvard Industries; Larry Cohen, CFO of The Griffin Group and past vice president of finance at Coca-Cola; and Charles Masson, vice president and director of Salomon Brothers Inc. We had worked hard all morning and while the lawyers were negotiating the last few details, we took a lunch break. Merv, Tom and Mat went to an adjoining room; the others headed out to lunch, leaving Charles and me alone. We joked about the way this whole thing had played out and talked about the last-minute haggling on compensation for those let go as a result of the merger. Management, the directors, everyone had made enormous contributions to the effort and the real winners would be the shareholders. While we were talking, I could not help but feel as if I had won the Kentucky Derby, as I remembered back to the time I took a gamble and bought 25,000 shares of Resorts International, now GGE, for less than 85 cents per share. When I calculated the return, I must have gotten a smile on my face because Charles asked why I looked so triumphant.

When I reminded him that I was the only independent director who owned stock before coming on the board, he also did some quick math. When it dawned on him how much I had made, he let out a hoot! I interrupted him and said, Charles, you do not know the best part. I bought it in my individual retirement account—it's tax free!" At that, he jumped to his feet saying, "I wish I had thought of that! Who said you had brain surgery!" At that moment the big conference room doors opened and the army of experts poured back into the room. Charles and I looked at each other, put a finger to our lips and whispered, "Sshh!" I saw the look in his eye and for the first time in many years felt a sense of pride, satisfaction and accomplishment. I could ride off into the sunset a winner. If we voted to accept the offer and if the thousands of shareholders accepted the deal—there were still a few ifs.

While I was daydreaming, the final issues were presented and reviewed. Everyone in the room looked to Merv to see if he had anything to add. Graciously he commented on the professional and impressive job everyone in the room had done. It was a moment of weightless anticipation! Without hesitation and with as much composure as I could muster, I made the motion that the board vote to accept the terms of the merger and sell GGE to Sun International. The motion was seconded without hesitation and the entire board voted unanimously to approve the merger. It was a Cinderella story for Merv, the directors, management and, most importantly, individual shareholders. Thousands of people owned GGE/Resorts International, most of them for up to 20 years and through two bankruptcies; they were the real winners. While everyone waited to hear whether the board of directors of Sun International had voted to accept the terms, Merv made a few complimentary remarks about the work everyone had done and lamented that the board would have to break up. I agreed in deeper terms than they could ever have imagined.

I noticed Charles sitting quietly in his chair while all the bankers and lawyers were congratulating each other. Merv noticed too and asked why he had such a perplexed look on his face. In a loud clear voice, Charles said, "I just cannot believe that with all the high-priced talent assembled in this room, there is one person who was smarter than all of us. And I just can't believe what he did." Everyone looked at Charles with curiosity.

"What are you talking about, Charles?" Merv asked.

"One person here had the courage to take a huge gamble and bought 25,000 shares of this company's stock for less that 90 cents a share."

"Who?" asked Merv.

"It was that Irish Catholic kid from Boston," Charles said and pointed to me. Merv and the others looked at Charles in puzzlement.

"What is so special about that? It was in the prospectus," Merv retorted.

"Merv, it is in his IRA account. Not only is the merger a stock-for-stock deal, meaning it is a non-taxable event, but he deposited it into an IRA, making the gain non-taxable." The room burst into conversation and smiles while I sat there reveling in glory.

As everyone shook hands and congratulated each other, Merv, Tom and Mat headed for a news conference and to meet Sol Kerstner, chairman and chief principal at Sun International. I asked Charles where we could get a good cigar and we headed down Fifth Avenue to celebrate. As we walked, I told Charles how much I thought he had contributed to the board and the deal; in fact, to the whole experience. I went on to say it was an honor to work with him and a pleasure to know him. He graciously thanked me and said that for the last year and a half he had sat in the board meetings and listened to what Jay, Vince, Tom and I had to contribute and was impressed with our intelligence and expertise. He said he had gone home and wondered how he found himself in such impressive company and confessed that he felt embarrassingly dumb at times. I told Charles that I too felt exactly as he did and, in fact, repeated the exact same words to Sue every time I came home from a board meeting.

"Charles," I said, "from one stupid shit to another, I have to congratulate you for doing such a fine job!" With that we smiled and shook hands and went our separate ways.

I bought a fancy cigar, sat down on a bench on Fifth Avenue, and smoked. Then I hailed a cab and went back to the hotel, gratified and filled with a sense of reward. I could not have picked a better way to end a business career. Sometime that January the shareholders of GGE voted overwhelmingly in favor of the merger of the two companies and the end of a long life for Resorts International/GGE—it became an asset of Sun International. The next morning, I went home to New Hampshire.

Chapter 32

In New Hampshire we proceeded to design and build our new home on 20 acres on a hill in West Campton. That same winter I eclipsed my skiing comeback with a 21-run, 72,000-vertical-foot powder heli-ski day, a record at the time. Over the next three years we worked on our property, clearing land and building stone walls. I had heard that Hermann Maier won a gold medal in the Olympics after training that way—if it worked for him, I thought it would work for me.

The only true regret I have as a result of my move and retirement to New Hampshire was that I would have to leave the one thing that meant the most to me in Massachusetts—Walter Mattson, his dojo and his students. His friendship meant more than I had realized. And after 550-plus hours of class and training, almost 11 months after the sale of GGE, I was invited to the November Dan tests and passed. I had sent Walter and my fellow students a letter thanking them for their vital role in my salvation. Walter surprised me by handing out my letter to all the students taking the Dan test, accompanied by his own letter of explanation. Although he had embellished my ski accomplishments, Walter's letter was the greatest compliment I had ever received. I gave up karate only to find myself studying tai chi with John Toy, one of the country's best teachers.

As the years have passed, I have accomplished more than any doctor thought possible. I have set records heli-sking the powder of Whistler and returned to winning-form ski racing. I have competed against younger and faster skiers and, on occasion, won. My crowning glory and the one event that really makes my story worth all the pain and anxiety took place in April 1999.

Ski season had ended and most of my gear was cleaned, tuned, waxed and put away. Then one night I got a phone call from my old freestyle buddy, Floyd Wilkie, who had retired from a far-more successful ski career than mine and had not skied for years. Incredibly he was encouraging me to call our friend Wayne Wong. Wayne wanted us to come out to an event he was organizing at Alpine Meadows. Wayne had talked Floyd into going, and Floyd wanted our friend, George Askevold, and me to go too. Hilton was providing the rooms and Wayne would make sure we were fed; all we needed was a plane ticket to Reno.

In no time flat and with little to stop us, we were on our way west. The event was Wayne Wong's World Hot Dog skiing festival and competition, a two-day contest. Day one was an individual event using the original bump and trick format. The second day would be a team event using the same format. We were going to compete against a lot of the great champions from the original three years of the tour. These guys were my idols. When I competed against these men—champions like Wayne Wong, Bill Oleary, Bob Solerno, Gordy Scoog and Roger Evans—I was 18 and most of them were in their late 20s. Now we were in our mid-40s to early 50s. After 27 years, 38 of the greatest Hot Dog champions of my time gathered, reminisced and competed. The weather was beautiful and the skiing awesome. I was a part of a historical event with some of the greatest freestyle skiers the world had ever known. Yes, life was good. I had surpassed all the hurdles in my life and had a second chance to prove that I too could be a ski champion.

With the exception of my pain and anxiety and half my eye-sight, I was in top physical shape. The martial arts had given me skills I never dreamed I would have; I was as strong as a bull. All I had to do was what I do best, and that is ski. On the day of the individual event, we had two runs in the morning and one in the afternoon. I felt stronger than I have ever felt when I skied, even though most of us had not skied moguls in 20 years. At the end of the day I had placed fifth—an incredible accomplishment at any age. Later that night all the competitors' names were placed in a hat and teams of four were drawn.

My team, Team Revo, consisted of Jim Garrison, one of the original Team K2 guys and an early movie star of ski movies like "Winter Heat"; Dave Sharpe, a pro racer from the Northwest and one-time member of Team Aslope; and a 30-year-old pro from the World Cup freestyle tour by the name of Curtis Tischler. The final member was Bob Howard, a champion ballet skier from the mid-1970s and the winner of the individual event. We actually bought the right to have him ski with us during the evening auction fundraiser for juvenile diabetes.

We had to ski four runs together and, with a plan conceived by Jim Garrison, we skied in tight formation one behind the other, a classic Dick Barrymore filming technique. Halfway down two of us peeled off—one right, one left—and I did a huge Nordic jump and Curtis caught a mogul to perform a daffy. When we reached the groomed portion of the run, we lined up and did a wave routine like at football games, then skied the rest of the run doing crossovers, 360 spins, Royal Christies, slowdog noodles, whatever trick came to mind. It was done without a hitch during the two final runs and we blew away all the other teams in the scoring.

While we waited for the afternoon's award ceremonies, a group of us who had hung together over the five days found the half-pipe and a bunch of snowboard jumps. The child in each of us would not let us go home without hitting some big air. In no time at all Rolf, Dave, Bob Bills, Gordy Scoog, Roger Evans and I found ourselves catching big air. All the young hot skiers and boarders were jumping with us. On one run through the jumps, I stayed behind a large group of kids watching. The guys went one after another over the series of three jumps and were definitely going for it. As they reached the second jump, one of the hot young pro freeskiers from K2 said, "Wo, dude, those old guys are really crazy!" That was one of the best things I had overheard in years!

I thought I had done all that I needed to do, my team had won the competition and it felt as if I had just won an Olympic gold medal. That afternoon I finally stood on the winners' podium, trophy in hand. Photographers took our picture as the first first-place team champions at a true champions' event put on by the greatest freestyle champion of them all, Wayne Wong, my friend and mentor. As I tried to hide my tears of joy, I took a hard look at where I was in life. Even though I live in pain, battling at times with deep depression and high anxiety, I believe I have been blessed. Not just for being alive, but for having survived a catastrophic illness and learning from the tragedy. I had the unwavering love, support and encouragement of the most precious thing in my life—my Sue. Without her I would have had no future or anything I held dear to my heart.

Some people say I am special—I do not think so. Some people say I have achieved a great accomplishment—I did what comes naturally to all of us and survived. When I graduated from college, my father asked what I wanted to do.

I said, "Ski."

He asked me, "How can you kids survive on skiing?"

I answered him by saying, "Dad, I am a survivor no matter what! We will make out fine!"

My story is proof that no matter what befalls you, our human spirit, our courage and our ambition contain the miracle of our survival. I believe this will be humanity's salvation. Endeavor to persevere, live your dreams, be honest with your actions and with others, and never give up hope.